BROKEN

MCGILL-QUEEN'S/ASSOCIATED MEDICAL SERVICES STUDIES
IN THE HISTORY OF MEDICINE, HEALTH, AND SOCIETY

SERIES EDITORS: J.T.H. CONNOR AND ERIKA DYCK

This series presents books in the history of medicine, health studies, and social policy, exploring interactions between the institutions, ideas, and practices of medicine and those of society as a whole. To begin to understand these complex relationships and their history is a vital step to ensuring the protection of a fundamental human right: the right to health. Volumes in this series have received financial support to assist publication from Associated Medical Services, Inc. (AMS), a Canadian charitable organization with an impressive history as a catalyst for change in Canadian healthcare. For eighty years, AMS has had a profound impact through its support of the history of medicine and the education of healthcare professionals, and by making strategic investments to address critical issues in our healthcare system. AMS has funded eight chairs in the history of medicine across Canada, is a primary sponsor of many of the country's history of medicine and nursing organizations, and offers fellowships and grants through the AMS History of Medicine and Healthcare Program (www.amshealthcare.ca).

BROKEN

INSTITUTIONS, FAMILIES, AND THE CONSTRUCTION OF INTELLECTUAL DISABILITY

Madeline C. Burghardt

McGill-Queen's University Press

Montreal & Kingston • London • Chicago

ISBN 978-0-7735-5482-5 (cloth)
ISBN 978-0-7735-5483-2 (paper)
ISBN 978-0-7735-5557-0 (ePDF)
ISBN 978-0-7735-5558-7 (ePUB)

Legal deposit fourth quarter 2018
Bibliothèque nationale du Québec

Printed in Canada on acid-free paper that is 100% ancient forest free (100% post-consumer recycled), processed chlorine free

This book has been published with the help of a grant from the Canadian Federation for the Humanities and Social Sciences, through the Awards to Scholarly Publications Program, using funds provided by the Social Sciences and Humanities Research Council of Canada.

Funded by the Government of Canada   Financé par le gouvernement du Canada   Canada Council for the Arts   Conseil des arts du Canada

We acknowledge the support of the Canada Council for the Arts, which last year invested $153 million to bring the arts to Canadians throughout the country.

Nous remercions le Conseil des arts du Canada de son soutien. L'an dernier, le Conseil a investi 153 millions de dollars pour mettre de l'art dans la vie des Canadiennes et des Canadiens de tout le pays.

Library and Archives Canada Cataloguing in Publication

Burghardt, Madeline C., 1964–, author
        Broken : institutions, families, and the construction of intellectual disability /
Madeline C. Burghardt.

(McGill-Queen's/Associated Medical Services studies in the history of medicine, health, and society; 50) This book is based on research conducted between 2012 and 2013 as part of research completed for the author's doctoral dissertation.
Includes bibliographical references and index.
Issued in print and electronic formats.
ISBN 978-0-7735-5482-5 (cloth). – ISBN 978-0-7735-5483-2 (paper). –
ISBN 978-0-7735-5557-0 (ePDF). – ISBN 978-0-7735-5558-7 (ePUB)

        1. People with mental disabilities–Institutional care – Ontario – History. 2. People with mental disabilities – Government policy – Ontario – History. 3. People with mental disabilities – Family relationships – Ontario – History. 4. People with mental disabilities – Ontario – Social conditions. I. Title. II. Series: McGill-Queen's/Associated Medical Services studies in the history of medicine, health, and society; 50

HV3008.C3B87 2018   362.3'09713   C2018-904613-9
C2018-904614-7

This book was designed and typeset by Peggy & Co. Design Inc. in 11/14 Garamond.

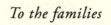

To the families

Contents

Acknowledgments

There are many people who helped me to bring this text from idea to completion. I thank my doctoral supervisory committee – Marcia Rioux, Geoffrey Reaume, and Nora Groce – for their scholarly advice and encouragement and for overseeing the completion of the original study. In addition, I would like to thank Claudia Malacrida and John Radford, who offered helpful insights and guidance at the end of that first phase of the journey and the beginning of the long transformation from dissertation to book. My colleagues and students in the Critical Disability Studies program at York University have been steadfast in their encouragement and for this I am grateful. I acknowledge the *Canadian Journal of Disability Studies* for an earlier published version of chapter 3 and portions of chapter 4. Chapter 5 is derived in part from an article published in *Disability & Society* 30 (7): 1071–86, copyright Taylor & Francis, available online: http://dx.doi.org/ 10.1080/09687599.2015.1076718.

Thank you to Kyla Madden of McGill-Queen's Press for her affirming spirit, and for her generosity of time and energy during the various stages of completing this text. Thank you to all at McGill-Queen's for their professional, helpful advice and communication. Thank you to two anonymous reviewers who provided vital feedback on earlier drafts of the text; through them I have learned a great deal.

I thank the many friends, neighbours, and community members who have accompanied me in this project. Though you are too numerous to mention individually here, know that I am grateful for your support and friendship. Thanks are owed to my large extended family, especially my siblings and my parents: being able to bring this project to completion with the accompaniment of my parents is a huge gift for which I will always be grateful. Enormous thanks are owed to Richard, Seph, Tonnán, and Raffi – my home crew, your interest and unwavering support kept me going through the months of listening and writing. Thank you for your steadfast faith in me.

Last, I thank all those who participated in this project and dared to share their stories with a stranger. Survivors, brothers, sisters, parents – you are all part of this text. Thank you for sharing your stories with me; may your generosity contribute in some way to the creation of a more just and inclusive world.

A Note on Terminology

Throughout this text, I employ the term 'intellectual disability' as a descriptor for the group of conditions historically associated with specific forms of intellectual and functional impairment. I have chosen this term due to its current use and recognizability, acknowledging that 'developmental disability' remains the predominant nomenclature in the United States, and that 'learning disability' is the preferred term in the UK. When discussing particular time periods in the text, historically situated conditions (Carlson 2010, xv) such as 'feeblemindedness,' 'mental retardation,' and 'idiocy' are occasionally referred to by their original terminology in order to situate the discussion in that era's discourse and language. For the most part, I forgo the use of quotation marks around these terms; this does not imply agreement with them, nor does it suggest that they are natural or unproblematic. For the most part, I have chosen to use 'people first' terminology (i.e. 'people with intellectual disabilities' as opposed to 'intellectually disabled people'), all the while acknowledging the vital point made by disability scholars of the importance of recognizing that people with impairments are *disabled* by the obstacles and oppression inherent to modern society (Oliver 1990). I use all of these descriptors aware of their historically contingent and problematic natures, and with no intention to perpetuate the suffering they have caused.

The term 'survivor' is used to denote the community of people designated as having intellectual disabilities who were institutionalized against their will. I was introduced to the term by a man who spent eighteen years in an institution, who reminded me frequently throughout our conversations that he did not 'live' at the institution, but that he 'survived' there. The term has been adopted by the community of people who have lived through institutionalization and continue to do advocacy work with and on behalf of others who suffered the same fate.

"If the law must now treat in a 'humane' way an individual who is 'outside nature' ... it is not on account of some profound humanity that the [outsider] conceals within him, but because of a necessary regulation of the effects of power ... 'humanity' is the respectable name given to this economy and to its meticulous calculations."

Foucault (1995, 92)

INTRODUCTION

The Asylum's Accomplice, or the Creation of Intellectual Disability

This book is based on research conducted between 2012 and 2013 as part of research completed for my doctoral dissertation. During that time, I spoke with institutional survivors and with members of their families in an attempt to gain some understanding of the impact of institutionalization on those who had been sent to live there and on those who carried on living at home in their absence. My research coincided with a sea change in institutional policy for people with intellectual disabilities in Ontario. On 31 March 2009, Huronia Regional Centre, the final remaining institution for people with intellectual disabilities in Ontario, was closed after almost one hundred thirty-five years of existence. In the wake of its closure, which signalled the end of the 'official' institutional era in Ontario, two institutional survivors, Marie Slark and Patricia Seth,[1] launched a class-action lawsuit against the Ontario government for abuses suffered while institutionalized and legally under government care. This action broke open the stories of other institutional survivors, leading to public expressions of institutional survivorship including, among other endeavours, two CBC radio documentaries,[2] several productions and exhibits from various arts communities,[3] and significant local and national media coverage.[4] The class action also led to a public apology from the Ontario government for wrongs committed,[5] a financial settlement for institutional survivors, and a commitment from the government to take greater responsibility for some of the aftermath of its institutional legacy, including upkeep of the institution's cemetery. Perhaps most importantly, the steps taken by the initial two litigants inspired a movement to speak the truth regarding what had happened to them and brought the stories of institutional survivors into the public realm, focusing attention on a piece of Ontario's history that had heretofore received little attention.

These developments were contemporaneous with my own deliberations about how best to respectfully bring into the public realm the stories of people who have historically been labelled, to varying degrees, as different, incompetent, and frequently inhuman, who have suffered enormously because of those labels, and who have generally had little opportunity to share their life experiences beyond what is asked of them in order to receive medical, educational, or other social supports. These deliberations were further provoked by my reflections on a funeral that I had attended prior to beginning the research.

The funeral was for a man who had lived most of his life at the Huronia Regional Centre in Orillia, Ontario. After leaving the institution at age thirty-seven, he had lived the last seven years of his life in a home in the community, with meaningful work, friendships, and an active social circle. He had come from a large family and his siblings were in attendance at his funeral. While I cannot presume to know what his brothers and sisters were thinking or feeling during those moments, I sensed unease, and I wondered if they were experiencing a disconnect between what they had been told about their brother when they were children – a young, 'retarded' boy who was sent away from home at a young age because he could not live at home any longer – and what they were now observing in the celebration surrounding his life and all that he had brought to the community around him. Could this be the same boy? My reflection on this possible disconnect led me to the questions which guided this project: to explore the impact that institutionalization had in the lives of families, not only on those sent to live there, although that phenomenon alone warrants deep and unflinching interrogation, but also on those who carried on at home in its wake. This project sought to explore one facet of lives that were touched by a regrettable historical process instituted and sustained because of the presumed differences between people, even within the same family.

In all, thirty-six interviews were conducted with institutional survivors, brothers and sisters, parents, former institutional staff, and key informants. Recruiting participants proved one of the more challenging aspects of the work, as concerns regarding confidentiality, as well as a reluctance from some to re-engage with what had been a difficult period in their lives, resulted in an understandable hesitation to discuss their experiences, particularly with a stranger. Moreover, while attempts were made to connect with more than one member of various families, this, too, proved difficult, resulting in a sampling from a total of twenty families, some represented by more than one member, others not (please see the Appendix for a list of participants). Despite these limitations, the stories brought forward by participants provide, at the least, a window into institutionalization's far-reaching effects in the lives of several families.

The purpose of this book is twofold. While the initial investigation had as its focus an exploration of the impact of institutionalization on family relationships and understandings of disability, another principal theme warranting exploration emerged: specifically, the relationship between influential historical moments, social and political discourse, and the construction of difference. This second broad thematic umbrella includes, but is not limited to, such concerns as classifications of intellect and the liminalization of those considered intellectually inferior; the complex relationship between power, decision-making, and their lived effects; the shared temporal and "political rationalities" (Foucault 1994, as cited in Chapman 2014, 25) which informed the incarceration of people with intellectual disabilities and other marginalized groups, including Indigenous peoples of Canada (Chapman, Carey, and Ben-Moshe 2014); and the position that institutionalization holds within the larger scheme of capitalistic labour and production. Thus, while people designated intellectually disabled and members of their families hold central positions within this text and the research which preceded it, their revelations necessitate a broader discussion which touches on areas of political, economic, and social concern.

I begin with an assertion, *de rigueur* in disability scholarship yet contentious within contemporary biomedical and political discourse, of the constructed nature of intellectual disability (Goodley 1997; Inglis 2013; Levine and Langness 1986). While I do not claim to disregard chromosomal and physical differences which set particular groups of people into distinction with one another, this book is premised on the idea that the political and biomedical designation of people as intellectually inferior has been of far greater influence in the history of intellectual disability than any physiological markers. Indeed, as the stories of institutionalized persons and members of their families began to come forward as this project unfolded, the influence of shifting linguistic boundaries, semantic manipulation, and political persuasions in the construction of intellectual disability, and the harmful cultural practices which resulted, became clear. The understanding of disability and the disabled person as a constructed entity, now considered a fundamental premise within disability scholarship (the lived realities of the limitations of impairment notwithstanding), has had input from a few influential theoretical bodies, two of which I introduce briefly here.

First, due in large part to the seminal influence of UK social model activists and academics, traditional, essentialist understandings of disability as body-centred, individually located, and independent of social influences have come under criticism in recent decades. The social model, first articulated in 1976 in a statement by the Union of the Physically Impaired Against Segregation (UPIAS), asserts that disability is not one's bodily impairment, but is rather the physical, political, and economic limitations imposed by society. While it has been critiqued by some (Hughes and Paterson 1997; Shakespeare 2006) for its inadequate acknowledgment of the corporeal limitations of impairment, the social model has had significant influence in the lives of disabled people by revealing the fallacy of the impaired mind or body as the root of one's disablement, pointing out instead prohibitive systems that limit people's access to the lives and services to which all people are entitled. The social model has inspired activism on the part of disabled people and has had considerable effect in political and social circles by drawing attention to the impact of oppressive systems and cultural understandings on the lived experience of disability. The social model, accordingly, assists in reframing a fundamental premise of institutionalization – that segregated facilities were necessary to deal with a problematic population – by suggesting that the problem, rather, lies in the systemic structures which prevented people with intellectual disabilities from living well with their families in the community.

The social model's emphasis on externally imposed barriers has exposed the extent to which much of the 'problem' of disability stems from cultural and social understandings of limitation in conjunction with oppressive policies and administrations (Oliver 1990). Examples of the influence of the social model can be seen in the implementation of two significant pieces of legislation in Canada, the Accessibility for Ontarians with Disabilities Act (AODA 2005) and the Accessibility for Manitobans Act (AMA 2013), which, despite their limitations, are initial attempts to address inequity within society using an anti-discrimination framework (Jacobs, De Costa, and Cino 2016). Similarly, the social model has had positive effects in the lives of people with intellectual disabilities by "turning attention away from the individual onto a society that excludes, discriminates, and stigmatises" (Goodley 1997, 372) and by reframing the ways in which supports for people with intellectual disabilities are offered (Williams and Heslop

2005). The positive effects of the social model have been unevenly felt in the lives of people with intellectual disability, however (Race, Boxall, and Carson 2005), perhaps due to that community's greater challenge in establishing a listened-to presence within the larger community of disability activism (Chappell 1998), and the reliance by some members of the community on others to speak on their behalf (Clarke et al. 2005). Moreover, the idea of intellectual disability as an undisputable and embodied phenomenon remains unchallenged in much current biomedical discourse, and the idea of social and cultural discourse contributing to its construction remains contentious (Vehmas 1999; Williams and Heslop 2005). Cultural markers of assumed and essentialist understandings of intellectual disability remain: the prioritization of intellect in a knowledge-based world; classificatory schemes such as intelligence tests that continue to have significant influence in the 'placement' of children with learning impairments (Kliewer and Drake 1998); and ever-finer designations of genetic variations that contribute to biomedical discourses of preferred embodiments (Scully 2002) – these all continue to promulgate essentialist and biologically based views.

The experiences of participants in this project, however, provide evidence of the constructedness of intellect and intellectual impairment and the instability in definitions and meanings which can result. One of the major themes arising from this project concerns the fluctuations, over time, in social and political understandings of intellectual disability, and how those changes contributed to shifts in families' understandings of their disabled sibling or child, to their relationships with each other, and to their family narrative as a whole. This had particular importance in regard to families' decisions to institutionalize and on how family members perceived their disabled child or sibling before, during, and after institutionalization. While fluctuations in definitions of intellectual capacity have resulted in significant harm to people with disabilities throughout history (changes in the functional threshold at which people would be considered to require institutionalization, for example), some of the narratives in this text suggest that discursive changes can also have positive effects, such as creating the social space to challenge assumptions of deficit and incapacity, and to critique the prioritization of intellect in the first place.

The second principal theoretical body which I employ to discuss the notion of the constructedness of intellectual disability stems from the work of Foucault and Foucauldian theorists, who draw attention to the discursive production of specific biological subjects (Carlson 2010, 15) and to the historical moments at which this influence was most keenly felt.[6] Foucault's (2006, 1995) central theoretical claims include the role of "biopower" in the categorization and segregation of marginalized groups of people; the influence of disciplinary administrative practices on the 'bringing into being' of the docile subject; and the role of institutions in the surveillance of 'problematic' populations. These claims are central to the idea that the "identity of the [intellectually disabled] subject was produced," not due to the indisputable evidence of biological deficiency, but "because this identity met certain requirements of contemporary social and political arrangements" (Tremain 2005, 10). Foucault's claims draw attention away from the assumed foundation of biological imperialism and suggest that persons with intellectual disability are discursively produced through the same mechanisms that are designed to discipline and control them. Thus, "the institution was not merely a response to a pre-existing problem, but was the way in which the problem itself was constituted" (Ingleby 1983, 147).

Further, Foucault's claims provide a genealogical way forward in the historical excavation of particular phenomena. Rather than examining chronological sequences of events, Foucault suggests engagement with their "historical ontology" (cited in Carlson 2010, 14), or "the ways in which the possibilities for choice, and for being, arise in history" (Hacking 2002, 23). The histories of particular phenomena, therefore, should not be considered linear progressions, but manifestations of the multiple ways in which power has influenced meanings, definitions, and discourse. For our purposes here, that includes calling into question the ontological assumptions under-lying the ways in which institutions came to be seen as essential tools in the management of particular groups of people (Carey, Ben-Moshe, and Chapman 2014). Thus, while it is important to understand the social and political conditions which contributed to the development of institutions (indeed, much of the first three chapters of this text is devoted to this objective), Foucault's ontological engagement requires considering insti-tutionalization as part of the defining of intellectual disability and a major contributor to its creation as a distinct, measurable, and, by extension, punishable category.

This text is divided into two main parts. Part I is a historical tracing of the development of institutions for people designated intellectually disabled. Chapter 1 begins with a description of five significant historical movements – the development of charitable responses to people with disabilities; the increasing prioritization of modern ideals of order, reason, and autonomy from the eighteenth century onwards; the influential rise of market capitalism and modern modes of production; the increasing reliance on scientific explanations for human diversity; and the role of colonization in the segregation and oppression of marginalized groups – all of which facilitated institutional development in Europe and North America. These five broad historical movements provide a framework for the subsequent analysis of location- and era-specific developments that contributed to the rise of institutions, particularly in North America. These include the eugenics movement of the late nineteenth and early twentieth centuries, fuelled by fears of reproduction in feebleminded and otherwise undesirable populations such as Indigenous peoples (Kelm 2005; Malacrida 2015; McLaren 1990); the influence of immigration policies that simultaneously encouraged and limited migration to Canada in order to ensure the establishment of "particular national formations" (Thobani 2007, 6); and the increasing use of intelligence tests which informed policy decisions with direct bearing on people's lives in the areas of education and home life (Gould 1996). Throughout, I draw attention to the overlapping "political rationalities" (Foucault 1994, cited in Chapman 2014, 25) between the rise of institutions for the feebleminded and other modern incarcerative projects, indicating the mutually reinforcing nature of much of the discourse surrounding the need for residential institutions in the nineteenth and twentieth centuries (Chapman, Carey, and Ben-Moshe 2014). Chapter 2 is a continuation of this historical framing, but begins to narrow the discussion to the geographic and temporal foci of this study through a discussion of conditions specific to institutional development in Ontario through the mid-late nineteenth and early twentieth centuries. Part I concludes with chapter 3, devoted to an analysis of the social, political, and cultural conditions which influenced families' decisions to institutionalize their children in the years following World War II, the time period relevant to the cohort of families who participated in this project. Noteworthy here are the significant features of Cold War tensions – namely, containment, conformity, and the threat of the 'other' – which, although primarily played out on the larger field of international posturing and politics, had considerable influence in the intimate and domestic rituals of everyday life.

Part II constitutes the heart of the book, accounts of institutionalization and separation as told by institutional survivors and by siblings and parents of institutionalized individuals. With the principal goal of illuminating the impact of institutionalization on family relationships and understandings of disability, this section presents participant narratives with an eye to reflections which shed light on those themes. Drawing from participants' stories, my analysis prioritizes the effects that years-long separations via policies of segregation, based on arbitrary systems of categorization and classification, had on relationships within families, and equally important, on people's understandings of the meanings of intellectual disability and the profound impact those meanings had in the lives of many thousands of people. Further, the stories of separation and brokenness as revealed in this text point to themes warranting deeper reflection due to their ongoing societal influence, not only with people considered intellectually disabled, but with marginalized individuals in general. These include the societal distribution of power, including its manifestation in the family, as well as the significant role that capitalist production plays in the ongoing classification of those considered different or deviant.

These broad analytical and theoretical pursuits may at the outset seem far removed from the initial encounter which inspired this project – the funeral of an institutional survivor and the reaction of his family – and indeed from the minutiae of domestic family life and relationships as described by the participants in this project. Yet the macro structures of economic efficiency, group surveillance, and segregation due to difference had significant impact on participants' daily lives, on their experiences of relationships within the family, and on their perceptions of intellectual disability. These effects were felt not only by those who were themselves institutionalized, but by all those whom institutionalization touched in one way or another, indicating the far-reaching impact of the segregative policies which allowed institutionalization to flourish for almost one hundred fifty years.

PART ONE

INSTITUTIONALIZATION IN CONTEXT

Institutions for the Feebleminded: Theory, History, and Context

In historical excavations, it is easy to fall prey to the lure of "presentism" (Fischer 1970, 135) and to evaluate the trends and practices of previous generations with current analytic tools, knowledge, and theoretical perspectives. While current understandings allow past mistakes to be revealed and grant moral clarity, such practices can prevent the analysis of events beyond the actions and decisions of groups and individuals, and can discourage consideration of broader social and political trends. In this project, the challenge was to consider not only the flawed decisions of policymakers, reform enthusiasts, and eugenics-inspired scientists who were major contributors to the establishment and proliferation of institutions, but to examine also the broad historical and theoretical movements which contributed to institutions' emergence and longevity.

To that end, I explore five fundamental historical developments which provide a metaframework for the examination of time- and place-specific social and political impulses that contributed to the rise of institutions. These include the long and contentious history of charitable models towards people with disabilities; the steady progress of modernity, including the philosophical priorities emerging from the Enlightenment, such as intellectual reason, order, and personal autonomy; the influential rise of market capitalism and modern modes of production; the increasing reliance on scientific explanations for human diversity, including the use of science as a tool to address issues of political and social concern; and the effects of colonizing practices on the segregation and oppression of marginalized groups. This broad historical perspective provides the scaffolding needed to understand some of the specific geographic, social, and political conditions which facilitated institutionalization in nineteenth- and twentieth-century North America, the eugenics movement being one example. All of these provide a backdrop for discussions in subsequent chapters concerning the development of institutions in Ontario, the reasons for their longevity, and the social and cultural context within which parents made decisions, or were compelled to make decisions, regarding institutional placement of their children.

Institutions as Charitable Response

Recent revelations of the mistreatment suffered by people institutionalized against their will have provided a bleak view of the lived experience of institutionalization in the nineteenth and twentieth centuries (see, for example, Ford 2017, Hutton et al. 2017, Malacrida 2015, Reaume 2000, and Scott 2017). This mistreatment counters original historical records of the motivations behind the development of institutions, which suggest that institutions were developed to improve both the living conditions and the capabilities of the people housed therein. That institutions culminated as horrible sites of containment and oppression does not belie the existence of evidence from the time that they were considered by the intellectual and political elite to be a humane way to house and support marginalized populations (Ferguson 1994; Trent 1994). In this section, while focusing primarily on the influence of charitable responses on the development of institutions for the feebleminded, it is important to note charity's position in the history of other forms of institutionalization, notably Canada's residential school system, both systems of incarceration that, despite significant differences, share interlocking histories and map, geographically and historically, one onto the other (Chapman 2014, 25).

From a historical perspective, institutions are one feature in the centuries-long tradition of charity towards people with disabilities. While charitable responses remain contentious within the disability community due to connected assumptions concerning people's need for external assistance from the able-bodied (Longmore 2010; Shakespeare 2006), they inform a significant part of our understanding of how the institutional response became so prominent. 'Charity' in its literal sense means caring for another, and thus is simply one feature of human interaction, but recorded charitable responses tend to be historically connected to religious observance and obligation. Known charitable practices can be traced to the early Common Era, although records of medical ethics concerning the charitable care of vulnerable groups exist from at least the fifth century BCE

(Jonsen 2000). Further, while scholars have illuminated the practice of charity as a component of communities throughout history (Porter 1997; Stiker 1990), my emphasis here is on charity's distributions and influences on institutional methods of care in Europe and North America from the mid-1800s onwards, drawing primarily from the Judeo-Christian tradition.

In most religious traditions, charity framed the care of people with disabilities as a necessary component of spiritual and ethical observance (Jonsen 2000; Metzler 2006; Porter 1997), and these obligations frequently overlapped with the practice of medicine and its accompanying body of ethics. Indeed, the relationship between healing, charity, and religious observation has historically been fluid, contemporaneous, and mutually sustaining (Porter 1997), and the 'curing' of people with disabilities has, at various points in Christendom, been considered evidence of God's existence and a way for people to achieve grace, and even sainthood (Duffin 2009; Metzler 2006). In the High Middle Ages (twelfth to fourteenth centuries) in Europe, the acceptance of and kindness towards people with disabilities was partly understood as an acknowledgment of the "infinite diversity of God's creation" (Stiker 1999, 68) and as respect towards people considered mediums for the Divine (Metzler 2006).

In his comprehensive history of disability, Stiker (1999) exposes the relationship between charitable responses and the development of institutional models of care. He notes the simultaneous development of the felt responsibility to perform works of charity within Christianity with the rise of institutions in Europe from the sixteenth century onwards. These responses were manifested primarily through the establishment of medical and educational institutions, often under the administration of a religious order, and established the tradition of an organized and ostensibly necessary response to the needs of people on the margins of society.

One European example is the work of Saint Vincent de Paul (1581–1660), who established a network of charitable almshouses in seventeenth-century France with the intention of caring for people who were poor, ill, or elderly, all embedded within a strong foundation of religious instruction. As Stiker notes, de Paul's objective was not only to provide relief to indigent individuals, but to "Christianize" (98) the poor, highlighting the personal and political motivations underscoring his work. The Christianization that underscored much institutional development in Europe was not confined there, however. In a process that Chapman (2014) links to other metanarratives of colonization and social elimination, the Canadian residential school system was also established as a system of Christianization, at least from the mid-nineteenth century onwards,[1] in which incarcerated children were forced to undergo religious instruction in the Christian tradition practised by the schools' founders, a process now understood as a form of cultural genocide (Churchill 2004).

Consideration of the nineteenth-century reformist movement also adds to our understanding of the complicated relationship between charity and institutional development in the UK and North America. In the mid-nineteenth century, social reform movements promoted the development of publicly funded institutions as a necessary and generous response to indigent people. Reformists, primarily from the middle-upper classes, advocated free access to education, humane prisons and asylums, and better work conditions, and demonstrated enthusiasm for "projects of social reform of every description" (Scull 1979, 55). In the zeal for social improvement, UK reformists supported the establishment of state-run institutions in the belief that centralized care would alleviate the "appalling" conditions (51) which until then existed in ad-hoc, individually organized facilities, or in situations where people were left to fend for themselves. Scull suggests that the trend to increasingly segregate those considered mad or deviant from the surrounding community, while assisting the move to capitalist production (discussed below) and to a more centralized organization of 'care,' was considered well-intentioned due to the immense contrast between newer state-run institutions and previous indigent and makeshift conditions in which people were, quite literally, "living in shit" (Scull 1983, 130).

Contemporaneous responses developed in North America. While in the early 1800s care for people considered feebleminded and mad had been primarily located within the family (Chupick and Wright 2006; Trent 1994) or in makeshift, privately run facilities, often with miserable conditions (Ferguson 1994), the mid-1800s saw a proliferation of publicly funded, centralized institutions. American reformists, imbued with a desire to bring order and respectability to the existing ad-hoc system of almshouses, pushed for the establishment of state-run, government-supported institutions and asylums. Their intention was to provide safe, curative environments within which individuals could be restored to full health (in the case of mad people), or could be trained or habilitated (in the case of the intellectually disabled) in the hopes of an eventual and successful return to meaningful roles in the community (Trent 1994). Indeed, the original intention of the mid-nineteenth-century reformers was to "prepare ... 'idiot' children for productive lives in the outside world" (Radford and Park 1993, 371). At the time of their establishment, institutions for the feebleminded in the United States (which developed twenty to thirty years before similar facilities in Canada) were intended, at least partially, for educative purposes (Carlson 2010; Trent 1994). A growing certainty in the power of education to transform individuals into productive members of society and a belief in the moral obligation to assist other members of the community, as well as the nascent acknowledgment of the right of all people to attend school, led to a rapid increase in the number of institutions for the feebleminded throughout the mid-1800s in the United States (Ferguson 1994; Trent 1994). Underlying this movement was the "perfectionist faith of many reformers that there was no limit to the improvement of humanity" (Tyor and Bell 1984, 15), made possible through both reformers' zeal and an assumed willingness for transformation on the part of recipients and their families. As will be explained in chapter 2, this enthusiasm was felt to a lesser degree in Canada, yet social reformers here continued to frame institutionalization as a humanitarian and compassionate response to the feebleminded well after institutions' establishment in 1876, despite their simultaneous positioning as necessary agents of moral and social control (Simmons 1982).

One example of the institutionalized charitable response towards the feebleminded in North America, as well as its subsequent decline into a custodial, incarcerative model, is the work of Édouard Séguin, a French expatriate who moved to the United States in 1848. Séguin established schools for the feebleminded with the conviction that feeblemindedness was caused by a lack of moral fortitude and "arrested development of the will" (Trent 1994, 46), and that "moral idiocy" could be transformed with the "guidance, care and restraint of the institution" (23), including the disciplined application of education and guided activity. Séguin's work was extremely influential in mid-nineteenth-century North America, and it was during this era of hopeful optimism that several institutions for the feebleminded were established. Historical records indicate widespread approval of Séguin's methods (Ferguson 1994), furthering the support for institutions as a humanitarian and worthwhile response to a population with the potential for productive and meaningful societal participation, if only given timely and appropriate care.

Similar, in terms of the originary impulses and discourses of beneficence that informed the surge in North American institutions for the feebleminded, was the concurrent establishment of residential schools for Indigenous children in Canada and the United States. What distinguishes the establishment of residential schools from institutions for the feebleminded is the particular colonialist discourse which justified the taking of Indigenous land and either the conversion or the extermination of the 'Indian' (Churchill 2004), who in the earliest centuries of the European invasion of North America were seen as a malleable template for Christianity or as eliminable due to their non-status as human beings (Chapman 2014). Accordingly, death-causing brutality within residential schools was justified by the necessity of conversion. While there are distinctions between the rationales which informed the differing mandates of Indian residential schools and institutions for the feebleminded, both were underscored by a belief in the promise of transformation of their residents: residential schools as a site of Christianization and white citizenry; institutions as sites to foster productivity and reasonableness.

This historical perspective provides an overview of some of the motivations behind long-term institutions. Movements with histories emerging from charitable discourses must be examined both in tandem with and in distinction from each other, and must be considered not only from the perspective of beneficent historical records, but as a result of developments that allowed the influence and political rationalities of ruling classes to continue (Chapman 2014, 33). The list of examples – seventeenth- and eighteenth-century almshouses, founded by people with religious and political intentions, and used as tools to evangelize large groups of people who were dependent on the institutions' shelter and amenities for their survival (Stiker 1999, 98); "the proliferation of schools for intellectually disabled or blind pupils, asylums, and Indian residential schools" (Chapman 2014, 33); the development of institutions for the feebleminded such as those at the centre of this study – these contemporaneous phenomena all trouble the notion of early institutional responses emerging from charitable impulses, and suggest instead that "they [were] the forerunners ... of what would become in our [twentieth] century the almost single formula for persons" marked by difference (Stiker 1999, 107). What may have originated as "practices of community responsibility" transformed instead into co-existing axes of "care and violence" (Chapman 2014, 30), features which remained part of institutional practices throughout their history.

Further, the establishment of institutions can also be attributed to larger economic and political factors; reformists' intentions for improvement emulated social changes as much as they were a desire for humanitarian transformation (Scull 1983). The influence of the onset of capitalism, which I address in greater detail below, is connected to the influence of charitable impulses in that the capitalist means of production hastened divisions between wealthy owners and poor, indigent, and frequently disabled labourers, now 'surplus' in the new industrialized economy (Carey 2009). Uneven wealth distribution saw the emergence of a ruling class that had the means to 'provide' for those 'less fortunate,' a development contemporaneous with understandings of disability as problematic and of people with disabilities as those in need of assistance (Davis 2010). Moreover, scholars point out that even when justified by charitable influences, the earliest institutions for the feebleminded served other, less generous intentions, such as allowing for increased surveillance over large assemblies of 'unusual' persons, which had heretofore been impossible (Borsay 2002), and "shaping the contours of care and control in order to ensure [professionals'] privilege and ... legitimacy" (Trent 1994, 5). Thus, these early institutions were "vectors of both assistance and repression ... intended not only to assist the poor but also for imprisonment ... confinement had social, political, religious, economic and moral meanings" (Foucault 2006, 51–2).

Ultimately, it was the idealistic proliferation of institutions that contributed to their rapid and dramatic demise. Despite reformists' initial optimism, their formative objectives began a lamentable shift in the latter half of the nineteenth century, such that by the turn of the twentieth century, the "original inspiration for the early institutions" in North America was more or less "obliterated" (Radford and Park 1993, 375). Their size, the increasing numbers of people being admitted, and a change in the definition of feeblemindedness from a malleable condition to one that could not be cured or habilitated led to a significant decline in the second half of the nineteenth century from a rehabilitative to a custodial model. By the end of the nineteenth century, incarceration as the principal method of intervention was well established in North American institutions, one that would remain in place for more than one hundred years.

Institutions as Pillars of Modernity

The establishment of the modern institution as a viable method to house and control the destitute and marginalized coincides with the heart of the late modern era in the middle of the nineteenth century. Emerging from the intellectual reforms of the Enlightenment in the eighteenth century onwards, this period was characterized by the pursuit of Kantian ideals including intellectual reason, order, and personal autonomy. The goals of modernity – to allow "the authority of intellectuals to provide universal standards of truth, morality and taste in alliance with modern state rulers in a joint effort to establish modernity as a fundamentally ordered social and political system" (Simons 2002, 29) – established a hierarchy of reason favouring the autonomous, well-educated, and sound individual. In an abstract sense, institutions, in their ability to house the 'unsound,' thus played an essential role in the "compulsive temporal and spatial arrangements of modernity" (Rhodes 2001, 69), and were a response to the "omnipresent subtext" (65) of reason, order, and progress.

The work of Michel Foucault is helpful in illuminating the role that institutions played in the developing modern state. According to Foucault (1995), institutions are sites of surveillance and control, considered necessary for the smooth functioning of the state. Surveillance creates the 'docile subject' through the combined forces of observation and repression, pervasive tools through which authorities can exert subtle yet exacting authority (Philo 1989). Surveillance "naturalizes and legitimizes" (Tremain 2002, 36) the limitations placed on conduct, and is the "modern interpenetration of power and knowledge" (Rhodes 2001, 65). Foucault's depiction of ultimate subjection – the prisoner who cannot escape the persistent view of the panopticon (Rhodes 2001), Bentham's late-eighteenth-century archetypal model of the prison (Park 1990; Philo 1989) – is an example of the surveillance enacted in institutional settings. Indeed, in her recent work on the Michener institute in Alberta, Malacrida (2015) likens the physical layout of the institution's wards to a panopticon, reflective of the deliberate effort on the part of administrators to ensure constant surveillance of institutional residents.

The surveillance and disciplinary control that institutions perform is exercised through what Foucault (1995, 144) calls "biopower," or systems which "qualify, measure, appraise, and hierarchize" individuals of interest, usually through the aegis of medical diagnosis and administration. Through the auspices of biopower, the human being becomes a subject of disciplinary power through measurement and categorization, and bears "the inscription of socio-cultural norms" (McLaren 2002, 91). Accordingly, those who do not bear the norms of "cultural inscription" (92), but rather its lack, are placed, physically and metaphorically, into liminal spaces – the prison, the asylum, the poorhouse – reserved specifically for purposes of

additional buildings, documentation suggests that until the institution's closure, overcrowding was an ongoing, endemic problem. The combination of political indifference and reluctance to implement positive change, as well as Orillia's historical position as the centrepiece of custodial care, meant that when other institutions were built between the 1950s and 1970s, the impetus was not necessarily to move forward in a positive way towards people with intellectual disabilities and their underserviced families, but rather to absorb Orillia's overflow. Moreover, as other long-term custodial institutions were built in the latter part of the twentieth century to address rising demand, crowding became a feature in those locations as well.

In Ontario, institutional admission patterns were not only influenced by negative policy considerations. Despite the government's stated intention that institutions were necessary for the care and protection of the feebleminded and for society, people's admissions were influenced by complex and interrelated factors including social class, geography, gender, and race. While some factors, such as gender for example, had continuous influence over the admission of people to institutions over generations, the reasoning underlying these factors shifted periodically in terms of direction and force as a result of changing social and political conditions. Thus, while the factors discussed below can be considered constants throughout institutional history, they have been informed by fluctuating and sometimes contradictory rationalities.

Class and Location

A family's socio-economic background had significant influence in regard to the institutionalization of a family member. This factor carried persuasion at both ends of the socio-economic spectrum, affecting people with means and without, depending on the time period within which the decision to institutionalize was being carried out and on other demographic categories occupied by the individual. As scholars have indicated (Malacrida 2015; Simmons 1982; Trent 1994), living without economic means has historically been as much a reason for admission as were concerns regarding feeblemindedness. In his history of intellectual disability in the United States, James Trent (1994) indicates that lower social class has always been a principal factor in people's designation as being intellectually disabled and requiring institutionalization. In his words, "the tendency of elites to shape the meaning of mental retardation around technical, particularistic, and usually psycho-medical themes led to a general ignoring of the maldistribution of resources, status, and power, so prominent in the lives of intellectually disabled people. [T]he economic vulnerability of these people and their families, more than the claims made for their intellectual or social limitations, has shaped the kinds of treatments offered them" (5).

This trend was also prevalent in Canada. Both Malacrida (2015) and Simmons (1982) have indicated the strong historical connection between a family's "poverty and dependency" (Malacrida 2015, 162) and the likelihood of admission, reflecting institutions' use as a dumping ground for those considered unable to contribute to the economy and with whom the government did not otherwise know how to intervene. This connection gained strength during the eugenic era, when fears concerning pollution of the social body encouraged the conflation of poverty, race, and incapacity in the public imagination and in political decision-making circles. The proliferation of 'helping' professionals, ostensibly to eliminate the dysfunctional behaviour associated with poverty such as lack of productivity and civic participation, played a key role in the identification of individuals requiring institutional care (Kennedy 2008; McLaren 1990). Moreover, the link between lower socio-economic status and institutional admission did not fade away with the strengthening of the welfare state in post–World War II Canada. As indicated by many of the participants in this study, referring agencies frequently remained committed to the conflation between poverty and intellectual incapacity until the end of the institutional era. Indeed, two of the former staff interviewed for this project indicated that as late as the 1960s and 1970s, there were many residents admitted to Orillia who "should not have been there," and that the motive for their admission was as much about their connection to family support services as it was a blurry diagnosis of intellectual disability.

As Radford and Park (1993) discuss, the growth of urban areas throughout the twentieth century also played a role in class-based admissions to institutions. Members of the social and political elite in Toronto, the largest urban centre close to Orillia, applied pressure on the Ontario government to promote segregation for feebleminded women of childbearing age, including "compulsory mental tests for immigrants, and stricter marriage laws" (384). Their calls were heeded; bowing to pressure, the Ontario government empowered physicians in 1919 to commit feebleminded women to Orillia. Urban centres also meant access to more highly developed and populated school systems, where education officials such as Helen MacMurchy enthusiastically identified dozens of schoolchildren for institutional placement. Further, urban settings may have created labour-related limitations on people with intellectual disabilities. While there is no evidence that feebleminded individuals in rural locations fared any better than their urban counterparts, it is possible that opportunities for inclusion were more numerous in rural areas due to family farms and smaller-sized, family-run businesses, and disabled people's contribution may have prevented or delayed institutional admission.

Economic factors influencing decisions to admit individuals have not been limited to those at the lower end of the scale. At the end of the Second World War, when government intervention enabled an expansion and strengthening of the middle class (Guest 1997), concerns about status within families of a higher economic standing began to play a role in decisions regarding family members with intellectual disabilities. As some of the sibling participants attest in the second half of this book, and as will be addressed in chapter 3, for some families, the birth of a disabled child, with attendant needs and costs, might have been perceived as a barrier to the attainment of a higher socio-economic status, now possible for the first time. The social embarrassment surrounding the birth of a disabled child, as well as the inevitable lifestyle adjustments this entailed, contributed to some middle-upper-class families' decisions to place their child into long-term custodial care. Further, by the middle of the twentieth century, eugenic fears were subsiding (McLaren 1990), and the public began to acknowledge other ways of accounting for the existence of feebleminded-ness as opposed to a reliance on outdated theories of genetic inheritance. Wealthy and established families, particularly in the United States, began to publicly reveal stories of feeblemindedness within their families (Carey 2009).[5] These testimonies concerning the existence of disability in families once considered exempt introduced new interpretations to the possibility of feeblemindedness and to the appropriateness of institutional care. As per most explanations concerning people's admissions to institutions, the reasoning provided for these decisions is complex. In some of the public accounts of the existence of disability in the family, institutionalization was framed as the location where the person would receive the best and most complete care, and thus institutionalization was considered the most loving response. However, as siblings suggest, these motivations were complicated by personal and family goals.

Economic differences between families also had bearing on how admissions occurred. People of lower status were historically sent to institutions through official channels and with little input into the decision, either through government warrant or through medical certification (Radford and Park 1993; Strong-Boag 2007). Admissions of individuals from higher-class families were usually made of their own volition (albeit often pressured through the influence of medical professionals and other persons of authority), and frequently by influencing local Members of Provincial Parliament (Simmons 1982). Thus, decisions concerning whether or not a family member would be admitted have historically been closely and complexly related to a family's socio-economic status and position in the community, which were, in turn, influenced by other factors such as race, including Indigeneity, and gender. As survivors' accounts will make clear, the reasons they were institutionalized varied; those who understood that their family had little to do with the decision were also those who recounted their families' involvement with social welfare agencies.

Gender

As introduced above, gender has historically been a significant factor in increases in the institutional population, particularly during the eugenic period in the first three decades of the twentieth century. Unfounded fears that feebleminded women of childbearing age threatened to pollute the general population due to higher rates of pregnancy and promiscuity led to Ontario government provisions which facilitated their detention (McLaren 1990; Radford and Park 1993). Because Ontario and Quebec presented stronger opposition to official sterilization laws than the Western provinces, primarily for religious reasons (McLaren 1990),[6] institutions became the tool of choice to limit women's potential reproduction. Yet the motivations for women's segregation, although couched in progressive medical terminology that emphasized personal and national well-being, can more accurately be seen as "middle class reformers' distaste for and condemnation of those whose sexual mores were different than their own" (Simmons 1982, 70). The disapproval directed at feebleminded women and their presumed sexual practices was a key directive in the call for increased custodial care. The impact that eugenic thinking and policy has had on women designated feebleminded, often through assessments based on subjective moralistic assumptions, cannot be overstated.

Other ways in which "gender figures into this story" (Carlson 2010, 64) can be seen in regard to assumptions made concerning women's roles and abilities. In subsequent chapters, we shall see that participants' reflections indicate that although gender continued to play a role in institutionalization, parameters around these presumptions shifted from eugenic concerns to ones of maternal inadequacy. While earlier guidelines frequently recommended single women's admissions due to fears of their reproduction, half a century later, concerns focused on the incompetence of mothers who were not considered 'up to the task' of raising a child with a disability. Although the final outcome, institutionalization, remained constant through different periods, as did gender as a contributing factor, the ways in which these constituted and informed each other shifted, and changed the ways in which institutionalization was approached and decided upon.

Race

Imbricated with all of the above factors, race has been a significant yet complicated feature of institutionalization patterns over the past two centuries. Attempts to disentangle racial factors from others reveal multiple possibilities, made more complicated in some instances by absence. First, akin to the eugenic practice of conflating feeblemindedness with poverty and low social status, in the early decades of the twentieth century in Canada, people of non-European origin (Thobani 2007), as well as those from eastern and southern regions of Europe (McLaren 1990), were more likely to encounter difficulties immigrating to Canada (Chadha 2008) and to be considered to require institutionalization upon arrival. Menzies (1998, 147) describes how the "burgeoning asylum system in B.C., as elsewhere, provided ... an ideal institutional site for the identification, containment and removal of these [dangerous] populations." However, historical records, including photographs, suggest that in Ontario, the majority of those admitted to institutions for the intellectually disabled were of European descent and, as discussed above, were admitted with varying degrees of socio-economic status and under varying degrees of duress.

The Eurocentric nature of the population in institutions for the intellectually disabled reveals two significant absences. The first is not really an absence, but is rather the parallel population of Indigenous children, who were sent to their own, all-encompassing sites of incarceration in Indian residential schools. While the two systems share some features, such as their "neat mapping" (Chapman 2014) one onto the other in terms of timing and their histories of abuse and oppression, they are distinct in others, as, for example, in terms of their mandates (the annihilation of Indigenous culture in residential schools; the segregation of the feebleminded in institutions) and reach (the grasp after the entire population of Indigenous children; the separation of the feebleminded from those considered normal). That attention to the overlap between these two sites of incarceration, in addition to their racialized distinctions, has only been paid within the last decade or so of scholarship is indicative of the concerned governments' success at keeping these two locations firmly separated from each other in both policy and the public imagination.

A further absence warranting some attention concerns the lack of non-European children in institutions for the feebleminded. While Chupik and Wright (2006) have uncovered ways in which Ontario families attempted to care for their disabled children at home in the early part of the twentieth century, thus providing a window into the care that existed outside of institutions, little has been written to date on the experiences of African-Canadian families, nor those of other ethnic origins who had a child with an intellectual disability. Uncovering convergent and divergent stories would be a worthwhile endeavour in the project of articulating the full history of people with intellectual disabilities and their families in Canada.

The above discussion provides some indication of interrelated factors which contributed to admissions to Ontario institutions for the feebleminded. Documents from the Ontario Archives suggest that increasing rates of identification through welfare services, combined with the government's ongoing lack of interest in initiating alternatives and the felt pressure for families to institutionalize, resulted in demand exceeding supply, a situation which remained in place for the duration of Ontario's institutional history (Radford and Park 1993). While consistent overcrowding could have provided an impetus for the exploration of alternatives, government reluctance to shift from a conservative, medical ideology with few community resources meant that institutionalization remained one of the few options for thousands of families seeking support.

Orillia: The Cornerstone
of Ontario's Institutional History

From its origins, the Orillia asylum became the template for long-term institutionalization in Canada. From a geo-historical and political perspective, Orillia was the "centrepiece of Ontario's mental retardation policy" (Simmons 1982, 131) and was "the central point from which mental handicap praxis ... diffused throughout Canada" (Radford and Park 1993, 377). An analysis of the historical and political reasons for the development of the Orillia asylum and its administrative relationship with subsequent institutions contributes to a clear understanding of the trajectory and longevity of institutions in Ontario and in Canada.

Simmons's (1982) detailed historical record notes that within one year of its opening in 1876, the Orillia asylum reached its maximum capacity. Despite additions in subsequent decades, the space available never kept pace with demand (30); throughout Orillia's history, there were long lists of people "clamouring for admission" (148–9), and this remained a constant feature until deinstitutionalization took hold in the 1980s and 1990s. Rates of admission fluctuated, however. Radford and Park (1993) note that the numbers of new admissions increased when new buildings were completed (for example, in 1891), and that increased early detection programs in Ontario schools led to an increase in the numbers of admissions of people under twenty years old. Moreover, people admitted via government-issued warrant were almost never released from the asylum, which contributed to the increasingly high numbers of residents. Due in large part to the government's lack of direct policy objectives towards people with intellectual disabilities, little was done to alleviate the overcrowded and poor conditions at Orillia, and almost no consideration was given to the possibility of providing alternate avenues of support so that individuals could remain at home with their families. Instead, the Ontario government chose to repair the existing structure, and eventually, when the problem of crowding threatened to overwhelm Orillia's capacity, to build more institutions.

The development of other institutions in the province, therefore, was primarily a response to Orillia's inability to house the large numbers of people whose guardians, state or family, were appealing for their admission. In the decades following World War II, in spite of the growing strength of the deinstitutionalization movement and an emerging discourse around the link between forced incarceration and the abuse of human rights, the

Ontario government continued to respond to the needs of people with intellectual disabilities through the construction of more institutions. More than a dozen smaller institutions were built throughout the 1960s and 1970s, and two massive institutions, Smiths Falls and Cedar Springs, were opened in 1951 and 1961 respectively, all on the outskirts of small towns, and all with the goal of acting as 'satellites' (Radford and Park 2003) to alleviate the constant pressure on Orillia to admit more residents.[7]

Although built almost one century after Orillia, the two large institutions were built with the same intention that had directed Orillia's original construction: to house large numbers of people in an isolated and custodial setting with no explicit plan towards their release or re-integration into the community. Smiths Falls and Cedar Springs were strategically located – one in the northeast corner of the province, the other in the southwest – thus, together with Orillia, creating a broad triangle that covered the most densely populated portion of the province. Their placement suggests an intention to cover as large an area as possible and to maximize the number of 'beds' available to people with intellectual disabilities in the province. Policy decisions flowed from Orillia's historical position: politicians were forced to make decisions when Orillia became overcrowded, and, despite increasing pressure from parent and advocacy groups in the latter half of the twentieth century to direct more funding towards community services, the government reacted by building more institutions with similar geographic and philosophical criteria. An additional point of interest is that many of these satellite institutions were established in former army bases and abandoned 'asylums for the insane' that had come under the control of the Ministry of Health. In their attempts to determine a solution for the 'problem' of the intellectually disabled, subsequent Ontario governments allowed Orillia to remain a template of intervention, and chose former sites of incarceration to perpetuate the custodial model.

Of equal importance is the place that Huronia occupied in the political and public imagination for over 150 years. Perhaps due to its status as the oldest and, at its closure, the longest-running institution for people with intellectual disabilities in Canada,[8] Huronia held a somewhat hidden and horrible mystique in the Ontario public's limited knowledge of institutions. While residents of all Ontario institutions have recounted experiences of oppression and abuse, it is interesting to note that the parents of some of the residents who were housed at facilities other than Huronia had the impression that Huronia was by far the worst of them. Indeed, one father, describing his son's admission to Cedar Springs near Chatham, claimed that although he was disheartened that long-term institutionalization seemed to be the only recourse for his son, he was also relieved that his son was not at Orillia. In his words, "when we got to the parts of Orillia they didn't want you to see, it was absolutely disgusting ... but he wasn't in Orillia ... if they'd said Orillia, I'd have said no." It is also noteworthy that the class-action lawsuit launched against the Ontario government in 2010 for abuses suffered by institutional survivors was initiated by two former Huronia residents. Thus, while Huronia was the template for the continuation of an oppressive, custodial model, it was also the site from which survivors first recounted their experiences of abuse in the road to gain recognition and compensation from the government, marking the beginning of a new chapter of self-advocacy in the post-institutionalization era.

Ontario's Institutions and the Economy of Self-Sustainment

In the work that has surrounded the recent class-action proceedings against the Ontario government, survivors have recounted horrific stories of oppression and abuse from their time spent behind institutional walls. Not least of these are their accounts of mandatory labour, which, although often framed under the auspices of therapy and rehabilitation, was frequently performed under terrible circumstances, and paradoxically contributed to their own incarceration. Working in the stores department and the laundry, keeping watch over younger or more disabled residents, institutional residents had no choice but to participate in the institutions' maintenance, a practice typical of the paradoxical relationship between one's confinement and one's contribution to it (Goffman 1961). Reaume (2000) has provided accounts of the work required of inmates in Ontario's institutions for people deemed mad, exposing the province's long history of forced labour within publicly funded facilities.

The work of institutional residents can be considered a microcosm of the larger template of the strengthening capitalist economy in Ontario and in other parts of Canada in the late nineteenth and early twentieth centuries. As discussed in the foregoing chapter, institutions served a particular purpose in capitalism's development from the mid-nineteenth century onwards. They provided a 'safe,' segregated site for those considered unable to contribute to a competitive, market-based economy, as capitalism's success depends on the active participation of able workers who can maintain the production/consumption continuum. Institutions provided a convenient site in which to house less productive individuals who, by their dependencies, could not be relied upon to provide the labour required to make profit possible.

Second, concomitant with the strengthening of capitalism, well-intentioned reformists in the mid-1800s initially saw segregated institutions as a way to provide asylum to feebleminded people from the dangers of a modernizing society, and as a site within which inmates could be habilitated or trained to undertake some kind of meaningful and appropriate work. It is from this second impetus for segregated facilities that theories of the benefits of institutional labour took root. As discussed in chapter 1, the work of the French expatriate Édouard Séguin in the mid-nineteenth-century United States is one example of the use of labour as a means of habilitation. Séguin's therapeutic interventions strove, through guided work, to provide inmates with productive skills and the capacity to return to their home communities. However, the good intentions espoused by administrators of the first institutions in the northeastern United States were short-lived. Rising admission rates, a gradual albeit reluctant acknowledgment that feeblemindedness was not as simple as a lack of moral fortitude,[9] and an unwillingness on the part of families to welcome their disabled family members back into their home communities were all impetuses for the eventual degeneration from an educative, curative model to an incarcerative one.[10]

The brief duration of Séguin's rehabilitative measures notwithstanding, they suggest at least some attempt at constructive intervention for the 'feebleminded' persons under institutional care in the United States. Institutions in Ontario, however, did not demonstrate a progressive mandate to the same degree. This could be due in part to the later establishment of institutions in Ontario, when reformist, rehabilitative models had already degenerated into primarily custodial models characterized by concern for protection of the public and segregation of the feebleminded. According to Simmons (1982), from the beginning, the Ontario government followed the asylum, and later the custodial model, and "never looked kindly on establishing a training school" (26), thus negating any attempt at educative intervention. In addition, Simmons suggests that public-sector funding of Ontario institutions meant that government priorities lay not in the well-being of institutional residents but in keeping institutional costs as low as possible. This tie to the public purse and the overriding concern to keep public costs at a minimum has always shaped policy concerning long-term institutions in Ontario and has hampered steps to ensure the well-being of those housed within.

The self-sustaining facility fits well under this mandate. By the turn of the twentieth century, institutions in Ontario were envisioned as sites of economic self-sustainment. A.H. Beaton and J.P. Downey, the two superintendents at Orillia during this era (from 1877–1910 and 1910–26, respectively),[11] realized that a well-run institution could, with a large pool of capable inmates, feed and clothe itself. Beaton considered Orillia a 'closed system' and strove to minimize and even eliminate the number of discharges from the institution in order to maintain a reliable and essentially imprisoned workforce. Downey's central preoccupation "seemed to be less whether prospective inmates were really mentally retarded and more whether or not they were good workers" (Simmons 1982, 104). Downey even imagined a 'corporate system' whereby various institutions in the province could support each other by meeting each other's material needs around such items as clothing, shoes, and produce, thus eliminating the need to barter with, and indeed to communicate with, the broader community. The "goal of efficiency became paramount" (83) and super-intendents prided themselves on their ability to maintain the institution as cheaply as possible. In the case of Orillia, per-patient rates were so minimal that they "[sank] to among the lowest in the world" (32). For the province's inspector of facilities at the time, John Langmuir, this was a point of pride, and the trend established a reputation for administrative efficiency that subsequent administrators sought to uphold.

Outward appearances of productivity gave the impression of well-run, organized establishments that provided meaningful employment to hundreds of individuals. This contributed to Orillia's decades-long reputation of being able to function with less money than all other institutions, including those in the northeastern United States (Radford and Park 1993; Simmons 1982). Administrators considered this an accomplishment, and felt it provided justification within political circles for the Orillia asylum's continued use. This also meant there was no great hurry to implement policy that would enhance opportunities for people with intellectual disabilities outside of institutional, custodial care. Orillia's economic efficiency, due to the use of inmate labour and to the rhetoric of the need for economic judiciousness, was one of the contributing factors to the provincial government's commitment to keep it open into the twenty-first century.

The Long Road to Deinstitutionalization

The road towards institutional closure in Ontario was a decades-long and arduous process, beginning in the late 1920s with an unsuccessful attempt at deinstitutionalization by Orillia superintendent B.T. McGhie, and culminating in Orillia's closure, the last Ontario institution to do so, in 2009. The process was marked by several years of debate between different groups of parents and advocates who claimed identical ideologies as their source of inspiration – a human rights perspective that included respect for their children's overall well-being – yet advocated for different outcomes.

The human rights perspective gained momentum in the years following World War II, a period characterized by concerns for social reform and by a renewed hope for global order within which negotiated and long-lasting peace might be realized after decades of uncertainty (Egerton 2004; Guest 1997). People who had survived the horrors of the war and had experienced significant personal loss were determined that notions of citizenship, essential to the establishment of a just and peaceful global body politic, must be expanded to include social and political rights for all persons, including people with disabilities and others who had historically been marginalized (Guest 1997; Simmons 1982).

The human rights approach to addressing the well-being of people with disabilities was manifested in different ways throughout this period. Some parents and advocacy groups drew on this framework by calling for institutional closure, an appeal grounded in the belief that all persons have the right to live at home with the supports necessary to participate meaningfully in the community around them. Importantly, parents who pushed for deinstitutionalization included both those who had resisted the pressure to institutionalize and had kept their child at home (usually drawing from the perspective that this was morally irreconcilable) and those who had reluctantly succumbed to that pressure (and thus were drawing from their family's lived experience). As one of the key informants interviewed for this study suggested, not all of the parents who had institutionalized their child wanted the facilities to remain open; their advocacy was based on the direct experience of institutionalizing a child and acknowledging the harm this had caused. Parents who had chosen not to institutionalize drew their assertions, rather, from the conviction that institutionalization was morally reprehensible in the first place.

A second group of parents, still drawing from a human rights frame-work, had institutionalized their children and continued to advocate for institutions to remain open in spite of the growing momentum towards their closure. The perspective from this group of parents was that institu-tionalization remained the best option for families and that efforts should focus on the facilities' improvement. This group had focused their ener-gies for decades, often through the auspices of local Associations for the Mentally Retarded, on pressuring the provincial government to address concerns regarding overcrowding, understaffing, and underfunding, rather than advocating that these funds be directed to community alternatives. Thus, although different groups of parents claimed a human rights per-spective as their source of inspiration, their interventions had varying goals and outcomes, a trend not uncommon in the history of the discourse of rights concerning people with intellectual disabilities (Carey 2009).

The distinctions between different groups of parents are important, as it indicates where parents located the 'problem' of disability. For those parents who saw disability as a problem, institutionalization was a reasonable solution and efforts to improve conditions at the facilities were a worthwhile endeavour. As one sibling participant in this study noted, the biggest source of his mother's disappointment was not his brother's institutionalization per se, despite any feelings of regret she might have had about placing him there, but that he had been born with a disability in the first place. Contrarily, for other families, the locus of the problem was not the disability but the decision to institutionalize and the resultant years of awkward separation and later struggles to deal with the emotional aftermath. These distinctions reveal the complexity underlying parents' motivations to institutionalize. Divisions between parents cannot be understood as a simple distinction between those who chose to institutionalize and those who did not; within these groups are multiple motivations, underscored by political, economic, emotional, and relational meanings.

Despite differences within parent groups regarding where efforts were best directed, the movement towards institutional closure grad-ually increased in strength and public awareness. A newspaper article by journalist Pierre Berton in 1960,[12] in which he described the "despairing conditions" at Huronia under which thousands of individuals lived and in which he called the public and the government to account, as well as two tragic incidents out of the Rideau Regional Centre in 1971 – one, a suicide by a resident on a work placement out of the Centre, and the other, a case of severe frostbite suffered by a man who was attempting to leave his fostered community placement – provided additional support to the deinstitutionalization movement. Following the incidents in Smiths Falls, Walter Williston was commissioned by the provincial government to table a report on the care and supervision of people with intellectual disabilities in Ontario. Williston's 1971 report recommended that "large hospital institutions for the mentally retarded be phased down as quickly as possible" (65) and that community-based family services be developed with clear directives and policy objectives (96).

Despite these windows into conditions at institutions and Williston's formal appeal to the government to immediately address the shortcomings of the institutional system, it was another thirty-eight years before the last institution closed its doors. This intransigently slow pace can be explained, at least in part, by the conservative ideology and its related economic priorities which dominated the political landscape in Ontario throughout the twentieth century.

Conservative parties governed Ontario for most of the twentieth century. Although the name of the party shifted during this time (from 'Conservative' to 'Progressive Conservative' in 1942, and then back again to 'Conservative' in 2003), it remained a right-leaning party throughout its tenure, and this had significant implications on the response to people with intellectual disabilities in the province. First, the province (as well as Canada, historically) has always adhered to a residual social welfare philosophy, which dictates that social welfare institutions provide resources only when individual sources of support, such as the family, are no longer able to sustain that role (Esping-Andersen 1990). Conservative governments in Ontario have consistently embraced the notion that the province has a limited obligation to provide care (Simmons 1982, 169) and that a lower level of service provision in public institutions encourages families to establish and provide necessary supports from their own initiative. This ideology also encourages, or at least does not discourage, a reliance on charities as a way for families to secure the support they need; charities, by providing care where the public purse does not, paradoxically provide a rationale for governments whose policies advocate minimal and individualized income support (Harvey 2005). Second, a conservative, residual ideology aligns itself with traditional disciplines such as medicine and education and is reluctant to invest in any services considered to have a social welfare function (Simmons 1982, 171). During the institutionaliz-ation years, increases in funding to community services for people with disabilities did not align with their main philosophical tenets and presented a role with which they were not "prepared to engage" (ibid.). For these reasons, successive conservative governments in Ontario were unwilling to alter their approach to services for people with intellectual disabilities for much of the twentieth century.

Moreover, there are political reasons for the government's long devotion to the institutional model. Records indicate that one of the principal meth-ods of admission for many persons with disabilities was through pressure to one's local Member of Provincial Parliament (MPP) (Simmons 1982, 165). MPPs seeking re-election were happy to oblige admissions requests when-ever possible as a way to establish favour with their constituents; the lowering of the volume of requests, moreover, gave opposition members less fodder to challenge the governing party in its intransigence regarding the development of policy or the provision of more institutional space (162). The locations of institutions were also political in nature, as they were closely tied to the economic fortunes or misfortunes of those geographic areas. Governing conservative parties knew that their largest constituent base lived in rural areas (173); hence, to locate institutions in rural sites or small towns ensured an economic boom in those areas as well as favour-able popular opinion and future political support. Further, by employing hundreds of local people as staff, institutions frequently became central economic mainstays of the communities in which they were located, and much of the opposition to institutional closure emanated from workers who feared unemployment.

For these reasons, the addition of more institutional spaces for people with intellectual disabilities remained a priority for successive conservative governments, and expansion continued throughout the 1960s and into the 1970s. That this growth continued in spite of growing pressure for the government to close down the large institutions and to provide more support for community care gave rise to a growing tension in disability policy in Ontario. This tension encountered a significant shift, however, when the jurisdiction for services for people with intellectual disabilities was transferred from the Ministry of Health to the newly formed Ministry of Community and Social Services in 1974. This transfer of care brought in a new era for people with intellectual disabilities: with a lessening of the authority of the medical profession, an influx of expertise from other professional disciplines, and an increasing awareness of the inherent right of all people to live where they choose, the prerequisites for institutional closure were in place.

The Postwar Years and the Setting of This Study

A century-and-a-half tradition of institutionalization in Ontario, an entrenched conservative political ideology, and increasing momentum towards deinstitutionalization through parent and advocacy groups was the context within which parents were making decisions about whether or not to institutionalize their disabled children in the latter decades of the twentieth century. The postwar cohort – those children born after the Second World War – comprises the survivors who were interviewed for this study, as they are the last group who experienced institutionalization at its fullest capacity, before sufficient political and financial support allowed community and home living to become a more viable option for families.

Yet the decision to institutionalize or to keep one's child at home was not a simple one. Competing ideologies around what was 'best' for the child were played out both publicly, in political, medical, and education circles, and within the intimacy of family homes. While parents increasingly began to choose to keep their children at home and developments began to indicate more strongly the possibility of institutional closure, there remained a sizeable number of parents who decided to institutionalize throughout the latter part of the 1900s. The political, social, and cultural pressures which contributed to families' decisions to institutionalize are the focus of the next chapter.

Choosing to Institutionalize: Politics, Families, and the Pressures of Cold War Conformity

The decades immediately following World War II marked the beginning of an era of renewed optimism and respect for human rights and a notable expansion of the welfare state in Canada. Calls for civic and social rights for all people characterized the strengthening of nascent social-political movements, such as the civil rights movement and second-wave feminism. These developments were contemporaneous, however, with growing ideological and militaristic tensions at the international level, known as the Cold War, which in turn influenced socio-economic and political conditions on domestic fronts. Although the opposing ideologies that characterized this era were played out on the global stage, they carried significant cultural weight and were felt at domestic and local levels. Thus, while this chapter addresses some of the broad ideological influences that marked the postwar era more generally, it also attempts to draw connections between those influences and the conditions of postwar domestic Canadian life, including the manifestation of power and decision-making in the family home. In particular, it examines how ideology influenced the treatment of marginalized populations in Canada during this time, including people with intellectual disabilities. This discussion lends some insight to the family narratives in subsequent chapters, as it provides the context within which post–World War II Canadian families were living.

This chapter consists of two parts. The first provides historical background on the Cold War years in Canada and discusses four Cold War phenomena – the 'containment' of external threats, conformity to normative standards, the re-emergence of traditional family and gender roles, and the strengthening of professional expertise – and their discursive and material connections to practices of exclusion, including institutionalization. This discussion includes an examination of Cold War discourses of fear and anxiety concerning the 'Other,' and their frequently devastating impact on marginalized people in Canada.

In the second part of the chapter, I explore this period in Canada's institutional history by interrogating its "historical ontology" (Foucault 1994, 316), or "the ways in which the possibilities for choice, and for being, arise in history" (Hacking 2002, 23). Thus, while this chapter explores the practical and discursive conditions that would have influenced parents to send their child to an institution, thus contributing to a more complete and nuanced understanding of motives and practices, it also opens up the possibility to mine a vein of enquiry which "explores the ways that certain kinds of questions and forms of discourse were made possible, and others discounted or excluded" (Carlson 2010, 17). This chapter thus addresses the conditions which allowed institutionalization to be sustained as a viable option in the public imagination, and explores the limits of possibility as understood by families of this era.

Social and Political Context

The approximately forty-year span following the Second World War was marked by the heated political and rhetorical contest of wills between the United States and the Soviet Union, each representing a distinct form of imperialism exemplified by capitalism and communism respectively. A principal characterization of this era is each superpower's attempt to achieve international dominance, particularly through space exploration and colonization, and through the possession and threatened use of a nuclear arsenal.

While the Cold War is generally understood as the military and political tension between the United States and the Soviet Union (Cavell 2004; May 2008; Whitaker 2004), the implications of the Cold War in terms of domestic and foreign policy were also felt in Canada (Whitaker and Marcuse 1994). Despite political movement to work towards a Canadian Bill of Rights, following the example of the Universal Declaration of Human Rights in 1948, consecutive postwar Canadian governments placed a "priority on fighting communism rather than advancing human rights" (Egerton 2004, 451). Prioritization of the Cold War within Canadian politics (Whitaker 2004) left little room for resistance to the rhetoric of external threat and the need for military preparedness. Notwithstanding pockets of anti-war resistance which began to demonstrate their position during this time period and continued to do so throughout the politically charged 1960s and 1970s, the general sentiment throughout the population reflected the government's priority to contain the perceived risk of the spread of communism (Brookfield 2012; Roberts 1989).

Scholars suggest, furthermore, that "Canada's Cold War was not simply an extension of the one waged in the United States," but that animosities "had a particular cultural dimension because [they] raised issues of national self-representation" (Cavell 2004, 5), and were *struggles for control of the symbols of legitimacy in Canadian society*" (Whitaker and Marcuse 1994, 24, original emphasis). Moreover, this time period was characterized by a "broad process of 'Othering'" (Cavell 2004, 4) marked by discriminatory practices that were already long-established in Canadian socio-political circles, but that became notably more pronounced during the Cold War. The Cold War, therefore, cannot be reduced to an ongoing tension between two superpowers (Whitaker 2004), but should be regarded as a time during which social and political discourse had significant influence on public and domestic life in areas beyond those powers' borders, including Canada.

In the sections that follow, I address four key ideological notions and practices and discuss their relationship to the phenomenon of sustained institutionalization practices in the years following World War II. These include 'containment' (Kennan 2012), considered the most effective tool to halt the spread of communism and its threat to the consumer-based, idealized lifestyle towards which postwar North Americans were encouraged to aspire (Brookfield 2012; May 2008; Runté and Mills 2006); conformity to normative standards, including the silencing and oppression of unseen yet ubiquitous enemies of the state (Cavell 2004) and the responsibility of citizens to contain this 'Other' linguistically and materially (Iacovetta 2004; Kinsman 2004; May 2008; Whitaker 2004; Whitaker and Marcuse 1994); the re-emergence of traditional constructions of gender, work, sexuality, and the family, which served particular social and political purposes; and the strengthening of the professional class and its role in the development of "a strong and flourishing nation" (Brookfield 2012, 53–4).

Threat of the Other and the Discourse of "Containment"

Containment, a term first coined by American diplomat George Kennan (2012 [1951]) in the late 1940s, refers to policies of restraint against the threat of Soviet expansion following the Second World War. A distinguishing feature of the Cold War, its principal ideological thrust was the containment of communism without resorting to either appeasement or military intervention – a 'middle ground' of diplomatic relations that would allow the United States to maintain control without increasing vulnerability in a time of international fragility. While diplomatic in nature, containment policies did not exclude strategies of military preparedness and discourses of self-protection against an unseen enemy. Throughout the Cold War, preoccupations with bringing foreign influences under control and preventing the spread of communism were also played out domestically through the establishment of protective social and cultural enclaves. Containment thus came to include the political and rhetorical support of cultural sites such as the suburban home and nuclear family within which citizens could find safety, security, and protection in a world considered imminently dangerous (May 2008).

Potential threats to domestic and political stability were not limited to foreign sources, however, and the menaces feared by political leaders included those perceived to emanate from within (Cavell 2004; Kinsman 2004; Whitaker and Marcuse 1994). Thus, while containment focused primarily on external factors, it came to include the official response to problematic 'Others' in the domestic sphere who were considered risks to the hegemony of capitalism and to the realization of an idyllic postwar future (Brookfield 2012; May 2008). The rise of internal turbulence, such as racial and civil unrest, the growing women's movement, and new configurations of the traditional family were as much cause for alarm for decision-makers as the risk of the spread of communism (May 2008). Nascent ideological movements, including the peace movement, were interpreted as threats to both the militaristic patriotism of post–World War II North America and the moral order of the modern family (Iacovetta 2006), and were opposed by political rhetoric which encouraged the upholding of traditional nationalistic, familial, and gender norms.

Canadian scholars suggest that government responses to these ideological and cultural concerns were the principal manifestation of the Cold War in Canada. For example, while subversive individuals and groups could all be considered suspect in the government's quest for foreign and domestic security, the harassment levelled at the gay community was particularly oppressive. Kinsman (2004) notes that the interrogation and arrest of thousands of gay men by the Royal Canadian Mounted Police (RCMP) in the 1960s is indicative of an overriding culture of surveillance and discipline aimed at those deemed a threat to Canada's national security (109). In an example of bizarre and tenuous logic, discrimination levelled at gay men and women during the 1950s and 1960s was considered justified in order to wean out of government service those who possessed a "moral or 'character' weakness ... these 'weaknesses' were defined as an inability to perform oneself as 'normal.' Because queers were defined as being outside 'normality,' they were seen as having something to hide, and [were] therefore subject to blackmail" by communist infiltrators (Kinsman 2004, 117).

This rationalized suppression of queerness, considered acceptable by many due to its moral undertones, facilitated a culture of discrimination against other marginalized groups. As Gentile (2000, 132) notes, "the notion of 'deviance' ... was a way to identify not only gays and lesbians, but also women [and other marginalized groups] who resisted or challenged the gender norms and social order prescribed by political and medical experts." While the queer community was the face, albeit hidden, of rationalized discrimination in light of the needs of the state, a generalized culture of 'Othering' became acceptable in the social and political milieu. In addition, Cavell (2004, 4) notes that while this historical period was marked by fears of the enemy within and without, processes of 'othering' were already "deeply rooted in the historical substrata of the nation," and the Cold War provided a convenient framework for the naming and surveillance of those considered different, practices already engrained within the Canadian political tradition (Kinsman 2004). Thus, while containment in the United States was the "overarching principle ... the key to security" (May 2008, 16) against the threat of communism, in Canada, the culture of containment could more accurately be described as "a culture of regulation" (Kinsman, as cited in Cavell 2004, 13).

These concerns were acted out in various ways. While the public face of the Canadian government's priorities concerned its position in the Cold War (Whitaker 2004), including the need to establish markers of "national self-representation" in contrast to its strong southerly neighbour (Cavell 2004, 7), there were parallel on-the-ground disciplinary measures, invisible to most, which acted as impediments to the establishment of a more inclusive and just society. As Panitch (2008) notes in her documentation of the work of activist mothers during this time period, any work initiated by parents in attempts to better the situation for their disabled sons and daughters was considered counter-cultural and, at times, troublesome. In general, public acceptance of and work devoted towards the inclusion of people with disabilities was under-prioritized and unrecognized. Government rhetoric that democracy and a long-desired lifestyle were threatened justified the use of control and regulation to monitor counter-cultural movements and gave precedence to the militarization of Canadian culture, lessening the support available for social initiatives.

Norms: Adaptation versus Resistance

Reification of the enemy (Kinsman 2004, 113) and the political priority to contain communism justified the identification and surveillance of people considered risks to national security. Those who questioned political decisions were considered unpatriotic and potential communist sympathizers, and deviance became suspect in the larger nationalist project of protectionism and preparedness. Ironically, 'peace' became a "contentious term," as it denoted action directed against government policy, and was "considered by many Canadians to be a concept more in line with communism than democracy ... to speak openly about peace was subversive" (Brookfield 2012, 76). Adherence to the status quo implied patriotism, while challenge, such as agitating for a reduction in violence-preparedness (ibid.), marked one as seditious, a trouble-maker (Whitaker and Marcuse 1994). Accordingly, the acceptable civic response during this era was acquiescence, not resistance (Roberts 1989; Runté and Mills 2006), and the general tenor of postwar life was distinctly "apolitical" (May 2008, 17). Social critique was not encouraged, particularly from marginalized groups such as women, who had much to gain from social change, yet instead played significant, if unwilling, roles in the maintenance of the Cold War ethos.

Although rooted in the militaristic milieu of post–World War II patriotism, the culture of conformity expanded into mainstream Canadian culture and consolidated the hegemony of the white, able, middle-class Canadian family (Gleason 1999a, 1999b). This era was witness to an explosion of data sets and intellectual and physiological standards to which children should be matched, and it became part of parents' obligations to ensure their children fell as close as possible to the average. Moreover, universalized standards became entrenched within patriotic discourse, as Cold War ideology extended to the kind of children who should be produced and their perceived ability to contribute to nationalist efforts (Helleiner 2001). Public health endeavours launched during this era, while ostensibly promoting reasonable lifestyles of healthy eating and exercise, also made discursive connections between health, capability, and the establishment of a strong postwar body politic (Iacovetta 2004; McPhail 2009). "Strong and able offspring ... [were] an essential ingredient to winning the Cold War" (May 2008, 96), and children who fell outside of the explicitly gendered (male), racialized (white), and ableist norms were "in a much more ambiguous relationship with nation-building" (Helleiner 2001, 150).

Contextualizing the Cold War family within the larger political agenda of conventionality exposes the impasse that some families would have experienced in the event of the birth of a child with a disability. In those situations, "inferiority was written on their bodies ... [and] the body was an inescapable marker from acceptable ... society" (Gleason 1999b, 122). In addition, "mothers were held accountable for the failure of their child to measure up to a normative standard of behaviour and independence" (Panitch 2008, 39). Those mothers who "insisted on their own or their family's respectability" (ibid.) in this milieu laid the groundwork for the parents-led activism and organizing that led to the establishment of associations for intellectually disabled children through the 1960s. Yet resisting the advice of medical and educational professionals and agitating instead for increased community services for children with disabilities would have been a difficult endeavour for many parents. In an era during which norms were aspired towards, deviance was suspect, and people's compliance was a demonstration of national allegiance, challenging expert advice, including the common recommendation to "put the child away," was as much an act of unpatriotic defiance as it was a demonstration of parental protection.

Cold War Families and the Regulation of Gender

Cold War ideology fostered the "symbiotic connection between the culture of the Cold War and the domestic revival" (May 2008, 13), and cultivated the re-emergence of a "conservative family ideology" (Iacovetta 2004, 78). Domestic containment, the nuclear family, and gender hierarchies became "part of the highly charged turf on which moral victories against communism were fought" (Iacovetta 2006, 174). Despite gains by first-wave feminists, including pre–World War II trends of later marriage, fewer children, and women working outside the home to support families hit by the Depression, the immediate postwar years were marked by a distinct reversal: marrying at a young age, having several children, and divisions of labour based on traditional gender lines (Brookfield 2012; May 2008).

North American families turned to conventional and distinctive roles: men worked outside of the home at hierarchically organized jobs, and women were encouraged to stay home as full-time homemakers, caring for children and organizing the running of the household (Iacovetta 2004; McPhail 2009; Runté and Mills 2006).

Marriage and family were central. The family home became a nexus of security and preparedness within the landscape of potential nuclear war and was an antidote to the perceived threat of familial breakdown due to rapid urbanization and modernization (Gleason 1997). With the chaotic uncertainty of no known location wherein this 'war' would be waged (Whitaker 2004), the "home front became the front line" (Brookfield 2012, 51–69), and successive Canadian governments encouraged a generalized preparedness in which family homes were secure enclaves, ready to withstand enemies from within and without (Runté and Mills 2006). Thus, a stable family home and a house "filled with children" (May 2008, 26) had as much to do with establishing a strong and secure state as it did with fuelling the romantic postwar notion of returning war veterans and their sweethearts creating a home together.

The return to traditional domestic arrangements was also part of a broader effort to ensure returning veterans' re-integration into regular civilian life with prescribed and restorative roles (Runté and Mills 2006). Efforts were made to ease men's resumption of positions as responsible and contributing citizens (May 2008, 86) and to restore their sense of masculinity and purpose. Domestic life "focused on the needs of the returning veterans" (ibid., 65) and women were encouraged to return to the home front to make room for their men, and to assume the role of the resilient home-builder and emotional sounding board.

The return to traditional roles and the centrality of the nuclear family exposes three possibilities that might have emerged within the family regarding the care and future of family members with a disability. First, the ideological dependence on traditional institutions such as marriage and family meant great efforts were made to ensure their survival (Iacovetta 2006). Women in particular worked hard to maintain their marriages, for they "had invested a great deal of their personal identities in their domestic roles and were not willing to abandon them" (May 2008, 38). Gendered domestic arrangements played a significant role in how decisions were made (McPhail 2009; Runté and Mills 2006), and scholars suggest that many women were likely to acquiesce within the relationship in order to sustain it (Brookfield 2012; Iacovetta 2006). Acquiescence in normative heterosexual relationships and the power differentials this exposes open up the possibility that the removal of a child with a disability was part of larger processes of marital survival and domestic order. That is, in the context and dynamics of the postwar nuclear family, removing a stressor – in this case, a disabled child – might have taken precedence over attempts to keep her at home, particularly if the family's life was already experiencing relational and domestic fragility (May 2008; Sherman and Coccoza 1984), a point that emerges in the siblings' findings in the next chapter.

Second, the re-emergence of traditional gender roles included assumptions regarding women's competence (or lack thereof) and the extent of their capabilities. Although women's realm was the home, men remained principal decision-makers within the family (Gleason 1997, 1999a, 1999b; May 2008; Thorn 2009). Women's absorption of domestic and childcare responsibilities, as well as cultural opposition to women's work outside the home because of the feared consequences of dysfunctional families and delinquent children (Gleason 1997; Iacovetta 2004; Thorn 2009), contributed to women's absence in the public arena and denied women the full extent of their authority (McPhail 2009; Runté and Mills 2006). Assumptions of incapacity reinforced the notion of women's limitations, particularly in areas considered physically and emotionally taxing. These assumptions, combined with the lack of community supports for children with disabilities and their families in the postwar period, reinforced perceptions that many women were not up to the challenge of raising a child with a disability, unassisted, in the home. The task of raising a child with a disability was considered too large, both physically and emotionally, for the limited abilities of most women. Typical of the generally apolitical milieu of this era, a frequent response to the difficulties women encountered was not to challenge the status quo and push for systemic change that might have alleviated the pressures they faced, nor to provide better opportunities for children with disabilities in the community, but to assume instead that families were better off placing the child outside the home into institutional care. As one of the parents interviewed for this project stated, "The basic reason that he went was that my wife couldn't handle him. And what was she going to do? She's got these three other children, and me, I'm not around that much, and he knew she couldn't handle him."

Third, through the public valorization of large, strong, and able families, parents were under pressure to ensure that non-disabled siblings were not impinged upon by the presumed burdens of a disabled brother or sister (Lobato 1983; Sherman and Coccoza 1984). Narrow, expert-informed parameters for the model family "pathologized those outside the ideal" (Gleason 1999a, 81) and provoked consternation when families did not live up to idealized expectations. Literature from the postwar period that discusses disability within the family concerns itself almost exclusively with the (principally negative) effect of a disabled child on his or her family and siblings, locating the 'problem' in its entirety in the child with the disability (see, for example, Farber 1959, Holt 1958, and Jordan 1961).[2] Moreover, postwar researchers on the family were silent regarding critical and structural reasons for familial challenges, and did not consider potential systemic changes, such as increased community support and funding, that might have improved situations for those affected by disability in some way.

Thus, throughout this period, families, and women in particular, were compelled to adapt to the status quo in terms of domestic and social arrangements, in spite of potential costs in other areas. This inclination towards adaptation explains the emergence of another Cold War phenomenon, the 'expert,' which had significant bearing on familial decisions regarding the care of family members with disabilities.

The Nuclear Family and the Role of the 'Expert'

Amidst fears of familial breakdown and the collapse of traditional values (Brookfield 2012; Gleason 1999a, 1999b; Thorn 2009), experts in professions such as social work, rehabilitation, and special education began to emerge as key players in the task of helping families to cope with emergent postwar issues. As experts secured themselves in the public realm, their expertise began to influence the culture and workings of the family. In alignment with the ideology of the time, most experts intervened using individualized, medically oriented approaches, and did not prioritize the consideration of socio-political factors.

Two phenomena explain professionals' emergence and their strengthening role in the modern Canadian family. First was the assumed link between strong families and a strong nation, and the connected assumption that the stresses of the age meant that families needed assistance in order to attain a reasonable level of normality and resilience. 'Well' marriages meant 'well' children (and vice versa), and the strength of the family imparted strength to the whole country (Brookfield 2012; Gleason 1999a, 1997;

Thorn 2009; May 2008). However, the traditional family was considered at risk due to rapid social change and the possibility of nuclear war. Perceived gaps in families' abilities to withstand these pressures created a space for the expert, willing to impart professional skills to families vulnerable to the threats of the age (Brookfield 2012; Gleason 1997; Thorn 2009). Moreover, while the role of helping professionals was ostensibly to assist families, they also reinforced hegemonic ideals of the white, middle-class, successful, and able Canadian family through the promotion of normative standards of behaviour, cultural practice, and embodiment (Gleason 1999a, 1997; Helleiner 2001).

Further, the relationship between the discourse around raising a 'normal' family in postwar Canada and the expert advice deemed essential to the task must be examined as symbiotic and mutually sustaining. The growth of several 'expert' disciplines during this era, not unlike the emergence of the institution itself, was part of the "social practice that actually [brought] itself into being" (Kinsman 2004, 109). Through the increasing identification and placement of children deemed in need of intervention, whether in special classrooms or segregated institutions, professionals played a role in creating the normative discourse which validated their own existence (Gleason 1997; Thorn 2009).

As professionals' expertise and authority expanded, families increasingly relinquished their internal authority to that of experts (Gleason 1997, 1999a, 1999b), and the pool of children deemed to require medical, educative, and psychological assistance grew wider. In this context, and in particular due to ongoing recommendations by doctors and other experts, long-term institutionalization remained a viable and often preferred option for postwar families with a disabled family member. Despite increasing efforts by many parents to ensure inclusion and services for their children and the work of many dozens of families who chose to keep their children at home, admissions to institutions continued to rise (Radford and Park 1993; Simmons 1982).

Second, a geographic phenomenon emerged which, although not normally considered in discussions concerning institutionalization, also contributed to a growing reliance on experts. The development of sprawling, suburban housing developments, dependent on large tracts of land, extensive road networks, and car ownership, was a significant aspect of Cold War life (Whitaker and Marcuse 1994).[3] The decentralized and expansive nature of suburban developments meant that for the first time in the modern era, extended families and their traditional lines of communication and support were suddenly distanced from each other (Thorn 2009). No longer was the expertise of parents and grandparents readily available to young men and women who were beginning families of their own (Iacovetta 2006; May 2008). Women in particular were affected, as they were isolated from peers and family from whom they might have gained practical and emotional support. Loss of the knowledge that would have been available to previous generations via more intense domestic arrangements, in combination with the figurative and practical distance between families, meant that many families did not have access to informal yet vital networks of support that might have sustained them while raising their children, particularly in light of the minimal community resources available at the time.

Women's absence from forums of public discourse and political critique, and gaps in shared knowledge and practical support, as well as isolating socio-cultural and geographic developments, left significant space in women's and families' lives for the opinions of experts to emerge (Iacovetta 2006; Simmons 1982; Thorn 2009). Indeed, "the reliance on expertise was one of the most striking developments of the postwar years" (May 2008, 30), and the link between adherence to professional opinion and one's moral and patriotic standing was encouraged via discourses of responsible citizenship and the respect and authority that experts commanded in the public arena (Iacovetta 2006; Thobani 2007; Thorn 2009). Moreover, as Trent (1994) and Simmons (1982) have suggested, the proximity with which professionals in the community worked with institutional supervisors and administrators as well as government officials responsible for their funding and oversight would have played a role in continued support for referrals to institutional care.

The trends discussed above suggest that families faced with decision-making regarding the care of children with disabilities had many influences with which to contend. Ongoing admission to institutions during the Cold War era was due not only to the lack of community support and acceptance of people with intellectual disabilities, nor to the hegemonic idealization of the strong, beautiful, and content family. Institutional admissions were also underscored in a very practical way by government policy which consolidated particular elements of Cold War life, including the development of suburban living and the resultant isolation of families and women, and the co-emergent authority of professional opinion and expertise.

Before moving to a more detailed consideration of the impact these factors had on families' decision-making, a distinction between different 'types' of families must be made. During the Cold War years, for families that otherwise fell within the hegemonic ideal of the white, heterosexual middle class, a child with a disability would have thwarted parents' imagined and idealized future, and the family would have had to grapple with the shameful ignominy of caring for a 'retarded' child. Social class and related discourses of public approval and humiliation, in addition to the influence of race as discussed in foregoing chapters, would have had some bearing on the decisions that families made regarding their children with intellectual disabilities. A large proportion of the families who made the decision to admit their children to long-term institutions were white and middle- to upper-class (Radford and Park 1993; Simmons 1982); the postwar upward mobility to which many of these families aspired would have been frustrated by the existence of a less-than-perfect child, a constant reminder of their failure to live up to the postwar ideal.[4] Despite these perceived limitations, in addition to a lack of community resources and support, families in such circumstances would have been able to maintain at least some semblance of choice.

For many families, however, the decision to place a child in an institution was not theirs to make. As Canadian scholars Strong-Boag (2011, 2007), Gleason (1999a, 199b, 1997), Helps (2007), Iacovetta (2006), and Helleiner (2001) have indicated, families from non-favoured demographic groups, especially those of low socio-economic standing, were more likely to be subjected to government surveillance under the auspices of child welfare services, and were more likely to have the decision to place their child in short- or long-term residential care made for them. The broad sweep of "children of adversity" included Indigenous children, placed in their own distinct system of incarceration via residential schools, as well as children from families living under socio-economic or functional duress (Strong-Boag 2007). In these cases, decisions to place children in institutions lay outside most families' control. What is missing from this discussion are accounts of racialized families of non-European descent whose disabled children remained at home; uncovering the decision-making undertaken in these families will add much to current understandings concerning which children ended up in institutions, and why.

Broad Discourse, Narrow Lives

The above discussion examines some of the socio-political conditions that shaped post–World War II Canadian discourse at national and domestic levels. The perceived need for order and preparedness in case of communist expansion and nuclear war justified a culture of regulation and militaristic government mandates, presented with expectations of little public resistance. Anxiety concerning the 'Other,' both real and imagined, encouraged families to ground themselves in the safety of domestic life and traditional gender roles and to rely on professional advice to ensure the well-being and stability of their children.

While broad, these discourses had an impact on people's daily lives, particularly those already marginalized in mainstream Canadian culture. Akin to the treatment of the gay community described above, people with intellectual disabilities and their families were one group who felt the ostracizing effects of a normative, ableist, and classist society. And while the internal decisions that families made might have been considered personal and private, they were, foremost, a reflection of the social conditions and influences that existed at the time.

These were the conditions within which parents attempted to make decisions about their disabled sons and daughters. It is tempting, in retrospect, to judge those parents who chose to send their child away to years of institutional life. Yet this kind of evaluation contributes to its own discursive construction – in this case, that of the 'bad' parent. Rather than participate in that process, by attempting to isolate and define the relative terms of 'good' or 'bad' choices and the characteristics of those who carried them out, my intention, rather, is to critically examine the conditions and practices that led to those decisions, and which prevented the practice of "imagining otherwise."

Thus, I return to the queries posed at the beginning of the chapter, to examine "the ways that certain kinds of questions and forms of discourse were made possible, and others discounted or excluded" (Carlson 2010, 7). That is, what were the historical conditions that allowed the choice of institutionalization to be made? To borrow a Foucauldian line of analysis, what prevented parents from imagining themselves to be other than what they perceived themselves to be? Or to imagine their children to be other than what they perceived them to be? What were "the ways in which the possibilities for choice and for being arose in [this particular time and place of our] history" (Hacking 2002, 23)?

Historical Ontology and the Limits of Imagination

This analysis is assisted by Foucault's (1984) assessment of the coercive nature of power, its existence as a "productive network that runs through the whole social body" (61) as opposed to a repressive tool. In the majority of cases, parents were not legally bound to institutionalize their intellectually disabled children,[5] but many of a higher socio-economic status chose to do so, despite having sufficient means to support their child at home.[6] Under the influence of power's coercive reach, many parents felt compelled to institutionalize without, in Foucault's estimation, an awareness of the persuasions underlying them. These decisions were made, not with attention to the effects of power running through them, but according to the administrative boundaries of what was considered 'best' for child, family, and state. Further, although all the parents in this study noted that they were reassured they were making the best choice, the right choice, the testimonies from some of long years of guilt and depression after the fact indicate that their experience reflected otherwise.

Moreover, it was not only the existence of particular social conditions that gave rise to the impulse to institutionalize, but their intentionality. Fear, conformity, containment of the enemy, and so on were not merely conditions governments felt they had to respond to, but were also tools utilized by governments to allow particular styles of governance to continue. For reasons discussed earlier, most provincial governments did not consider it a priority to introduce changes to the ways in which people with intellectual disabilities were cared for. Institutions were a "convenient" (Radford and Park 1993) way to maintain one aspect of society as the government wished it – efficient and well-organized, with a potentially demanding group out of sight – and it served them well to not introduce the radical changes that closing institutions would have necessitated. Throughout Ontario's long institutional history, government efforts were not directed towards encouraging families to imagine otherwise, but to consider institutionalization as a primary choice for both personal and societal reasons. As this chapter has indicated, the concerns of the postwar era, while touted as the reasons for regulation and control, also supported the government mandate of the continued use of institutions.

Finally, it is important to loop Hacking's (2002) call to examine the ways in which we constitute ourselves back into the larger picture of the circumstances outlined in the earlier sections of this chapter. Questions emerge, not only about the families who decided to institutionalize a child, but about assumed societal practices that contribute to ongoing oppression. That is, at different points in history, how have people been encouraged to 'create' themselves in ways that support larger projects which, although purportedly designed for the 'greater good,' cause destruction in individuals' and families' lives? In what ways do we continue to constitute ourselves such that oppression is sustained? How do governments encourage this kind of self-constitution in order to meet their own ends? And finally, where are sites for challenge and resistance located? While there are no easy answers, Hacking's and Foucault's approaches provide us with the tools to "imagine ourselves to be other than we are" (Carlson 2010, 17). If we examine phenomena such as those outlined in this chapter with the "historico-critical attitude" that Foucault (1994, 316) espouses, then we remain open to the possibilities of imagining other, better futures. By acknowledging the ways in which we constitute ourselves (Hacking 2002, 2), we are compelled to respond to the points of resistance that emerge and to alter the patterns of injustice embedded in the history of people with intellectual disabilities.

Critical analyses, while potentially instructive, do not alter the oppression and abuse that many Canadians suffered during the peak of our institutional history. While it is too late to change the fact that thousands spent decades of their lives in institutions, institutional survivors have themselves taken steps to ensure that "historical conditions of possibility" (Tremain 2002, 33) for ongoing segregation and oppression are interrupted.[7] It is in survivors' own re-constitution of themselves as persons who can live where they desire, without government restraint, that other possibilities can be imagined.

Institutions as Sites and Processes Revisited

The previous chapters have provided an overview of the historical and contextual factors that contributed to the development of institutions as a principal method of intervention with people with intellectual disabilities in the nineteenth and twentieth centuries. From this historical discussion, three themes emerge which allow us to move from an examination of institutions as edifices to a deeper interrogation of their effects in people's lives. First, institutions were sites, material locations that carried a visible and tangible presence in the communities in which they were located. Within these buildings, people were incarcerated against their will, injustices

happened, memories were created. The importance of institutions' phys-
icality has become evident in recent years with the surfacing of competing
claims regarding potential prospects for their ongoing use.[8] While some
community groups have articulated a desire to convert these massive structures into cultural centres or seniors' residences, many survivors strongly
suggest otherwise. While for survivors, the desire to establish and maintain
cemeteries for those who died while under institutional care is essential
in the quest to recognize each life that underwent institutionalization,
many have stated that the buildings must not be used for entertainment
or cultural purposes.[9] Survivors' resistance to the idea of transformation
from sites of confinement to places of recreation lays bare the buildings'
contentious nature and the need to recognize both their materiality and
the pain they encompass.

Second, institutions emerge from the foregoing historical discussion as
processes. Institutions were not only the physical locations within which
people were housed, but they were part of the discursive construction
necessary for the "creation of the feeble mind" (Trent 1994) upon which
they depended. Institutions were one part in the process of naming, cat-
egorizing, classifying, and ultimately constructing individuals as people
requiring the confines that institutions provided. Thus, institutions are
not static entities, but are active agents in the process of creating the
population in need of its buildings, the regimes contained therein, and
the professionals who ran them, all aspects of institutional life upon which
survivors reflect in the next chapter.

This leads to the third thematic thread, the tension between two of
institutionalization's principal features: fluidity and fixity. While institutions were tangible structures, their bricks-and-mortar materiality was
also a reflection of theoretical and philosophical currents that existed
at particular historical moments. While buildings generally appeared
unchanged (despite alterations and renovations that attempted to suggest otherwise), justifications for institutional use were prone to intense
fluctuations, depending on current philosophical framings and understandings of the people they were designed to 'serve.' From the product
of charitable impulses to the provision of refuge and asylum, to sites of
educational and vocational transformation, to storage sites for society's
"flotsam and jetsam," institutions' outward purpose has shifted notably
throughout their existence. Institutions, and the people they held, were
a phenomenon whose definition and stated purpose has historically been

altered to meet the needs of popular discourse and government mandates. Further, the many permutations of the motives which justified institutional use point to the ways in which people's identities and abilities were made variable in order to 'fit' into the institutional model, a fluidity that ultimately had significant impact on many thousands of lives. However, while institutions' stated purpose and meanings have historically fluctuated, as have professional claims of advances in the kind of care and intervention they provided, the fundamental reason for their existence has remained secure: the incarceration of thousands of people against their will as a result of classification systems based on arbitrary measurements of intellect and personhood.

The historical framing of institutions leads, finally, to the impact they had on the lives contained therein. It is with the group of people most affected by this process – institutional survivors – that we begin to examine the tangled consequences of its long history.

PART TWO

STORIES

The effects of institutionalization can be thought of as ever-widening circles of influence moving outward from an inner core with survivors at the centre. This cascade of effects (Barad 2007) is an appropriate metaphor for the pervasive nature of institutionalization's impact, moving outwards from those most deeply affected, touching siblings, parents, and others in the families' circles.

One of the principal foci of this project was to examine the relational impact of institutionalization: to examine its effects on the spaces between individual participants, on their understandings of each other, and on what each person saw him- or herself becoming as a result. In order to do that, it was necessary to first examine the reflections from each group of participants before moving on to consider points of commonality and divergence. Accordingly, the chapters that follow present the findings and analysis from each group of participants separately first; the text then moves to a deeper interrogation which seeks to find patterns of intersection and overlap between and among the different groups.

In an attempt to respect the pattern of effects that emerged from participants' reflections, I begin with survivors, who carry the deepest and most painful lived experiences of institutionalization. From there, I move from sites of immediate and intimate experiences of institutionalization to those gradually more removed – to siblings, parents, and then former staff and key informants. I recognize that my choice to present siblings immediately after survivors is contestable. Indeed, parents can be considered closer to the children who were institutionalized than their siblings; they were undoubtedly closer to the decision to institutionalize. However, in light of the comments siblings made regarding the impact of this decision on their lives, a removal and a rupture not fully understood as children yet vividly felt long after the fact, it seemed more appropriate to place siblings' reflections immediately beside those of their institutionalized brothers and sisters. The intention here is not to minimize parents' experiences of loss, but rather to respect the pattern that seemed to emerge in this particular group of participants in this one, unavoidably limited study.

Chapters 4 to 6 contain direct phenomenological accounts of the lived experiences of survivors, siblings, and parents respectively. Each group describes what they remember of institutionalization in their families' lives and what this period of separation has come to mean to them individually and within their families. In chapter 7, former staff and key informants provide observations from the perspective of those who did not experience institutionalization directly, but had particular insights into its impact on families. Notable in this chapter are the discrepancies that emerge between the narratives of former staff and those of survivors. There are marked differences between these two groups of accounts, as survivors' descriptions of the institution as "the worst place I ever lived" contrast distinctly with former staff assertions that it was "the best place I ever worked." These divergences are explored in some detail as an example of how power differences are manifested within and between different groups of people, and are dependent on status and assumptions of capability. Chapter 7 serves as a segue to the analysis in chapter 8, which examines what happens when groups' reflections are laid one upon the other such that lines of intersection, areas of overlap, and points of discord emerge. It is through this study of commonality and divergence that some of the deeper lessons of this project are revealed. These include the discursive production of intellect and the intellectually disabled person, and how these processes affected familial understandings of the person designated as such within their family; the impact of power distributions within the family on people's interpretations of decision-making and its aftermath; and the role of institutionalization in capitalist methods of production and consumption. Thus, as was suggested in the opening pages of this book, while its primary purpose was to explore individuals' experiences, the study unavoidably opens up discussions of power, status, and personhood due to the points of friction and confluence that arise when participant groups are examined relative to each other.

4

Survivors

"It wrecked me sadly"
– Sean,[1] institutional survivor

The discussion that follows is based on the accounts of five men and four women who were institutionalized in one of Ontario's institutions for the feebleminded sometime between 1948 and 1973. These men and women lived in institutions from between six and thirty-five years, with an average of more than seventeen years.[2] Although a small group, their stories have breadth, as they represent a range of experiences in terms of the admitting authority (parent, social welfare agency, or medical authority),[3] the reasons given for admission, and the site of institutionalization (all three of the large institutions in Ontario – Huronia, Smiths Falls, and Cedar Springs – are represented in this cohort). They also provide depth of experience, as survivors describe institutionalization as the most central and formative aspect of their lives thus far. At the time of her interview, for example, one sixty-seven-year-old woman had spent almost half of her life in an institution from the time she was age five or six; four others had spent one-third of their lives institutionalized.

Before discussing the major themes that emerged in survivors' narratives, it is important to note the overriding tenor of their reflections. Without exception, all of the survivors in this study spoke of their institutionalization as a time of sadness, confusion, and loss. All of the participants described this period of their lives as an unhappy one, during which the burden of being designated a rejected 'other' was inescapable. Each imposed routine, each day separated from their families, each incident which gave evidence of their lack of control and agency, together were constant reminders of the oppressiveness and wretchedness of their situation. One of the most oft-repeated sentiments I heard while speaking with this group was that they did not like living in the institution, and that their lives are much better now.

Survivors' reflections are divided into two main sections. In the first, survivors' experiences of oppression, abandonment, and exclusion are presented. These reveal the extent of the dehumanizing processes to which they were subjected, and illustrate the profound sense of abandonment they experienced as a result of being left to this fate by their families. This unavoidably reads like a list of harrowing experiences; while unpleasant, it serves as a starting point for the analysis that follows. In the second part of the chapter, the discussion moves into a more comprehensive look at the impact of these experiences on survivors' relationships with members of their families, as well as their observations of some of the broader social-political forces that influenced their incarceration.

Oppression

The recent emergence of survivor accounts of the lived experience of institutionalization provides a window into the extent of the oppression and abuse they encountered (Ford 2017; Hutton et al. 2017; Scott 2017). These range from a persistent atmosphere of regimentation and lack of freedom, to experiences of dehumanization via disrespectful admission procedures and forced labour, to the ubiquitous culture of violence that marked many encounters in the institution. In the sections that follow, I discuss each of these in turn, as they provide the backdrop to survivors' experiences of abandonment, one of the central characterizations of their institutional experience.

Regimentation

According to the accounts given by survivors, every detail of life within the institution was prescribed in exacting detail in order to support its overall efficiency. Residents' desire for choice and volition was subservient to the larger goal of maintaining the running operations of a huge administrative machine. Efficiency, or the "handling of many human needs by the bureaucratic organization of whole blocks of people" (Goffman 1961, 6), was paramount. As one of the former staff noted, "A big place works. That's where you do economies of scale," indicating a prioritization of large-scale efficiencies over the individual needs and choices of residents. All survivors described the dearth of opportunity to make their own choices, to determine their own schedule, what to wear or eat, and how to spend their leisure time. All clothes were taken from them upon entry; food was portioned out; days were ordered in exactly the same fashion, day after day after day. Joe noted, "It wasn't a different day; it was the same day. I guess every day was the same day." One example of this repetitive, assumed regimentation occurred in the lack of acknowledgment of people's birthdays. Some of the survivors stated that birthdays were not celebrated in the institution; this contributed to survivors believing that their birthday was identical to every other day, and indeed, that their lives were not notable to any great degree. One man indicated that upon discharge, he did not know when his birthday was, as it had never been celebrated or even acknowledged.

Concomitant with the overriding regimentation were feelings of power-lessness. Survivors learned that attempts to voice complaints, to argue for change, or to make even simple requests were usually fruitless, as they would not make any difference within the highly structured bureaucracy of the institution and its military-like culture. In the desire to create order out of the inevitable chaos of huge numbers of people being housed together in unfavourable circumstances, there was not room for individual requests or fluctuations in schedule.

Dehumanization

The rigidity with which the institutions functioned meant that facets of daily life within which dignity and respect for self and others are normally imbued were overruled by the importance of schedule and discipline, part of the dehumanization process (Malacrida 2015) which survivors encoun-tered as soon as they entered the institution. Several survivors spoke of the lack of dignity with which most of the tasks of daily life were carried out. Marie recalled, "There was no privacy. When we'd go to the bathroom, there was no cubicles. It was all just one room with toilets." For residents with more involved physical disabilities, 'slab' baths were used, a method in which residents were laid down flat on washing tables without curtains and were hosed down in front of the other residents. Survivors spoke of beds being crammed close together and of sleeping in a room with several other people. Sean stated, "you didn't know whose bed was whose."

Dehumanization also included processes that incessantly wore down survivors' understanding of themselves as meaningful individuals and challenged their sense of worth as human beings. These were particularly evident in admission procedures and in survivors' experiences of insti-tutional labour. Joe and Peter, in painful recollections of their arrival at separate institutions, spoke of being forced to strip themselves of their clothing in front of admissions personnel and to surrender personal belongings. Joe described his arrival at the institution at the age of twelve: "It was scary for me just to get out of the car ... and when I went in there, I went to the admission ward, and when you go into the admission ward, they *[pause]* ... they strip your clothes and you're naked and you're standing there, and they measure you, you know, to see what are you wearing, your clothes are all gone and they give you new clothes, their clothes, like prison clothes." Peter spoke of his new, blue suit "that I had just bought. I had the blue suit on [when I went to the institution] ... I never saw that suit again." The confiscation that these men experienced echoes another of Goffman's (1961, 140) observations of total institutions: when one becomes an institutional resident, one is "stripped of almost everything," materially and figuratively. This was their introduction to the extent to which the administration of the institution would suppress individuality and autonomy. Moreover, the forced nakedness to which these men were subjected is a blatant example of an abuse of authoritarian power. The threat of exploitation, present as soon as the child is exposed, would ensure complete obedience.

All of the survivors referred to some aspect of institutional life that wore away at their sense of humanity and well-being. Many referred to the absence of anything personal: closets were communal, and residents were assigned two outfits which, it was made clear to them, were not really theirs, but belonged to the institution. Hilary,[4] Pat, and Marie referred to 'ticking dresses,' a kind of uniform allocated upon entry that was uncomfortable and depersonalized: "I only had two dresses, and they never let me wear my clothes – 'ticking' dresses." Hilary also referred to the institution-wide shaving of heads, a strategy employed to prevent the possible spread of lice. Meals were communal and rushed, with no option for personal preferences. Pat described meal times: "A lot of the food was poor quality ... You only got to have ten minutes to eat, because thirty-one of us would line up and get our tray to sit down ... If I was at the end of the line, which I was quite a bit, by the time I sat down, I didn't have time to finish. You got ten minutes to eat, five or ten minutes, to eat your meals."

This lack of opportunity to demonstrate agency in even the simplest daily tasks was one of the visible elements of the dehumanization processes to which institutional residents were subjected. As Malacrida (2015) notes in her history of the Michener Institute in Red Deer, Alberta, dehumaniz-ation was also invoked via a culture of constant surveillance. Institutions, according to Malacrida, were built "to offer surveillance and control over large populations, reducing the need for force in keeping individuals acquiescent" (68). Moreover, through the normalization of surveillance, even when residents were not being watched "they came to learn that they must act as if they were being watched or could be caught at any moment" (69). Thus, while surveillance may not always be a visible feature of institutional life, its effects are felt via its potential and the subsequent self-regulation it imposes.

Negating people's humanity was also evident in survivors' description of the labour they were forced to do while institutionalized. In his extensive historical research on the degradation suffered by institutional residents through forced labour, Reaume (2006, 2004, 2000) notes its double injustice: first, inmates had to work under horrible conditions and with no compensation; and second, paradoxically, the labour they performed contributed to the upkeep of the institution in which they were incarcerated.

The participants in this study provided a striking example. Notably, half of the participants reported doing the institution's laundry. Survivor accounts of the worst part of this menial task – cleaning residents' excrement out of sheets and clothing in the basement of the building – reveal two important points. It is indicative not only of the cost-saving measures that institutions' administrators made use of, justified by residents' otherwise "unemployability" (Reaume 2004, 467) and the feeling that they should bear some of the responsibility for the institution's upkeep, but also of the poor regard that institutional administrations exhibited for their residents. The task of having to clean up the excrement produced within the institution is reminiscent of Douglas's (1966) work on the liminalization of waste in order to preserve the cleanliness of the community. In this case, institutional residents were forced to deal with human dirt, the "by-product of the creation of order" (161), as part of the organized effort to sustain the institution.

Violence and Abuse

"I got a lot of wrong done to me
and a lot of harm done to me." (*Marie*)

The dehumanizing encounters and humiliations described above were underscored by a culture of violence and silence that simultaneously fostered and kept hidden survivors' experiences of degradation. All of the survivors referred to the violent atmosphere that permeated the institution. "It was rough," Graham[5] said. "The men's staffs used to talk dirty. Yeah, talk dirty, and I didn't like that either. It was disgusting. And they used to do this *[indicating an obscene gesture]*." While this kind of communication was disrespectful and dehumanizing, it also carried the potential to escalate into physical violence. Survivors explained that throughout their daily routines and in all avenues of communication, there was an ever-present threat of physical or emotional violence if one did not adhere to the conformity of institutional life. "I got beaten up by some of the staff. Nobody stopped it … if you even looked at one of the staff the wrong way, you got beat up," Pat reported. "We weren't allowed to talk back … I got into trouble every day for something … Stupid little things, you know?" added Marie.

Survivors noted that staff also facilitated an atmosphere of violence by inciting residents to act violently towards each other. Almost all of the survivors referred to the frequent bouts of aggression between residents. André[6] recalled, "there's too much fighting going on … They fight in the morning, the afternoon, and night. That's too much!" Pat noted, "The staff beat you up. And they instigated fights between us too." While distressing, the logic behind these tactics make sense in the larger picture of institutional life: it is more difficult for a group of oppressed people to resist their oppressors if they are not united; inciting violence between residents was a way for staff to maintain control and to "prevent residents from supporting each other" (Malacrida 2015, 102). Violence between residents also justified the ongoing use of institutions and harsh punishments such as solitary 'side rooms.' Residents acting out against each other, regardless of the circumstances, allowed supervisors and decision-makers to maintain the high levels of supervision and punishment typical of the institutions in which these survivors lived.

The violent atmosphere was frequently manifested as direct abuse against institutional residents. The motivation behind the abuse appears to be a combination of an extreme prioritization of order, a heightened and grossly ill-defined demand for respect from staff, and the misinformed and anxiety-ridden understandings of disability that imbued relationships between staff and residents. Many of the survivors indicated that they sensed the fear and misunderstanding that many of the staff felt towards residents, a fear that translated into aggressive and inhumane treatment. As Marie explained, the presence of people with disabilities challenged some staff's understanding of humanity, which seemed to justify the poor treatment they gave to residents: "They probably didn't think we were human or that we had any feelings or anything or that we wouldn't know what was going on. Thought they could get away with it."

Frequently framed as punishments for misdemeanours residents had committed, mistreatment included various forms of disrespect and cruelty. These included verbal ridicule from staff; different meals for staff and residents; minimal time to eat meals; being sent to lie under benches for speaking out; staff instigating fights between residents; 'digging for worms,' that is, being forced to lie on the floor with one's hands tied behind one's back and to rub one's face on the floor; scrubbing the floor with one's own toothbrush; being sent, naked, to isolation rooms; being forced to walk in front of the class with pants down; 'climbing the walls,' that is, being made to stand in a corner with one's hands over one's head; and accounts of sexual abuse in one's bed or in the shower. This partial list gives some sense of the pervasive culture of fear and violence in the institution and suggests the despair many residents must have felt in knowing they had been left to these circumstances.

The abuse was usually contextualized as 'deserved,' justifying its administration. This corresponds to what scholars of institutionalization have described as one of the effects of the super-structure of institutions: regimentation, punishment, and abuse are warranted in order to maintain their overall functioning. Essentially, the institution, as designed, could not operate save for strict adherence to schedule and the use of punishment on residents. Moreover, the defilement residents experienced (Goffman 1961, 43) ensured that any hope they might have had of maintaining a sense of self within the institutions was negated (16), lessening their potential to act as threats to its operation. What is striking, moreover, is the specific cultural location of the abuse. Although not proven, it is unlikely that institutional staff would have committed the same kinds of atrocities on their own children, even for similar misdemeanours, once away from the institution. Yet there appeared to be a low level of tolerance for 'misbehaviour' when it occurred in the institution. This raises questions about the implications of institutionalized care, not only in terms of residents, but also in regard to the moral and ethical reasoning that is engendered in caregivers when situated in an institutional model, a point that will be discussed in more detail in chapter 7. Last, the narratives above imply that the reason why residents were mistreated was because they were residents of institutions, that this status was warranted, and that it rendered them undeserving of humane care and relationships. Institutionalization brought into question the humanity of people with intellectual disabilities, demonstrated by the abuse residents experienced.

Abandonment

> "They looked at me like I was a monster. It was
> abandonment and rejection." (*Pat, in reference to her family*)

Survivors' recollections of oppression and abuse were made more difficult by the realization that they had been left to this by their families. Interviews suggest that survivors' most overwhelming sense of loss and rejection was embedded not only in the dehumanizing experiences described above, but in the recognition that those closest to them, willingly or not, had been part of the decision to send them there. For many survivors, acknowledgment of this abandonment remains a tangible and painful thread in their lives.

Abandonment was felt the moment survivors realized they were being left behind. All survivors spoke poignantly about the moment when they first fully understood that they were being deserted by their families, often at the door of the institution, most often as children. André recalls, "I was not happy at all. I started to cry. I held back tears and I didn't know what to do, and I didn't like it. Said good-bye, and after that, I didn't know what to do with it." Pat described her incredulity when she realized her family was not going to stay with her: "I sat on the floor and I cried. I said – Mom, aren't you going to stay with me? – And she said – No. I've got the kids in the car and Dad to look after … I honestly thought they were going too. I assumed Mom and Dad would at least stay with me. As a little girl, I didn't understand. They *left* me. They abandoned me … I was scared, being left with strangers." Survivors also describe this transaction as confusing, for most had not been told it was going to take place, and for the most part no explanations were offered. There were some exceptions: Sean explained that his father had admitted him to the institution after his mother had died, when he felt that he could not sustain the care Sean needed. Peter described the medical advice that had led his family to believe that the institution would 'cure' him of his epilepsy, a misguided and ill-informed recommendation that resulted in Peter being institutionalized for almost twenty years.

Moreover, survivors were astute in recognizing that they had been abandoned not only by their families, but also by the state. For those children whose families of origin were under surveillance prior to institutionalization, usually through the auspices of Children's Aid, the state played a key role in facilitating the transition from home to institution. In a heart-wrenching example, Marie, who stated she also has Indigenous heritage, explained how she came to know some of her siblings after meeting them for the first time at the institution where she had been sent: "I didn't believe she was my sister at first, because somebody mentioned that my sister was here or something like that … I thought I only had one sister because that's all my family would talk about, was my one sister. They never said anything about another sister." The state had intervened with this family when Marie was very young, and by sending several children away to institutional care, had prevented Marie from establishing even a basic understanding of who her family was and the reasons for her institutionalization. Thus, Marie's experience of abandonment must be contextualized not only as an act from a family deemed unable to care for her, but as a part of the larger bureaucratization of 'care' which acted readily on those families considered dysfunctional and inadequate, and whose situations were complicated by social disadvantage and racialization (Strong-Boag 2007).

Finally, survivors described the experience of coming to realize that the state's abandonment went beyond participating in referrals to the institution. Joe described learning of the government's awareness of the extent of abuse in provincial institutions, an awareness not met by corresponding action on behalf of residents: "Yeah, the government knew. And I was so upset inside. I was overwhelmed to hear – the government knew about this? And they didn't do nothing about it? They took away our vocation, they took away our dreams, our hopes, everything … these people knew what they were saying and doing. Because if they didn't, why would they keep it a secret then?" Joe's observations point out the government's culpability in all that happened in institutions, as children were sent as wards of the state whose care was entrusted to the government. For Joe, the government's failure to uphold its end of this fostering agreement was the ultimate abandonment, for it was primarily through government policy and decision-making, enacted through professional avenues such as medicine and social welfare, that families had been convinced to allow their children to be institutionalized.

Exclusion

In their accounts of being left at the institution, survivors also spoke of specific experiences of exclusion. By exclusion, I refer to survivors' prohibition from the decision-making, rituals, and milestones of everyday life, as well as their being barred from communal spaces where mainstream society functions, relates, and creates culture (Dorn 1999; Young 1990). The loss and grief survivors experienced via exclusionary practices, even seemingly minute ones, was profound. Besides the removal of control over everyday and taken-for-granted decisions, such as what to wear and when to turn the lights off, survivors also expressed the loss of life-giving practices that they had enjoyed before being institutionalized. André described his participation in his family's sing-alongs, a ritual that disappeared as soon as he entered the institution. Hilary spoke of her love of knitting, something she did not have access to while living in the institution: "They never let me have my knitting. I used to stay inside every day and sit in my room." Brian[7] described his recent pleasure in going to the video store, choosing a movie, and watching it at a time that suited him, a significant contrast to the institutional experience of staring at a TV perched high above the room, fixed at a station that staff had chosen. These are small, concrete examples, and probably seemed insignificant in the midst of administrative concerns to keep the institution running. However, they indicate the extent of the removal of meaningful praxis from people's lives. Bearing in mind the silence with which most residents would have held the knowledge of the rituals dear to them, there are undoubtedly infinite examples of survivors feeling excluded from practices in which they had engaged prior to entering the institution.

At a more abstract level, survivors' accounts allude to their exclusion from larger forums of public discourse and community engagement, in particular those discussions that had bearing on their future. They were unable to contribute to what Runté and Mills (2006) call primary discourses (695) or avenues of power and decision-making that directly influenced their lives. Despite increasing recognition of the rights of all people in the post–World War II landscape and the gradual implementation of legal frameworks to ensure the inclusion of marginalized groups, traditional power structures continued to dominate decision-making on behalf of people with disabilities. Patriarchal and medical opinion were the principal contributors to primary discourse, and "secondary" or "companion" discourse (Runté and Mills 2006, 700), relegated to women, children, and people from marginalized communities, did not carry equal authority (Young 1990). At the time, there were few expectations that people with intellectual disabilities would have anything meaningful or reasonable to contribute to decisions regarding their own future. As Marie noted, "we were not allowed to have an opinion."

This indifference to the potential value of survivors' contributions has its root in historical assumptions regarding 'incompetence' and an individual's ability to make decisions involving their own care and the future direction of their lives (Levitz 2003; Mosoff 2000; Stefan 1993; Ward and Stewart 2008). The presumed superiority of intellect, which continues to be contentiously defended by scholars (see, for example, Harris 2002 and Singer 2011) despite scholarship that points to its non-essentialist and constructivist nature (Gould 1996), has been and continues to be a limiting factor in the lives of people with intellectual disabilities (Enns 1999; Marzano-Parisoli 2001).

Survivors expressed awareness of the connection between presumptions of incapability, the indignities they suffered while institutionalized, and their exclusion from the fundamental rights deserved by every person. As Pat noted, "We were not allowed to talk back. We had no rights. We weren't allowed to think for ourselves." At its most extreme, survivors who had little or no contact with the 'outside' world and with members of their own families referred to an experience of non-existence: by the world not knowing they were there, and no-one but the institutional staff acknowledging their presence, they had little experience of identity or meaning. Joe summarized it thus: "They locked us up. Nobody wanted us in the society. That's what we felt. Nobody wanted us, so they locked us up."

Finally, this discussion gives rise to another area of exclusion, one about which survivors were not aware. As researcher, I became aware of those aspects of family life that had transpired in survivors' absence and about which they knew nothing. Survivors missed out on a great deal of what went on in the family home, and for the most part they were not aware of those developments. One family explained that they had two Christmas celebrations: one, several days or weeks prior to Christmas with their institutionalized daughter who came home for that celebration; the second, a celebration on Christmas Day with the extended family in which their daughter was not included. The first one they called "Nora's[8] Christmas," distinguishing it from the actual Christmas, and marking its distinction as the celebration for the absent family member. This distinction must have been maintained at some expense, for the investment in organizing two Christmases would be significant, yet it must have been considered worthwhile even though it barred one family member from participating. The demarcation between these two celebrations is a difficult reminder of the delineation between people with intellectual disabilities and those without; what is perhaps more poignant is Nora not experiencing or even knowing about the family's other, 'real' Christmas celebration. There was a gap in Nora's understanding of her family, an unnamed piece of her story that she was not allowed to partake in and perhaps was not even cognizant of.

In another case, Muriel and Vici discovered only recently that Vici's brother Rob, who had lived in an institution more than thirty years earlier, had believed all along that Vici had also lived there. Rob's misperception was brought to Muriel and Vici's attention when they began to talk in their home about the class-action lawsuits being launched against the provincial government. Vici recalled: "Rob was talking and talking about [the institution] and did *this* [*demonstrates hitting*]. And then, trying every possibility in my brain of what he could possibly be talking about … and then I finally said – *Did you think I was hurt? – Yeah – Did you think I was at* [the institution] – *Yeah*. And then I had to sit there and say – *No, I was here. I stayed home. I got to stay home.*"

In another example, André and Peter spoke of attending their fathers' funerals while living in an institution. Neither of them was able to attend to their fathers nor to visit with them in the days and weeks leading up to their deaths. Rather, they were allowed to mark their fathers' deaths by leaving the institution only long enough to attend their funerals, followed by an immediate return to the institution. Peter observed, "That was the only time I got to go home. I didn't go home for visits for eighteen years. The only time I went home was when my father died." Similar to the previous example, one can presume that there was much these men missed in the time leading up to the deaths of their fathers, and in their lives prior to that, including partaking of any insights their fathers might have shared and the opportunity to say good-bye. This removal from the 'normal' cycles of family life, even in more intense moments such as family celebrations and deaths, has meant that survivors continue to live with spaces in their family stories that will never be filled on account of their own absence from the family home. These gaps contribute to the painful points in family relationships with which several of the survivors continue to struggle.

Abandonment and Exclusion
in the Context of the Family

Many of the survivors were aware of the reasons their families used to explain their institutionalization: the number of other siblings at home; the dearth of community resources and supports for people with intellectual disabilities; their parents' anxiety regarding how to raise a child with extra needs; and the influential involvement of medical and child welfare authorities who directed the placement of children identified as having a disability. Many of them also recognized that their 'difference' and their families' feelings of inadequacy in knowing how to deal with it were the underlying reasons they had been institutionalized, reasons difficult to come to terms with due to their proximity to people's sense of identity and well-being. The compassionate understanding that many survivors have towards their families does not lessen the severity of that decision, nor did it make their lives while institutionalized any less difficult. And despite the forgiveness that many survivors feel towards their families, they simultaneously continue to bear the wounds of their abandonment.

Survivors described a range of experiences of abandonment and exclusion within the context of their families. These varied from interruption and disruption in family relationships to situations of extreme brokenness. All of the survivors stated that relationships with their families were, at the very least, strained and unnatural because of the intermittent and infrequent nature of their contact, and because of the inability to interact in the normal, day-to-day manner of regular family life. This was true even for the five participants whose families came to visit on a somewhat regular basis. The rigidity of the institutional setting, the limits placed on families regarding how often and when they could come and visit their family member, and the real and metaphorical distance that institutions created within families disallowed the development of the depth of relationship that would be considered normal between parents, children, and siblings. Visits happened in a designated visitors' space during a designated time, allowing the institution to temporally and spatially control the connections between residents and family members and to limit the extent of the relationships that families might have endeavoured to maintain. As Peter explained, "The thing was it [the visit] was too short ... You had so many things you wanted to say and not enough time to say it in."

Further, all of the survivors whose families did visit remarked upon the distinction within their families regarding who came. Visits were primarily from parents; in five cases, survivors were not visited by a brother or sister for the entire duration of their institutionalization. Thus, within many families and for decades, siblings had no contact with each other. This had some bearing on the kind of understanding siblings developed of each other and on how they related with each other later in life, when the forced distancing from institutionalization became the obligatory reckoning, through deinstitutionalization, of a familial bond, untended for decades. André spoke of his parents' desire to absolve his siblings of any responsibility from maintaining contact with him while institutionalized, as his mother felt it was a responsibility that siblings should not be obliged to carry. This stance, exhibited by many parents towards non-institutionalized siblings, suggests an acceptance of predominant discourse around 'normal' family functioning. The parents' desire to ensure a 'healthy' upbringing of the non-institutionalized children included distancing them from the institutionalized child – perhaps to protect siblings from the shock of the institution, perhaps in an attempt to not 'burden' siblings with feelings of guilt or responsibility, or perhaps as a misguided attempt to protect them from the institution's contaminative potential (Douglas 1961). For the most part, survivors were unable to articulate why their siblings did not come; to them, the decades of distance reinforced their self-knowledge as someone undeserving of the affection and attention of others.

Further, four of the survivors, Graham, Hilary, Sean, and Peter, reported that they each had an older brother who came to visit many years later once the brother had left the family home and had re-established contact with his institutionalized brother or sister. Despite the small sample size, the observation that only brothers attempted to re-establish contact with an institutionalized sibling while he or she remained incarcerated is of some interest. While far from conclusive, it suggests that some time- and gender-specific discourse might have influenced who was encouraged to venture into the institution. While girls and women might have been discouraged from entering what was considered a dark and dangerous place – in regard to both the physical manifestations of the institution itself as well as the unpredictable encounters with the unknown sibling or others in the institution – boys and men might have been allowed to manage those relationships in ways that they desired, including venturing into a previously hidden part of the family story.

Six of the survivors stated that the damage caused to family relation-ships went beyond the disruption described above and has resulted in a brokenness that persists, years after their leaving the institution. In the most extreme cases, some survivors lost contact with their family altogether. Joe, who had been in foster care prior to being admitted to the institution, stated, "it was like I disappeared from the planet. No-one knew where I was, not even my family." Eighteen years after being discharged, he was reunited with his mother and brother. Peter also spoke of his mother's lack of knowledge that he had been discharged from the facility; two years after he was discharged, his mother finally learned that he was "out." While this can be blamed in part on the institution and its inadequate communication with the family, the breakage between family members as a result of long absences no doubt also played a role. Finally, two of the women, Pat and Marie, spoke of the ongoing brokenness and difficulty that exists in their families, a direct result of being sent to live in an institution. Pat, in reference to her attempts to forge relationships with family members during and after her institutionalization, stated, "it [the rejection] happened too many times growing up, and I couldn't bond with any of them … I quit trying."

The experience of brokenness in family relationships is not limited to survivors. In the chapter that follows, many of the brothers and sisters of institutional survivors express sadness at the significant gaps in their family stories left by years of separation. While all families experience absences in their family narrative to some degree – few people know all the details of the lives of other family members – siblings and survivors together noted the gaps they have experienced, and their powerlessness in accessing the years that were lost to each other. In situations in which the institutionalized individual was unable to speak, the breakages in family narratives are particularly hard to bear.

However, although most of the survivors stated that they did not fully understand why their families decided to institutionalize them, and that they had been hurt by this, they also demonstrated a surprising lack of rancour towards their families. Save for the two women mentioned above who remain angry towards their families, all of the survivors stated that their deepest desire upon leaving the institution was to re-forge connections with members of their families and to be included in the relationships they still consider most dear to them.

Survivors: Recognizing the Errors

The introductory chapters of this text take a constructivist stance towards feeblemindedness and discuss the role this has played in the lives of people with disabilities. Many survivors from this project, in particular those involved in the self-advocacy movement, were aware of the influence that constructivist discourse had on their institutionalization. Four of the survivors stated that their families or the Children's Aid Society misread their abilities and behaviours and that this misreading played a role in their admission to custodial care. Marie stated, "They made me out to be worse than I really was." Joe gave an insightful explanation of the state's role in the measurement and construction of intellectual incompetence and the resulting recommendations for institutionalization. He stated, "I was a normal person before I went there ... my IQ was 78, so why did I go there? ... They said *mild moron range of intelligence, borderline range.* And I say to the government – shame on them. Giving us labels ... these were labels that weren't even true ... And me, I was normal. That's what I'm saying – there was a lot of normal people that went into the institution."

Moreover, these four survivors noted that constructivist discourse had a significant impact on the state's assessment of their families. Their families were deemed incapable of caring for their children, and they lacked access to the skills and resources needed to resist the discourse of incompetence levelled against them. All of these cases were, notably, within families with a lower socio-economic status, suggesting a conflation between socio-economic circumstances and recommendation for institutionalization. Two of the families had Indigenous status, thus compounding the discriminatory grounds under which their children would have been assessed as requiring state care (Aylward 2010). Seemingly 'substandard' living conditions and Indigeneity contributed to authorities' recommendation for institutionalization, a recommendation to which families were obliged to acquiesce. Thus, rather than survivors' seeming lack of ability being the principal reason for placement, societal interpretations of intellectual disability and interrelated discourses of familial incompetence were principal driving influences.

Further, all but two of the survivors stated that their parents believed that the institution would be a better place for them, an observation that was indeed confirmed when this research was conducted with parents. Sean noted, "My father said he felt that I would be safer there ... but I wasn't too keen." Peter said, "Dad saw it as the best place for me." The faulty reasoning behind their parents' decisions was a difficult truth for many survivors to come to terms with, and it contributes to the overall tragedy of institutionalization: first, that they had to live in an abusive and harmful environment, and second, acknowledging the misguided decisions and limitations of their parents and society that had placed them there.

Ontological Meaning

Survivors' experiences of abandonment and exclusion, while they connect to the potential for abandonment relevant to all human experience, are particular to their histories and thus need to be identified and understood. When survivors ask themselves why they were sent away to an institution when their brothers and sisters were not, ontological questions concerning the nature of being and the meaning of their lives emerge. Their questions force examination beyond family circumstances and point to a more difficult discussion concerning the fundamental value of people's lives, particularly those considered different.

Hughes (2007) has addressed these concerns in a heartfelt essay in which he discusses the "negative ontology of disability" (678) and the reality that people with disabilities continue to "have to make a significant effort to establish their human worth" (677). Hughes points out that despite repeated efforts by disability scholars to remind non-disabled individuals of the "universality of impairment" (679) and the ubiquitous nature of human vulnerability, people with disabilities remain in the precarious position of having to repeatedly "make a claim to humanity" (678).

Statements made by institutional survivors in this project indicate that Hughes's concerns remain valid and continue to plague survivors' emotional and psychological processing around why they were forced to spend so much of their lives in undesirable and abusive situations. Indeed, as discussed in previous sections of this chapter, there are few satisfactory answers to questions concerning one person's abandonment instead of another's, for it was only people's differences, considered anxiety-provoking enough to warrant institutionalization, that justified their incarceration.

Moreover, reflection on the ontological implications of institutionalization reveals the arbitrary nature of the boundaries which necessitated it, an arbitrariness that has ongoing and universal implications. While the historical record continues to describe institutionalization as a phenomenon which has affected particular groups of people, the flexible boundaries that have characterized it are also a warning of its potential to reach in directions previously not considered. What protective wall of able-bodiedness and intellectual capacity do the majority of people rest behind, unaware of the historical flexibility that characterizes their borders? Questions that survivors ask concerning the reasons for their institutionalization should not be limited to those who have lived through it. They must also be asked of those who assume immunity, indeed, the majority of people, forcing an acknowledgment of the universality and unknowable extent of human variation, as well as the universal vulnerability to the power of government preferences and the policy used to enact them. Thus, survivors' questions are not necessarily unanswerable, but are a reminder of how disability serves more as a point of human connection than as a justification for segregation.

Labelling and Resistance

Struggling with these questions reveals the labelling to which survivors were made to submit. Even if, while grappling with the ontological questions discussed above, survivors were able to transcend the assumption that the institution was their rightful place because of their difference, they still had to carry the weight of knowing they had been labelled in such a way.

Realizing that they had been sent away because of their 'difference,' however, also gave survivors a site from which to resist. Many survivors in this group, while recognizing the powerlessness of their situation, did not acquiesce to the nomenclature assigned to them, nor to the reasoning provided by families and administrators, but fought against it in order to not give in to the assumption that this was the place where they belonged. Pat described being punished for "talking when you weren't supposed to," or "looking at the counsellors [staff] the wrong way." This did not deter her, however, from ongoing attempts to resist authority when she felt it necessary to do so. According to Pat's friend Marie, who lived at Huronia at the same time, Pat "got it worse, because she … had more courage to speak out." Joe resisted the confines of the institution by attempting to run away by hitching a ride on a train. He was caught and was returned to the institution. Joe recalls being designated a trouble-maker because of his actions; he was the problem, not the institutional method he was trying to escape.[9]

Moreover, survivors described the resistance and advocacy work they have undertaken since their release from the institution. After his release from the institution in 1978, Peter co-founded People First, Canada's foremost advocacy group for people with intellectual disabilities, and one which pushed tirelessly for institutional closure for almost three decades. Drawing from his own experience, Peter was determined that no-one would have to "live through the life I had. I don't want anybody to have to experience that. I feel that anyone can live in the community with support, whatever it happens to be." He is determined that deinstitutionalization is a process that is done carefully and well: "Close it properly so that people can get the proper support in the community. Sure, it may take a bit of time, quite a bit of time. But closing it properly is better than dumping people on the street."

Similarly, Joe draws from his experience to teach college students who are training to become developmental service workers. Joe has written an account of his institutional experience, including his reflections on the responsibilities of government and society to participate in the care and support of all members of the community, regardless of ability. He writes: "I want to tell people about my story, and to other people who were in the institution that were not able to tell their story. I am putting my past behind me, even though it affects my life so much, and forgive everyone no matter what they did to me. I want to make sure that this type of punishment and abuse doesn't happen again to any human being. I want to tell people what happened, so that the world will be a better place and so that I can make a difference in the world … I know that someday I will die, but I will rest well because I actually did something to help the community. Speaking up to the world for what I believe." Joe suffered profoundly as a result of his institutionalization, but he has chosen to educate young people about its devastating effects, and about the possibility of moving on, forgiving those responsible, and building a life. Both he and Peter have married, have meaningful work, and live in their own homes in the community.

Also, in 2010, two survivors, Marie Slark and Pat Seth, launched a lawsuit against the Ontario government for abuse and mistreatment experienced by people while institutionalized in one of Ontario's institutions for the feebleminded. As a direct result of this action, the government gave a formal apology to all institutional survivors in the Ontario legislature in December 2013 and offered a financial settlement as compensation. While the compensation can only be considered partially successful, as the application process for funds was tedious and inaccessible for many survivors and remains unfinished, this was a major milestone in the history of the treatment of people with intellectual disabilities in Ontario and paved the way for other class actions for the treatment encountered at other institutions.

These survivors have demonstrated particularly notable work on behalf of institutional survivors and towards the creation of communities which are better able to support people of varying abilities. As Peter explained, "We all benefit from the fact that people aren't in institutions." More than any other group interviewed for this project, survivors recognized that it is not impossible to simultaneously acknowledge differences and remain committed to building an inclusive society. Many other survivors, while not undertaking work with as much of a public face, continue to advocate on behalf of themselves and their peers by carrying on in ways that a few decades ago would have seemed unimaginable for people with intellectual disabilities: living in the community, working, participating in family life, sustaining long-term relationships – thus challenging in unobtrusive yet persistent ways the labels that earlier led to many years being spent in institutions.

Survivors: Pawns in the Capitalist Enterprise?

Foregoing chapters have discussed the co-emergence of capitalism and institutionalization. In this context, institutional residents can be seen as tokens of exchange that allowed certain aspects of a market-based system to continue. Historically, excluding people with intellectual disabilities was an efficient way to ensure adequate production in the mainstream, yet this segregated system was not opposed to residents' contribution towards institutions' upkeep. Moreover, institutionalization and the classification upon which it depends has historically supported and relied upon an entire class of professionals whose role would be greatly diminished if it were not for the socio-political construction of various impairments and their 'need' for intervention (Trent 1994). The assumed nature of the need for institutions contributed to an unspoken discourse in which families were expected, and often encouraged, to surrender their child to the state. This allowed the leaving of children to institutions to be seen as the unfortunate consequence of an ill-fated life event, rather than it being considered an essential role in institutions' ongoing success. Thus, people with intellectual disabilities were not only subjects of the "manifest" or spoken discourse of institutionalization (Foucault 1972, 25), one which promoted its benefits, but were also affected by the "repressive presence of what [the discourse] does not say" (ibid.) – that is, that they played a vital albeit unwilling role in its upkeep.

In this process, people with intellectual disabilities became commodities, objects of exchange between families and the state to ensure institutional survival. As commodities, they satisfied institutions' need for workers, allowing institutions to thrive. They satisfied institutions' need for bodies, as this justified the need for staff, charged to care for those bodies. The movement of people with intellectual disabilities into institutional care legitimated the need for institutions in the first place.

Survivors who participated in this study did not express the idea that they were playing a role within the system, nor that institutions held a function in the larger establishment. Their stories were focused, concise depictions of the lived experience of having survived a difficult period in their lives. While historico-critical analysis of the interconnectedness between institutions and the maintenance of market systems is helpful, particularly as governments look towards other ways of supporting people with disabilities in the community, it is essential to acknowledge that the abandonment of people with intellectual disabilities was not only a hypothetical exchange of goods, but was simultaneously a real and painful experience. As survivors have emphasized, their existence at institutions was not only as figurative placeholders or as captive workers, but was tangibly and corporeally felt through instances of psychological and physical abuse, oppression, and punishment.

Conclusion

This chapter has presented survivor accounts of their removal from their families and their placement in an institution. From their stories of mistreatment and their experiences of abandonment, three threads emerge that inform efforts to understand what happened, and challenge society's ongoing insistence on the classification, marginalization, and segregation of people considered 'different.' The first is the historical arbitrariness of the distinction between those considered intellectually sound and those considered otherwise. History has repeatedly demonstrated patterns of removal for arbitrary distinctions of difference; survivor accounts that ask why they were chosen to leave their families and that challenge measurements of intellectual inferiority reveal the inadequacy of explanations used to justify people's separation and segregation.

Second, survivor accounts alert us to the mechanisms underlying the movement of the care of people with intellectual disabilities from the family to the state. Survivors' narratives give some indication of the multiple, frequently conflated factors that contributed to institutionalization, including race, socio-economic status, the fear of difference, coercion, and so on. However, they also point to larger social processes, usually unchallenged, that justified the role of the state in taking control of the care of people with intellectual disabilities, at least during this era in our history. While the post-institutionalization era has seen the introduction of client-centred forms of support, including increased control over one's personal finances, the ease with which the state assumed control over many thousands of individuals is a cautionary tale regarding policy that will continue to have an impact in the lives of people with intellectual disabilities.

Third, and perhaps most importantly, survivors' stories give a direct indication of the felt impact of institutionalization in people's lives. Existing at the core of institutionalization, survivors' stories are the starting point for the narrative interpretation of institutions' "cascade of effects," a process which went beyond the institution and into the lives and homes of the families who had sent them there.

Siblings

"He was a secret"
– Margaret, sister of an institutional survivor

Eleven siblings of institutional survivors participated in this project, two men and nine women. Ideally, the study would have included complete family constellations – parents, institutionalized children, and non-institutionalized children from the same family – in order to give a thorough view of the impact of institutionalization within particular families. The realities of recruitment dictated otherwise, however, and the reflections here consist of a combination of accounts from twenty different families with various configurations of relationships (see Appendix). Although the project was unable to investigate the experiences of all of the members of any one family, it reflects a range of experiences from all three groups, some of whom are sisters and brothers, others who are parents and children.

Before launching into an analysis of siblings' reflections, it is important to note some demographic features which have bearing on how their accounts can be understood. All of the siblings who participated in this project were from either middle- or upper-class families. In all except for one of the siblings' families, there were two parents at home, although the extent of parents' presence within the family varied and is discussed in more detail below. All of the siblings who participated are well-educated and employed or retired, the majority in professional, educational, or service occupations. All of them are white, and all come from families that voluntarily institutionalized a child, which, as discussed in foregoing chapters, are two mutually reinforcing features of institutional admissions in the latter part of the twentieth century. This precludes a robust analysis including racialized perspectives or those from siblings whose families were forced to institutionalize their child;[1] these absences are evidence of the work that remains to be done in completing the historical record of institutions in Ontario.

Three principal themes emerged from siblings' narratives. The first involves siblings' perceptions of their family's makeup and presentation to the 'outside' world, both in terms of having a family member with a disability, and in terms of their parents' decision to send their brother or sister to an institution. By necessity, this includes an examination of the family stories that siblings perceived were being created by and around their families, some of which were complicated by family conventions that dictated what, how much, and in what situations certain details could be divulged. The second theme concerns siblings' descriptions of the impact that their brother or sister's removal had on their families. While their accounts portray a range of experiences and emotional after-effects, from profound loss to a less tragic sense of inevitability, all of them suggest that the institutionalization of their brother or sister has had a significant effect on their family story and has shaped their lives to some degree. Third, all of the siblings recounted, to varying degrees, some breakage in family relationships as a result of institutionalization. For many of the siblings, this breakage continues, evidenced both by the unfillable gaps that remain in their family stories, and by the ongoing psychological and emotional work many of the siblings continue to do in order to come to terms with the more difficult pieces of their family histories. As Michelle[2] stated, "this has been my life journey."

The predominant tone underlying the siblings' accounts was anger. Eight of the eleven siblings expressed significant anger with respect to their parents' decision to institutionalize their brother or sister. While the most evident explanation for their anger includes a profound sense of regret and loss for a relationship that never had the opportunity to flourish, siblings also expressed anger in regard to the emotional and sometimes physical consequences of their siblings' institutionalization, many of which they did not come to recognize until adulthood. While in some cases, anger was directed at the 'system' for its inability to care adequately for their brother or sister, and siblings acknowledged that their parents had had few options in regard to the care of their child, the majority of siblings expressed disappointment in their parents for the choices they had made. Indeed, in at least seven cases, siblings suggested that the parents' decision to institutionalize a child was an example of their general inadequacy as parents and their lack of commitment to a challenging situation. Far from a self-centred anger, however, many siblings also expressed anger on behalf of their institutionalized brother or sister, who, they recognized, had suffered to a far greater degree than they had, a situation that most siblings felt powerless to change.

Family Presentation

"I was always one of two children,
before *and* after he was born, to the world."
(Marilyn, sister to an institutionalized boy)

Many of the siblings who participated in this study described living in a family in which there was more than one family story, a family whose composition and history bore more than one 'truth.' A disconnect existed between the family's public presentation and their authentic constellation and lives together.

Siblings described a range of divergences, ranging from some inconsistencies between what others were told about the family and what was really being lived, to a complete denial of the existence of a family member with a disability. At the less severe end of the spectrum, for example, two siblings, Abigail[3] and Gregory,[4] described their family's depiction of their brother's institutionalization not as something that they *could* not talk about, but rather something that they "just *did* not talk about." Similarly, William[5] stated that the fact that they did not often talk about his sister Hilary and her institutionalization did not constitute a burden; rather, he experienced it as a regular feature of his family's life.

Other siblings, however, described a larger discrepancy between the family that was presented to the outside world, and the one that was lived in the home. Colleen, for example, described a situation in which some friends knew about the existence of her disabled brother and his institutionalization, yet revealed that this was not always an easy truth to live publicly, particularly in her teenage years. She described one phone conversation with a friend in which she claimed to have only two brothers, when in truth she had three. While she was not forbidden to speak of her institutionalized brother, and indeed her family was one of the ones interviewed for this study that visited the institution regularly, Colleen explained that she was simply "tired of having to explain this aberrant family to people." Faced with this prospect, Colleen avoided explaining her family's situation to someone unfamiliar with it, an omission that she continues to reflect upon more than forty years later.

Five of the remaining siblings described situations of greater intensity, in which their institutionalized sibling was rarely spoken of, and their family's presentation to the outside world gave the impression of a family with fewer members than the reality. Three participants, Michelle, Olivia[6] (sisters), and Carmen, explained that their families did visit their institutionalized siblings, and in Michelle and Olivia's case, even had their sister home for some holidays during her institutionalization.[7] Despite these two families' attempts to maintain connection with their institutionalized child, few people outside of their families knew of their existence. Carmen reiterated Colleen's experience that this was particularly true in her teenage years: "My [high school] friends never knew ... My friends couldn't come to the house ... They never came. This was not a story to be shared." In these cases, the family member's institutionalization was not exactly denied within the home, but there was a gap between the true story and the story within which the daily life of the family was carried out.

Along the spectrum of incongruent family narratives, three women, Margaret, Marilyn, and Erin,[8] recounted particularly difficult situations. Margaret described the lack of story around her brother Johnny. She explained, "He was a secret. So, once he was institutionalized, he was never spoken of in a family context, *ever*. I knew of his existence ... [but] we never talked about him." This explains why, according to Margaret, her youngest brother, who was an infant when her brother Johnny was institutionalized, did not include Johnny when talking about their family: "My youngest brother barely knew Johnny ... how would he even know Johnny existed? ... He had no memory, and there was no family talk." As an adult, the youngest brother "had not bothered to tell his wife that Johnny had existed ... because he was that irrelevant to his life, in his opinion."

Marilyn also described a family that functioned on the premise that her brother was no longer part of their family and was not to be discussed. Contrary to what her parents might have wished in keeping details of her brother from her, Marilyn described ongoing attempts to fill the gaps that she knew existed in her family story. Marilyn knew of her brother's existence – she was made painfully aware of his removal from their family the moment her mother returned from the hospital without the baby she had so looked forward to taking care of – but it has only been through a life-long process of picking up fragments of information about her brother that she has gradually been able to put together a picture of who he was and what kind of life he lived. Through sometimes unkind comments from neighbours, as well as more recent information from an uncle who knew her brother's whereabouts and maintained contact with the institution where he lived, Marilyn has slowly constructed the story of her brother's life – a story which has brought with it the need to come to terms with the losses that his removal engendered.

In one extreme case, the difference between the public portrayal of the family and its actual makeup was so marked that a younger sibling was not even aware that another child existed. Erin describes how her youngest brother Kevin[9] did not know he had a brother, and this discrepancy remained unspoken for many years. In her words, "I was in a family that actually had five people; Kevin was in a family with *four* people. It was a totally different family from his perspective." Such care was taken to protect the false version of the story that Kevin was not present at his brother's funeral, a ceremony that took place in the family's own living room. Rather astonishingly, the parents somehow managed to arrange their child's funeral in their own home, and simultaneously prevented one of their children from attending. Erin recounts: "And so, when David[10] died, Kevin went to other people's house overnight. He didn't know. And so, while we had a funeral in the house, Kevin was at a sleepover at someone's house." As can be expected, when the unknowing brother finally learned the story in its truthful entirety as an adult, any trust that had existed in the family underwent significant breakage, and it remains "a hurtful topic between us … there's a whole bunch of stuff about the fact that I didn't tell him."

These examples suggest a spectrum of experiences concerning the ways in which families chose to represent themselves. At one end were those families who lived their stories with a certain degree of honesty: while they were not necessarily open about their institutionalized family member, they also did not deny the person existed, and oftentimes, friends and family knew. At the other end were those families whose knowledge of an institutionalized family member was not divulged outside of the family home, and sometimes not even within the family home.

In all of these examples, the families' functioning, one in which their external presentation was different from the reality, became normalized within the home and became the accepted code by which the family lived (Pelias 2008). The normalization of a discordant family narrative often had significant repercussions within the family, including situations in which the young siblings of an institutionalized child felt responsible for the story's upkeep.

Protecting the Story: Precarity and Navigation

Siblings reflected on the reasons why their families had protected untrue or partially true narratives and their own motivations for participating in them. All the siblings who came from families with a higher socio-economic standing, or a desire to achieve one, indicated that their parents' desire to maintain some semblance of success and normativity in status-conscious postwar society was a significant factor in their decision to remove their disabled child from the family home. The disabled child was an encumbrance, an obstacle to the desired goal of a successful and beautiful family, a point which emerges with greater clarity in parents' reflections in the next chapter. As Margaret stated, "It was very shameful. And so he was a secret." Carmen described her mother's desire to maintain a particular image: "If you're from a family like Mom's, you don't have a handicapped kid ... I think there was a lot of shame around having a handicapped person in those days ... I think class was a big player there ... There were people who were very well off, very wealthy people who just didn't bring the kid home ... and people didn't talk about that at all." The practice of sending children from upper-class families away from home for schooling also normalized a disabled child's institutionalization (as was the case in three families); in other families, aspirations towards that kind of status became a motivating factor in their decision.

Margaret, Marilyn, and Erin also explained that their siblings' institutionalization, the discourse that was shaped around it, and their participation in those dynamics may have also served a protective function in their home to prevent an already-fragile marriage from dissolving and the family from falling apart. In the context of postwar normativity, the survival of the marriage was essential and frequently depended on sacrifice somewhere else in the family (May 2008). As Margaret noted, her parents' marriage was "terrible," and "the household was a mess, an absolute mess." Her mother decided, when her brother Johnny was three, that if his needs were to be met, "the whole family would have to be sacrificed for the household to work around him." Rather than do that, and thus end the functioning of the family as they knew it, Johnny was sent away instead. Erin described what she thinks was a 'deal' between her mother and her father in regard to her brother's institutionalization and its ongoing secrecy: "The decision to institutionalize ... I tend to chalk it up to my father. And I tend to feel like my father said she couldn't visit him because she would get too upset ... I think that was the deal ... basically they had to disengage and that was the basis of their continued marriage."

Many of the siblings described feeling a responsibility towards participating in the family's secretive narrative, even when they were very young. Erin remembered, "I was a kid, a good kid, and I did what I was supposed to do." Marilyn described what she now believes was her motivation for maintaining the family secret: "I was afraid to mention it [brother's institutionalization]. I didn't want [my parents] to be losers, so I tried to bolster them by just evading. I was afraid of destabilizing my family ... you hold on to your image of your family against the world, right?" She feels that she participated in the story her parents created as a way to ensure her own safety and protection. She notes that children are dependent on parents for survival and learn early on what it might take to prevent the only institution they know from falling apart. These siblings' participation in their families' public presentation, even if it wasn't true, is one such example.

The felt need to protect secretive elements of their family story led many siblings to experience their family home as a precarious place that required ongoing navigation. They described the precision with which they had to conduct themselves in the home for fear of breaking the fragility of the untruthful narrative, and of upsetting the balance between their family's public face, their parents' well-being, and the knowledge of their family's actual composition. Discourse was managed and there were rules regarding its boundaries; some things were permitted conversationally outside the home, others, not. As all of the siblings were children or youth when their brother or sister was removed from the home, this discursive management was the context within which they learned to function and from which they grew into adults.

Thus, many siblings describe the care with which they had to interact with others for fear of breaking open the narrative of an institutionalized brother or sister. Erin stated, "My teacher didn't know ... I knew that we were not discussing this with anybody else ... I don't remember talking about it to anybody, really." Michelle recalled that even though some of her friends knew she had a sister with a disability, "I was so isolated ... I had one friend in grade five who had a brother ... whose family had him admitted to an institution ... But then the same year, her family moved ... so that was kind of the end of that." Even as children, they knew that speaking beyond the boundaries could have harmful repercussions. Erin explained, "I was careful. If I provided this information when I shouldn't … this huge thing was going to unravel." This was true even within the family home: when she and her brother were older, if the story of her institutionalized brother was raised in her mother's presence, her mother would cry, and "I always felt like she would never stop."

The precariousness of their situation, in combination with feelings of isolation in the knowledge of a disabled brother or sister who lived away from home, both contributed to what can be described as a feeling of powerlessness. While parents had some control over the design and praxis of their family story, siblings were left to determine how to manage it. As children, much of siblings' lives revolved around school and neighbourhood situations over which they did not have complete control, and they intersected with divergent circles of people without the shared history of an institutionalized brother or sister. Siblings interacted in these circles not always certain who 'knew' and who didn't, creating anxiety about whether or not they could share their family's story, and about others' reactions should the true story come out. In addition, siblings explained that the precarity of the family narrative and their participation in it has resulted in long processes of reconciliation, both between themselves and other members of their families, and with regard to their own role in the fabrication. As Erin explained, she continues to struggle with the fact that she participated in the 'untruth' of her family story by withholding information from her non-institutionalized brother, despite the fact that she was three years old at the time.

Absence/Presence

Regardless of the degree to which family members knew and spoke about the institutionalized child's existence, all of the siblings recounted some element of heaviness in the family home, a sense that the person's absence was not an absence in the typical sense. Siblings referred to the "felt" and often significant presence of their missing brother or sister despite the child's invisibility, a phenomenon Goodall (2005) likens to the power that unspoken family secrets can hold within family narratives, a power that increases the longer the secret is held in abeyance. The physical absence of the individual from the home did not remove them from the family narrative; rather, their absent persona maintained a presence that often grew in figurative scope and size in spite and because of their absence.

Carmen explained, "There was always a darkness, always a heaviness to that absence." Carmen also experienced the absence/presence of her sister as a feeling of the institution and all its residents directly in the home. She stated, "When it's your family … it's as if the whole institution moves into your house. So, that person isn't there … you go from one little person who's moved, to a place of thirty-eight hundred people who somehow come home with you … it's an emotional place that travels." Ironically, in Carmen's parents' hopes for a more stable and presentable home life, one person was removed and in her place, thousands of others took up residence. Colleen named this phenomenon as the proverbial "elephant-in-the-room kind of thing … this thing that was never discussed, never acknowledged." Despite parents' best intentions that the removal of a problematic individual would assist in establishing a safe and stable home, many siblings found that their removal gave rise instead to a strange situation in which the person was present without being seen.

Reasons

All of the siblings interviewed for this project were young children when their brother or sister was sent away. For that reason, and typical of the time period, they were not party to any of the discussions or decisions concerning their sibling. Most of these siblings describe growing up not knowing why this had happened, but have retrospectively arrived at what they believe are partial explanations.

Many of the siblings who came from middle-upper-class families felt that their parents' aspirations towards an upper-class lifestyle were contributing factors. Typical of these aspirations, Margaret noted that it was common for families of higher socio-economic standing, particularly of British heritage, to send their children away to boarding school. This gave a sense of normalcy to three families' decisions to institutionalize their disabled child. Gregory drew parallels between his own experience of being sent away to school and his brother's institutionalization: "One of the things that made it not so strange … I spent relatively little time at home in Toronto, and so I wasn't at home with my parents that much more than Graham was."

Another reason was families' intellectual aspirations. Five of the women described the overlap they experienced between their family's social standing and the felt need to demonstrate intellectual achievement. Margaret noted, "there was this thing around intellect that was a really big deal in my family ... intellectual competence was really important." Erin stated, "In my family, unless you had intellect [and] you demonstrated intellectual capacity at a very high level, you didn't have value ... the brightest and the most intelligent among us were the ones who rose to the top of the value ladder in my house." Michelle described the demarcation between different categories of children in their families: "So, there were the 'smart' kids – my sister Olivia and me – and the 'dumb' kids" – her disabled sister and an adopted brother. This protection of the image of the bright, competent family explains in part why some families, particularly those striving for a solid rung on the socio-economic ladder, would have guarded the knowledge that they had a child with an intellectual disability and had decided to send him or her away.

In addition, more than half of the siblings described their parents' belief, supported by medical and sociological perceptions at the time regarding the negative impact of children with intellectual disabilities on family life, that the removal of the problematic child from the home would allow the remaining children to flourish. Siblings referred to parents' perceptions that they would have more time, attention, and energy for their other children that would otherwise be 'used up' by the disabled child if he or she were to remain at home, an assumption contradicted by siblings' recollections (below). This perspective continues to be reflected in mainstream medical literature, which prioritizes discussion of the effect of disabled children on the family from the perspective of non-disabled family members, with a general focus on perceived negative effects.

Institutionalization's Effects

Success and Achievement: "She was an anomaly"

Siblings' understanding of the reasons for institutionalization overlap closely with its felt effects, ranging from feelings of needing to provide evidence of their own intellectual and material success to witnessing institutionalization's impact on other members of their family.

Siblings recounted that the perception that institutionalization would lead to more space in the home for them to flourish often had the reverse effect. They spoke of feeling tremendous pressure to 'do well,' both to make up for their parents' experience of loss around having a child with a disability, and to support the narrative of justification for institutionalization that existed in the home. That is, if the remaining siblings were to underperform academically and socially, with the biggest 'drain' on family resources removed, then parents' rationale for institutionalization for the sake of the other siblings would be brought into question.

Parents were particularly desirous that their remaining children demonstrate a sound intellect, as if the presence of intellectual brilliance in some members of the family would provide evidence that the child with the deficit was an anomaly, a 'freak' who was not representative of the family's true capabilities. This happened most frequently in families in which intellectual and academic achievement was considered an essential indicator of success. Siblings describe feeling this pressure acutely. They knew their parents expected them to do well in all areas of their academic, social, and extra-curricular lives. Michelle stated, "I had to be the smart one, and the successful one … it's like I compensated for Nora." She went on to describe feeling responsible, not only to perform well, but to be grateful to her parents for providing her with this opportunity. She stated, "I know she [mother] made that decision for us, which is a heavy, heavy thing to carry. You know, she did it for us – thanks, Mom – the thinking of the time was – the other children will suffer."

Some siblings reported that this atmosphere contributed to a fear that if they did not fulfil their families' expectations, they could potentially meet the same fate as their institutionalized brother or sister. Erin described her fear of being sent away: "You know, if you don't do super well, we'll ship you off – there was this sense of very, very high expectations of us. And the undercurrent of all of those high expectations was – if you don't fit into this category, you're expendable, right? We had an expendable child." In a more extreme case, Margaret recounted being sent to Australia (her mother's country of origin) for six months, without her family, at the age of five, after her brother had been sent to an institution. Although Margaret now interprets this as a likely response to her mother's exhaustion and the need to lessen the demands on her within the household, as a young girl she interpreted this as punishment for not having lived up to her parents' expectations. "My take on it [institutionalization] was that I did not understand Johnny as having a disability. I understood Johnny as being bad … And so my take on being sent to Australia was because I was bad … so, you've got to really watch out, or you get sent away."

These situations point to a theme that appears throughout other participant narratives that were part of this study: a lack of critical analysis of the factors contributing to institutionalization beyond the 'deficits' of the person in question. While parents might have felt tremendous relief when their remaining children demonstrated 'sound' intellect (and consternation when they did not), this was not founded on a critique of the context or situation within which their family was located. That is, for many of the families in this study, the non-disabled children's success was probably as reflective of the relative comfort and socio-economic advantage of their situation, as it was evidence of the anomalous nature of disability's presence in the family.

Derogatory Discourse: "It's the right place for her"

Another major effect of institutionalization within the family as reported by siblings was the use of derogatory language to refer to the institutionalized child. In part to defend parents' decision to place their child in an institution, some siblings described a disdainful narrative around people with intellectual disabilities in the home. Michelle spoke of this in regard to her sister Nora: "to us she was a mongoloid." She described the attitudes with which she was surrounded as she grew up: "So much [of my fear] had to do with the attitudes I grew up with about disability and about Downs ... like, how ugly ... well, I guess the words were – she was retarded, right? There was something wrong with her genes, with her chromosomes ... so she was never going to be able to do the things that we would do ... she would be with her own kind ... it was better for her. I think I had an attitude of superiority ... I just saw her as this defective person."

Carmen spoke of hearing her mother refer to her institutionalized sister as someone who "ruined our lives." Carmen attempted to formulate different explanations for her mother's comments: in one, she reasoned that her sister's ruinous presence was directly related to her disability; in another, Carmen assumed that if her handicapped sister was able to 'ruin' her family, surely she could as well – did this also mean that she might be sent away to a facility far from home? Derision, therefore, also created uncertainty.

One of the effects of this disdainful attitude was its hindrance of the development of authentic relationships between siblings. The limited portrayal of people with intellectual disabilities did not encourage non-institutionalized children to develop accurate perceptions of their institutionalized siblings, nor to establish healthy and formative relationships. This discourse worked so long as the disabled sibling remained in the institution, and so long as public discourse continued to support institutionalization as a viable method to house people with intellectual disabilities.

While parents might have attempted to convey that the institution was the best place for their disabled child, little could be done to alter the institutions' foreboding and often frightening presence in the lives of some siblings. Indeed, siblings described their visits to the institution not as something that helped them to better get to know their brother or sister, but as difficult encounters that confirmed their impression that the institution was a dark and dangerous place, and that their sibling was an unknown stranger. For example, Carmen described her visits to the institution where her sister Dore-Ann lived as "incredibly rough. Those kids were like something out of Dickens. They were so strong and they would push ... there was like a pack of kids. And they'd grab cigarettes out of people's hands, and puff on them, like it was really a rough and ready place." Olivia recounts, "I know I used to be scared going to the institution. Everyone would want to come up and touch you ... I remember seeing someone tied with a skipping rope to a chair and things like that."

Moreover, Michelle noted that their sister Nora's visits home did not necessarily improve the family's bond with her. Michelle explained that Nora's visits served rather to remind their mother of her self-perceived failures: that she had had a child with Down syndrome, and that she felt incapable of raising her. Nora's occasional return to her family home underpinned her mother's impression that she did not have the heart or the skills needed to care for a child with a disability, and that there were others who were more suited for and more capable of the undertaking.

Thus, although the institution was framed as the right place for these children, and some parents attempted to forge relationships between institutionalized and non-institutionalized children, the distance created because of institutionalization, as well as an ongoing discourse that the institutionalized child did not belong in the family home, all added to the difficulty in establishing normal, regular relations between brothers and sisters.

Once deinstitutionalization began, many siblings were asked to participate in the relocation of their brother or sister into community settings. Many found themselves in the awkward position of having to get to know a brother or sister they had barely met and had not seen for years; as Margaret noted, "He has no idea who I am." For many, this was a difficult moment, as they were forced to reconcile earlier perceptions they had formed about their sibling with new understandings that portrayed their brother or sister in a more favourable light. Through this process, siblings became aware of the role that public discourse had played in their understanding of their brother or sister: as children, it had served the family well to perceive their sibling as someone who needed to be segregated and institutionalized; as adults, they had to adjust this perception as institutions closed, and families were called upon to play more active roles in the well-being of their now-adult family members.

A Desire to Know

A third major effect of institutionalization on siblings was an unrequited desire for more knowledge of their brother or sister. Marilyn described her attempts to learn more about the brother she was never permitted to know. She recalls feeling confused when her mother returned home from the hospital without the baby she had looked forward to: "I wanted to know where he – if he's not coming home, where is he? Who is looking after him like I planned to?" She described a specific incident in which she attempted, while still a young child, to learn the whereabouts of her brother: "We were at some friends' cottage in the area.[11] We went to a restaurant in Orillia, and I went with this other family. And I remember leaving the table and going to a public phone booth and looking up the phone number of the place [the institution], just to know it was real. I wasn't going to call, although I think I wished I could have. But I just wanted to know that there was such a place, and it just brought it closer to me, just seeing it in the phone book." Marilyn's desire to learn more about her brother continued into adulthood, when she took a job in the institution where her brother had lived, partly, she realizes now, in an attempt to fill the vacuum of knowledge that her parents had left vacant around her missing sibling. She was determined to find out as much as she could about her brother – "it was absolutely, I had to do it." That she was denied the opportunity to see and touch him, save only for his funeral when she was thirteen years old,[12] remains for her a devastating piece of her family story.

Erin also recounts her desire to learn more about her brother, whom she did not see between the time he was institutionalized and his death a few years later. Although she was present at his funeral, she does not know where he is buried, and this lack of knowledge has plagued her since she was a child. Her continued but unsuccessful attempts to find his grave have, in her words, "intensified as time went on" and it remains an unfinished part of her family story.

Less tangibly, but equally importantly, other siblings describe the long process of coming to terms with the realization that they may never learn the full story of their institutionalized brother or sister. Colleen explained that due to her brother's limited ability to communicate and her family's inability to determine the whole story of his institutional years, despite her desire to know what happened to him, she will never know his story fully.

Effects on Mothers: "It came out everywhere"

Another significant observation siblings offered concerns the impact that institutionalization had on their mothers. Although siblings understood the decision to institutionalize as being made by both parents, it is notable that this group of participants spoke more about the impact of institutionalization on their mothers than on their fathers. This could be due to a number of factors, although none of them can be claimed with absolute certainty. Perhaps mothers were more expressive in their responses to the removal of the disabled child and thus their feelings were more known; or, the participants in this study (mostly women) spent more time with their mothers than their fathers and thus were more observant of her emotional status; or, fathers truly were less affected by the disabled child's leaving. What is clear is that this particular group described mothers who expressed high levels of emotional effects from this process, and fathers who seemed to maintain greater emotional distance.

All of the siblings noted that their mother carried some regret or sadness about the situation; what was not clear was whether the mother felt regret about deciding to institutionalize a child, or about having had a child with a disability in the first place. The ways in which this sadness was carried also varied between women, hence having varying impacts on the family.

Three of the siblings described mothers who bore the situation of having a child with an intellectual disability and their subsequent decision to place him or her in an institution with quiet stoicism. For these women, the child's disability was an unfortunate life event that needed to be dealt with. These were women who did what they felt was expected of them by their social position and felt obliged to heed the advice of educational and medical authorities. Gregory stated, "One of the great regrets of my mother's life was Graham ... that was one of the greatest sadnesses of her life ... [yet] my mother would be very determined to do the right thing, to do what she was, in effect, told to do. Quite strong on 'ought' ... she would have made her decision based on what she felt was best for all of us." William described his mother's religious foundation as a way to accept her situation and to come to terms with the decisions she had made: "Her faith meant a lot to her ... Part of her understanding of how she lived out her faith was to accept the life that was hers to live. Now, that meant accepting her children, that meant accepting Hilary, and accepting some problems that we had in our own family that she couldn't do anything about." For these women, doing what they felt was best for their family, including accepting others' advice, was paramount, even when this was difficult.

The remaining siblings described their mothers as deeply emotionally affected from the situation in which they found themselves, with sometimes debilitating effects on the family. Colleen described her mother's life-long depression after admitting her son to an institution: "I don't think my mother ever recovered from having to let him go. My mother then went into a serious depression. Even suicidal ... my mother never recovered." Michelle and Olivia noted that although their mother felt that others were better equipped emotionally to provide the care her daughter needed, she still suffered "years of self-recrimination" for having had a child with a disability and then feeling incapable of raising her. Indeed, Michelle felt that her mother allowed her heart to "turn to stone" in order to cope with her own sense of failure; accordingly, her mother expressed relief when her sister passed away, as her death signified an end to years of self-criticism. According to Michelle, "I think for my mother it was a tremendous relief. When Nora died ... most of us went in and were with her and touched her and said good-bye and cried and everything ... my mother didn't do anything. She just left the room. Didn't touch her, nothing."

Three other participants describe their mothers as 'criers.' They describe growing up fearing that once their mothers started crying, they would not stop, and the family would be left to cope on their own with an emptied-out and disengaged mother. Marilyn described her mother's emotional fragility, which surfaced whenever discussion about her son in the institution arose. Marilyn now recognizes this as a form of neglect; in those moments, while Marilyn was still a child, her mother was incapable of responding to her needs. In particular, Marilyn remembers, when she was thirteen years old, the family attempting to make funeral arrangements after learning of her brother's death in the institution, "and my mother refused to go to the funeral home. And it was that scene again of her emotion and everything ... she should have been there with me. We should have done it together."

Carmen described her mother's gradual slide into a dark place after her sister's institutionalization: "Mom had no capacity to cope ... she became an insomniac, very, very teary, just more and more incapacitated." She recounted that her mother's emotional struggle with the situation was lived out every week, when Carmen and her parents made the trek to the institution where her sister lived. On the drive home from the institution, "she would sit in the front seat with her head down," an example of what she describes as her mother's unending sorrow. "There was no way that Mom could feel better. Whether Dore-Ann was at home, or whether she was in the institution, or whether she was driving, or whether I was driving, she never got herself out of the funk of her feelings of having had Dore-Ann. She could never turn the story ... she would just never do it. Mom's ploy was to put her head down and cry ... that was her signal to all of us – I'm not going there."

Erin also described her difficulty in knowing how to respond to her mother's intense bouts of emotion: "My mother was a huge crier ... and the most difficult thing I experienced with her is, I always felt like she would never stop. She would grab onto me, she would hold me, she would hug me, and she wouldn't let me go."

Mothers' reliance on their daughters took other forms as well. Siblings who describe their mothers as experiencing their situation with a high level of emotional intensity recall being thrust into positions of responsibility and emotional leadership within the family at a young age. Colleen explained: "One of my memories is my mother sitting on the couch feeding Martin[13] [baby brother, prior to institutionalization] and directing me to open a can of soup and put it on the stove. I'm five years old. And then, her being so angry with me because it went dry ... I remember thinking – *I'm just a kid. I don't know how to do this.*" Others referred to role reversals. Marilyn, for example, recalled the significance of the moment when her mother returned from the hospital without her baby brother when she was four years old: "I see that as a turning point in my life, where my job was to look after my mother after that, not her job to look after me. Because she was this vulnerable person, I was supposed to be strong." Carmen spoke at length about her role as family facilitator in light of her mother's incapacity: "I was the decision-maker in the house, probably from the time I was twelve or thirteen. I just did it. It didn't occur to me there was any choice. So, that became my role. Part of my job was to keep my parents happy. It was my role in the family to facilitate everybody else, getting them up and getting them moving, sort of trying to keep everybody else's spirits up a little bit. As for my mom, it [having a child with a disability] just drowned her, and my role was to keep her swimming."

Marilyn provided an interesting insight here. She stated that while it was perhaps important for mothers to cry, it seemed that some were crying more for themselves than for their children. "They've cried and cried and cried over the years. But maybe a little bit more for themselves – because they lost a child, or they had to deal with this, and other people didn't. The sort of 'why me' questions that anybody asks. They've cried and cried and cried ... but maybe the mothers should start to cry for their children, that's what they should have done." She noted that these women remained devastated over the birth of a child with a disability, and they were not able to "turn the story around" and use that sense of loss to work for something better for their children. Perhaps the "great sadness" to which some siblings referred had more to do with the mothers' own loss, never fully resolved, than about the suffering of their children.[14]

These vignettes reveal a sad irony. If, by placing their disabled child in an institution, parents had hoped to locate their disappointment and grief away from the family home and tuck it out of sight, they were sadly mistaken. From the stories these siblings have shared, mothers carried their grief with them, and seemed to experience an emotional entrapment at their own and others' expense. Erin described her mother's grief as something that "came out everywhere, because it came out nowhere." With her son's existence a secret to almost everyone, there was nowhere Erin's mother could safely express her sadness, and thus, according to Erin, it seemed to be "everywhere." Moreover, parents' dreams of creating a beautiful and successful home by removing the troublesome family member proved misguided when the emotional toll on the family is considered. What the parents had perhaps not taken into account was the impact that the child's removal would have on the family, the negative effects of which resulted in unusual home situations in which children keenly felt the absence of their sibling and felt the need to sustain and encourage the entire household at a very young age.

Loss and Rupture

Echoing survivors, siblings referred to breakage in family relationships and stories, acknowledging that there are entire chapters of their lives that remain unknown to each other. While this is true to some degree in all families, there is an added sadness here, as many survivors do not have the communicative capacity to describe that period of their lives with those close to them. Colleen, whose institutionalized brother did not communicate verbally, juxtaposed what she knew of him with what she knew of her other two brothers: "With my other brothers ... I know big chunks of their life stories, and I know lots of things about them that my parents didn't know. And I don't have that with Martin. I don't have that shared history. There's a whole bunch of stuff that I just don't know." This was particularly difficult for her when she suspected that Martin was being sexually abused in the institution yet felt powerless to intervene: "to know that he had been so horribly harmed and nobody could even say to him – *I know what happened to you* – as a big sister, that's really hard." Similarly, Abigail told of her surprise when her brother Graham, years after leaving the institution, described its violent atmosphere and the rough treatment he had encountered. She, as well as the rest of her family, had been assured that he was receiving "the best of care." Indeed, this theme of not knowing is one that appears repeatedly throughout families' experiences: because of the lack of family contact (and, frequently, the highly supervised nature of families' visits), and because of some survivors' lack of verbal communication, most families never knew the nature or extent of their experience.

Breakage between family members was intensified when an institutionalized family member passed away. Marilyn recounted that the only time she saw her brother was at his funeral when he was eight years old. As he had never come home as a baby, she had never had the opportunity to touch him, speak with him, play with him. While his funeral confirmed this gap in her life, she also recognized the role it played in her understanding of the situation: "this was the realest it got ... there was a role to that, as strange and horrible as it was." In a process from which she continues to learn, she confessed that it took her many years to tell her own children about her brother, their uncle who had existed but was absent from the family story.

For Erin, the gap in her knowledge of her brother remains, and her grieving for him remains unfinished. Although she was present at the secret funeral that her family had for him, she does not know where her brother is buried. Far from allowing her to put her brother's life to rest, this 'not knowing' perpetuates the absence that his life symbolized. With no physical place to which she can direct her attention, she continues to grieve: "I would just say that my own personal experience of grieving him, which I have done my whole life, without any of the information, like in a vacuum of information … it's all about the things that I should have done or could have done … if the only thing I have left to do is some kind of assurance that he is properly buried and remembered, then that's what I can do … I can't do anything. I don't, I have nothing left to do." She goes on to suggest that the lack of recognition of her brother, in life and in death, disallows him from participation in the larger story of the human family. "He's unremembered in lots of ways … he's like the hidden kid. So, how do I unhide him? How do I bring him into the light? … How do we deal with all these invisible people? … He wasn't even permitted to be known by people in such a way that he could live on."

Michelle described her distress over her family's disagreement regarding her sister's final resting place. While her parents determined that it would be best to scatter their daughter's ashes, Michelle felt that, after a lifetime of being denied the opportunity to claim any place as her own, her sister's ashes should be buried. Her parents' refusal was devastating. "To me, it was a re-enactment of the very thing that had happened in the first place, when they took her away." Michelle has reconciled herself to the fact that this fracture in understanding between herself and her parents is one that will never be reconciled. "There are some things I really can't share with my parents. They will never get it, and, you know, I can never share that part of myself with them. That was so hard."

For Michelle, the brokenness she experienced in her family as a result of her sister's institutionalization also took on a physical manifestation. Her sister Nora was institutionalized at age two; Michelle remembers this as the removal of a playmate without explanation, replaced by talk that painted her sister as someone with a deficit who needed to live away from home. As an adult, Michelle began to experience this loss in an embodied way, feeling intense pain in one part of her body, eventually learning with the help of therapy that the pain was a manifestation of the burden of sadness and guilt that she felt around Nora's departure. Only after Nora had died, and Michelle had taken steps to ritualize her leave-taking, did the pain in one part of her body cease to haunt her. While this is an extreme example of grief's manifestation, it is illustrative of the potential depths of the wounds caused by a child's unexplained and sudden removal from the family home.

In general, siblings acknowledged a loss of relational possibilities due to the removal of their brother or sister. "The whole family was robbed of him, and he was robbed of us," said Colleen. Siblings describe the gaps in their family stories and understandings of each other as experiences of loss, loss of friendships that could have thrived had they been allowed to exist, and loss of a complete sense of self which emerges through our interactions with one another (Gibson 2006; Price and Shildrick 2002; Shildrick 2009; Thomas 1999). When the numbers of families affected by institutionalization are accounted for, the magnitude of the loss of unrealized relationships is of tragic proportions.

Relief

Most of the stories recounted above paint a picture of the loss that siblings experienced at the removal of a brother or sister. Some of the siblings, however, described a feeling of relief that entered the family home once a child was institutionalized. This usually occurred when the home had been fraught with some chaos or instability in the first place. Margaret explained that her brother's institutionalization was motivated to a large degree by the need to remove one stressor in an already-dysfunctional situation. Her brother's lack of presence in the home was an "unaddressed absence" that "added to the terribleness" of an overwhelmingly poor family dynamic. Accordingly, she did not miss her brother: "it didn't haunt me at all"; it was simply another element of the "huge stress" of a complicated family life. Abigail, whose brother was institutionalized when she was a teenager, also indicated that not having her brother at home was a relief, and that she "would have found it very difficult to cope with living with him." She referred to her embarrassment around her brother for a certain period of her young adulthood: "I did sort of shut him out of my life. He wasn't on my radar. I didn't want him on my radar."

Carmen, while aware of the poor conditions at the institution where her sister lived and the devastating effect her institutionalization was having on her mother, noted that she did not really miss her sister during her growing-up years: "It wasn't until the end of the 90s that I was able to say – I actually have a sister … [still] I can't honestly say that I look at

Dore-Ann with any love." Thus, the sense that the family missed out on a significant relationship was not the experience for all siblings. Even while knowing that institutionalization was not a good thing in essence, some stated that they did not miss their sibling, and that the family situation would not have necessarily been better had it not happened.

Ongoing Repercussions

While most of the stories recounted by siblings revolve around their childhood years and the impact that institutionalization had on their families while growing up, they also describe its cascade of effects (Barad 2007) and ongoing repercussions. Regardless of circumstance, all save one of the siblings in this study noted that the birth of a disabled child and the subsequent decision to institutionalize him or her was generally experienced negatively within the family, with emotional characterizations ranging from disappointment to shame to secrecy. These are experiences that siblings continue to come to terms with as adults and to reconcile within the larger context of their family. Michelle's experience of physical pain as the manifestation of her sister's absence/presence, and Margaret and Marilyn's acknowledgments of their career choices – psychotherapy and social work respectively – as evidence of their need to psychically integrate their own upbringings, are examples of some of the ways that the experience of institutionalization has played out in other people's lives. As Carmen noted, "When you think about that baggage, somehow when one of your family members goes there, that becomes part of what you carry. There's just no way around it … I still carry all those years."

Vici, a woman whose observations stood apart from those of the other siblings, made one of the more distressing observations in regard to institutionalization's ongoing effects. Vici's experience was somewhat different, primarily because her brother Rob was institutionalized for a shorter time than most (approximately one year), and she has maintained an open and honest dialogue with her mother[15] about the process. Since young adulthood, Vici has worked tirelessly as an advocate on behalf of her brother and others with intellectual disabilities, and has done significant work in ensuring better lives for people now living in the community. However, when she reflects on what she imagines for her life in the future and what she might wish to aspire towards, she states, "I don't really deserve a good life for myself." In light of what her brother has suffered, Vici struggles to believe that she deserves to feel content with her life. While this is one example of the way in which someone has been affected by institutionalization in their family, and is not the way the other siblings in this study have coped with 'survivor guilt,' it is nonetheless indicative of the potential for seepage of one family member's negative experiences into the lives of those closest to them.

Conclusion

Siblings' stories provide a rich account of what transpired within families as they experienced institutionalization. For many of the siblings, the institutionalization of a brother or sister was, principally, a reflection of their parents' (mis)understanding of disability, and of their assumptions concerning the impact of a disabled person on the future of their family. As will be explored in greater depth in the next chapter, parents' perceptions of disability were instrumental in their decision regarding whether or not to institutionalize a child. Accordingly, many of the siblings' reflections convey anger towards their parents, who were seen as the driving force behind the decision to institutionalize.

However, siblings' reflections also reveal the complex web of factors that contributed to institutionalization. For some siblings, the institutionalization of a brother or sister was one feature in an overall situation of dysfunction. As Marilyn pointed out, "my parents were not very good parents for many, many reasons"; in her opinion, their decision to institutionalize her brother was one example, albeit the most devastating one, of their inadequacy as parents. Some of the other siblings noted that their parents' emotional self-centredness would have been challenging in any family situation, but was particularly limiting when disability was introduced into the equation. Further, siblings' acknowledgment of the role of families' socio-economic aspirations, particularly in white, middle-upper-class families, the rigidity of gender roles, and the lack of social support typical of the era provide insight into the larger, multifaceted milieu within which families were attempting to function. The next chapter, reflections from parents, deepens these insights and readily exposes the connections between intrafamilial factors and societal expectations.

Two final points emerging from sibling narratives require address. The first concerns the role of gender and its impact on the experience of institutionalization within the family. The findings from this study suggest that the sisters and mothers of people who were institutionalized suffered extensively from the experience, more so than did their male counterparts. Sibling accounts identify the suffering their mothers endured after having made the decision to institutionalize, manifested through relentless stoicism, regret and sadness, and, in some cases, depression that lasted the rest of their lives. Sisters also described a deep struggle with this piece of their family history. They indicated that their parents' decision to remove a brother or sister from the family home has been a significant marker of their identity and of the role they have carried within the family, and that it has resulted in an ongoing emotional and reconciliatory journey. In contrast, the brothers and fathers interviewed did not outwardly express the same depth of emotional anguish. In general, siblings spoke of their fathers' distance from both the process and the manifestation of the decision to institutionalize, a position encouraged by the societal expectation for men to assume non-domestic roles outside of the family home. As Margaret noted, "He was absent. He was very present [to his work] professionally. And absent in the home. He absolutely never spoke about Johnny; he absolutely did not visit him."

In order to adequately address gender concerns, however, methodological considerations must be taken into account. More women siblings (nine) than men (two) participated in this study, and from a research perspective, it was easier to recruit women than men. Seven of the nine women were immediately willing to participate in the project (indeed, some of them sought me out once they learned of it), and three men who were contacted for potential participation declined the invitation. Moreover, the fathers and brothers who participated in this project appeared significantly more composed and less emotionally distraught by the recounting of their experiences than were the mothers and sisters. These behaviours reflect the tendency, addressed in the literature, towards greater female representation in qualitative research (Polit and Beck 2008), as well as issues of gender socialization (Affleck, Glass, and MacDonald 2013, 156) and men's felt need to present an "essentially masculine self" (Schwalbe and Wolkomir 2003, 56) in interview situations. Taking these considerations into account, conclusions concerning gender from this particular group must be undertaken with caution; at the least, they emphasize the depth of emotion that most of the women brought to the interview.

The second major theme requiring address stems from the first and concerns the distribution of power and the relationship between power and one's experience of institutionalization within the family. As part of an inverse pattern that emerges at different points in this text, siblings' accounts suggest that the further removed one was from the nexus of power and decision-making within the home, the more suffering one seemed to experience. At the core of this were the survivors, who had no input into decisions made about their lives, yet suffered most profoundly as a result. So, too, did many of the siblings in this study suffer significant emotional distress as a result of their parents' decision, one to which they had no input. Thus, at least within this particular group, to be a sibling meant not having power or input when institutionalization was introduced into the family. This entailed a powerless yet compulsory participation in a family marked by the removal of a disabled child, as well as managing several difficult life tasks. These included the subsequent decades of separation; the naming of the disabled child, frequently the sibling's only playmate until that time, as 'different' in order to justify their removal; years of navigation within an unclear family make-up and the accompanying uncertainty regarding acceptable family discourse; and often an emotional re-connection with siblings much later in life, made obligatory by institutional closure. All of these moments in the lives of their families were difficult turns with which siblings had to grapple, all the while holding no authority in the decisions that directed them. It is possible that a larger study, with more participants, and with more variant socio-economic and racial backgrounds, might reveal a more diverse range of experiences in terms of how power was experienced around the decision to institutionalize. What emerged from this group was that the further one was from the decision which set into motion the removal of a family member, the more emotional suffering one seemed to experience. In this group, siblings' anger seemed to reflect many years of incapacity in front of an ongoing and frequently distressing family narrative.

The theme of power re-emerges in the chapters that follow, indicating its relevance in both the lead-up to and the aftermath of institutionalization within the family. And as the parents' narratives in the next chapter indicate, the power we are concerned with here is not necessarily a power of domination, the definition with which most of us are familiar, but is, rather, the subtle exertion of the extensive hand of coercion (Tremain 2005, 8–9), indicating the need to examine not only parents' stories of what transpired in the events surrounding their child's institutionalization and its aftermath, but also the direction and conduct of power's manifestation within the family.

6

Parents

The recruitment of parents who were willing to participate in this study was one of the most challenging aspects of the project. By the time I undertook the research in 2012, many parents who had institutionalized a child in the postwar years had already passed away; the ones I interviewed were all well into their eighties and nineties. Thus, the pool was small, and, as with all the groups of participants in this study, their accounts must be interpreted as a window into one aspect of a phenomenon as opposed to a comprehensive picture. In the end, I interviewed six parents who had institutionalized a child and two who had had a child with an intellectual disability but had chosen not to institutionalize (Appendix).

Three principal themes emerge from the parents' narratives, themes that simultaneously reinforce and contradict those from siblings.[1] These include systemic issues that prevented parents from securing adequate support, the influence of gender roles, and considerations involving the family. Yet within these thematic areas, parents' reflections varied significantly; these variances were largely dependent on parents' perceptions of disability, and their self-perceptions regarding whether or not they felt capable of raising a child with an intellectual impairment. Thus, while factors such as the amount of support a family received, where they lived, the number of children they had, and their household income might have had some bearing on each family's decision and subsequent experience, findings here suggest that these factors were deeply interrelated with parents' interpretations and understandings of disability, and with their own assessment regarding how best to respond to it within their own family. Moreover, parents' perceptions were in turn interrelated with and heavily influenced by broader social discourse and preferences around constructions of intellect, domestic roles, and so on. For these reasons, and due to the small sample size, patterns in parents' responses were difficult to discern; what became clear was that parents' feelings about institutionalization were deeply connected with how they regarded disability and how it should be addressed. The discussion that follows will address each of the above-named three themes in turn, followed by some discussion on this underlying and influential feature of parents' perceptions.

Systemic Obstacles: "There was no choice"

All of the parents interviewed for this project identified government policy and the absence of community resources as key factors in their decision to place their child in an institution. For reasons discussed in foregoing chapters, especially the economic and political priorities of successive conservative governments, there was little administrative impetus towards the establishment of supports for people with disabilities and their families throughout the first two-thirds of the twentieth century, other than the expansion of existing custodial institutions (Radford and Park 2003, 1993; Simmons 1982; Strong-Boag 2007). Gradual increases in the numbers and visibility of people with intellectual disabilities in the community and within family homes did not correspond to an increase in government funding for services, nor to policy that would ensure people's inclusion in non-segregated education, work, and regular civic life until well into the 1970s (Buell and Brown 2003).

Almost unanimously, the parents in this project stated that their decision to institutionalize had been at least partially based on the lack of resources and support. Bertram[2] stated, "Well, it was a lot of work for my wife ... there wasn't anything here. There wasn't support for anybody. And she said, '*I can't keep doing this all the time*' ... it ended up that he was accepted down at [the institution]." Muriel, who spoke openly of her regret for sending her son to an institution, noted, "There wasn't a choice; there was nothing." Gregory, one of the siblings, stated, "I don't think my mom ever regretted sending him away; I think she regretted that there weren't other choices."

In addition, the social and political climate during this era did not make it easy for families, particularly mothers, to create alternatives for children who fell outside socially accepted definitions of normalcy (Gleason 1997; Helleiner 2001; May 2008; Panitch 2008). Students with disabilities were generally not allowed to attend school, except for those schools established within segregated institutions (Carpenter 2007; Odell 2011). Until 1974, any funding for children with disabilities was housed within the Ministry of Health, and thus did not make provisions for community and social support. If parents felt inspired to create their own systems of support for their children, including educational opportunities, they were on their own.

The lack of possibilities, in combination with a climate not conducive to the development of alternate resources, left parents with two alternatives: keep their child at home and assume full responsibility for their care without support from the government, financial or otherwise, or surrender the role of parent and allow the child's care to be subsumed by the state via admission to a government-run institution (Simmons 1982). It was difficult for parents to imagine or construct alternatives that fell somewhere in between, and many parents who struggled to care for their child on their own eventually chose the only other option available to them. Audrey, a mother who did not institutionalize her son, stated, "I don't think parents had a choice – if nothing or an institution – that's not a choice."

Some parents recalled bureaucratic steps that were put in place with the intention of creating inclusion, but ironically made it more difficult for parents to choose alternatives other than institutionalization. Muriel and Bertram described the frustrating situation that developed after 1969, when school boards took over the administration of segregated schools that had been initiated by parents' associations.[3] While this was considered a positive step towards inclusion, it also contained a bureaucratic caveat with significant implications, as Muriel explains: "The school boards had taken over the segregated schools that the associations had started. However, they also inherited the admission criteria that you had to be toilet trained. I fought that ... anyway, they wouldn't let Rob go to school; that's what the rules were. And the doctors wouldn't sign and the school board wouldn't change ... I didn't know how to do it ... And so I said okay. So, my husband and I walked Rob up the five-eighths of a mile corridor at the institution."

Muriel and her husband reluctantly admitted Rob temporarily to an institution until he gained the self-care skills necessary to meet the admission criteria to attend school. Due to the promise of an integrated and publicly funded education, they felt resigned to admitting him on the grounds of benefiting from a rigorous toilet-training program conducted by professionals in the institution. Muriel was acutely aware of the implications of this requirement on more than just her son: "you know, the numbers of kids that were sentenced to go to places because they weren't toilet trained ..." Notable also is the popular conviction of the need to make use of a professional training program (in this case, conducted by professionals from a nearby university) to help a child establish a skill that the family might have been able, with some support, to teach on their own. This persuasion of the need for professional expertise, what Trent (1994, 5) describes as a manipulation of the "contours of both care and control to ensure personal privilege and professional legitimacy," reinforced the general belief in the supremacy of institutional care over that which parents could provide.

Many parents felt constrained by the administrative limitations they encountered when attempting to forge a support network for their children. Yet parents' decisions to institutionalize did not necessarily mean that they did not engage in activism on behalf of their sons and daughters. Five of the six parents in this group whose children lived in an institution were also active in their local Association for Retarded Children, at least for a short while. Two of the parents in particular referred to their work of attempting to improve the conditions within institutions. Agitating for improvement in the care and environment within institutions was a common feature of parents' activism throughout the 1960s and 1970s (Carey 2009; Panitch 2008; Simmons 1982) and was one way parents felt that they were contributing to their child's care, despite having made the decision to institutionalize. It is interesting, in retrospect, to reflect on the ways in which these parents demonstrated their concern on behalf of their children. Feeling limited by the restrictions of the age, they acquiesced by sending their child to an institution, yet continued to work on their child's behalf. These two parents were clear, however, that their activism would not have extended to keeping their child at home.

Those parents who decided to keep their children at home thus provide an interesting counterpoint. While the bureaucratic labyrinth often made institutionalization the easier option, many parents chose instead to work for years, often in isolation, to establish meaningful and alternate support systems for their children. This was not easy; the social and political milieu, in combination with the fact that parent networks did not yet exist, made it difficult for families to connect with and to act as resources for each other. Parents had to work against the "collective practices" (Bourdieu 1990, 54) and official avenues that made institutionalization an easier option.

Toddy and Audrey, the two women in this study who kept their children at home despite circumstances akin to those of the other participants, felt that they had the social and emotional resources to consider other options and to resist the professional opinion and bureaucratic obstacles that favoured segregation. They presented as women who were strong-willed, and described being well supported in their marriages and families, willing to educate themselves about the political and social aspects of caring for their children, and prepared to act on their behalf in order to effect change.

Toddy and Audrey both stated that they and their spouses were in absolute agreement that their child would not be institutionalized. Toddy remembered: "We decided we're not going to treat her differently, she's always going to be at home ... Ray and I had the chat about institutions and whether that was an option. But I knew, and Ray said – never, ever, will I let her go to an institution. This is her home; she's going to live here with us. So, that was out of our head. Institution was not in our head." Indeed, both women claimed that the support of their husbands was instrumental in the decision to keep their children at home. Audrey explained: "I wouldn't have been able to place [my son in an institution], and neither would Fred. I know I was very fortunate. I had ... my husband and I were absolutely together on these things all the way through."

Further, these two women were committed to self-education about their children, about disability, and about the policies and political conditions preventing people with intellectual disabilities from engaging in the broader community in a just and equitable way. Audrey believes that knowledge and a commitment to act on it are the tools needed to instigate change, and that people's unwillingness to engage with the political and historical elements of disability is one of the reasons why improvements in the lives of people with disabilities remain painfully incremental. She believes that parents are frequently more concerned with the "immediate" without recognizing that the immediate is a "result of that history ... [and] what's wrong with the system." Audrey's husband was a librarian who contributed to her efforts to secure information about her son's disability; while aware of this fortuitous relationship, she also stated: "It's your job to read it ... you have to read it. Fred did all the finding, and I had to do all the reading; that's how I got started. I decided to start at the beginning, so I started with the history."

Toddy explained that much of her activism stemmed from the desire to have her daughter Janie benefit from all the opportunities available to her five other children. Anger fuelled much of her work against government limitations: "When it came time for me to look at schools, or to decide where to put Janie to school, I had trouble then. And then I started to get busy." Despite feeling intimidated by walls of bureaucracy, she decided to establish a school her daughter could attend: "It just kind of gets your back up. I said – I'm going to have to get a per diem for these kids. And I wrote a letter to the Minister of Education, and I got an appointment in Toronto, and I went by myself. I was brave as a lion when I think about it, because I was just quaking in my boots … but I did it and it worked. And I got a per diem … I kind of knew how to write, and I was strong. And you get strong when you think there's an injustice. Injustice makes you strong … I was just in a rage. And there was no fooling around. I mean, they were all men, they were listening to me. And I said – I'm not leaving here until I have a commitment from you guys. And I want it now. And I'm starting this school. And I got it."

While Toddy and Audrey are aware of the commitment involved – "it's been work; it's still work. It never ends; it never ends" – their statements suggest that besides having support at home, these women also had a clear sense of their own capabilities. This self-awareness and self-confidence emerge as key distinctions between parents who decided to institutionalize their child, and those who did not. While parents' understandings of disability were relevant with regard to the decisions they made on behalf of their children and how they responded to systemic limitations, equally important was how parents viewed themselves, their roles as caregivers, and what they believed themselves capable of, thus necessitating an examination of the social constructs which had a particular bearing on how parents, especially mothers, regarded themselves.

Gender, Mothers, and Narratives of the Self

Foregoing chapters have discussed gender constructs and the rigidity of gender roles post–World War II, the time period of this study. In brief, men held positions of greater power and authority both within and outside of the home. Women occupied a more limited field, making the establishment of identity outside of caregiving roles, the seeking of non-domestic meaningful engagement, and the testing of capacities more difficult. Findings from this project suggest that these gender divisions had some bearing on parents' decisions regarding institutionalization, not only because decision-making frequently defaulted to men, but because of assumptions regarding women's (in)capacities. Many of the mothers recounted being told they were incapable of carrying out the demanding work of caring for their disabled child at home. This assessment came both from external figures of authority (especially medical doctors), and internally, from the women themselves, suggesting ubiquity in the social and cultural discourses which defined and delimited women. Louise[4] stated repeatedly throughout the interview, "The doctor said that I wouldn't be able to look after her." Louise, despite deeply desiring to keep her only child Harriet[5] at home, obeyed the doctor's orders and had her admitted to an institution. Moreover, Louise was completely dependent on her husband or the children from his first marriage to travel and visit her daughter. Although she had a driver's licence, Louise did not feel comfortable driving to the institution to see her, nor was she encouraged to do so, and thus only went when others could take her. For Louise, a large part of her experience of being a mother was framed by understandings of incapacity. Her life, she believed, contained two major failings: she had borne a child with disabilities, and then was considered incapable of caring for her.

Moreover, while some families were aware that it was difficult for mothers to raise their disabled children on their own, there was little critique within these families, reflective of the lack of critique within society generally, regarding how things could be done differently. For example, Bertram believed that his wife was not capable of caring for their son with Down syndrome at home: "The basic reason that he went was that my wife couldn't handle him. And what was she going to do? She's got these three other children, and me, and I'm not around that much, and Martin [child with a disability] knew she couldn't handle him." It is notable that Bertram foregrounds his wife's (in)capacities in their decision, as opposed to the circumstances surrounding their home life. Assumptions that the difficulties in the home were located within the 'problem' of the disabled child and in the mother's inability to cope with him were supported by the gender and domestic arrangements of the time, arrangements that saw men carrying purposeful roles in the public sphere, frequently with long absences from the home, and women carrying private roles of domestic responsibility. There existed little critical discourse suggesting that difficulties in caring for a child with a disability were linked to socio-cultural and systemic factors and that more diverse domestic and labour arrangements would have better served everyone's needs (Brookfield 2012; May 2008). Gender roles thus reinforced the difficulties that many women faced and likely contributed to decisions which led to children's placement in institutions.

Louise in particular described her situation as one in which a challenge to normative arrangements would not have been considered. She described feeling resigned to the decisions of authority figures; she did not interpret her decision to place her daughter in an institution as a choice, but rather as something that was inevitable. "I didn't feel like [it was a matter of choice] because … we prayed a lot and everything. And I just figured that the good Lord was going to have her go to the place that she was supposed to go." This somewhat fatalistic perspective contrasts with that expressed by Toddy, above, who decided to fight the provincial government for education funding: "*I started to get busy.*"

Women's lack of role in the public sphere may have been a contributing factor to the slow pace of change in policy concerning people with intellectual disabilities in Ontario. In all of the marriages described in this study, men worked long hours outside of the home, while women stayed at home in the roles of mother and homemaker. Mothers absorbed almost all of the care of the child with a disability in an environment with limited support. Women were also minimally represented as elected officials; those making government decisions may not have been as invested in making changes to an unsupportive system, as they would not have felt its effects to the same degree. In addition, the constructive changes that began in the 1970s to provide greater inclusion for children with disabilities did not significantly threaten men's roles, publicly or privately. While positive changes began to be implemented in the community, the position of men remained generally untouched throughout – they maintained their role, their work, and their public face. The changes that began to be introduced had far greater implications for women and their children with disabilities.

Further, inherent to mothers' roles typical of the era was the assumption that women would support their husband's work and public countenance. Betty[6] described her need to have an ordered household so that she could host social gatherings, at the last minute if need be, in order to support the public facet of her husband's work. Betty stated that she and her husband circulated in an environment in which the presence of a child with a disability would be detrimental. "Well, we used to do a lot of entertaining, because Owen[7] [had an important position]. So, when he got to a certain position, we were having dinner parties for these people who had come from [overseas], they tend to visit around, and they were rather official ones, and you had help putting them on, and so on … I was fully co-operative in what his position was, and what that kind of entailed …

So, we were having people from other [important roles], and they would come to visit and so on, and we would be putting on parties for that, so it was easier, you know, I mean it fit in better with how our lives went." The role of hosting was simplified by her daughter's absence and allowed her to fulfil her obligations as a diplomatic wife without restraint.

Last, it is important to consider some of the parents' expectations concerning the public image they were projecting of themselves to the wider community. Drawing on Goffman's "dramaturgical metaphor" (Riessman 2003, 7) and from Judith Butler's (1990) work on performativity, Riessman (2002) suggests that people in public forums "do not reveal an essential self as much as they perform a preferred one, selected from the multiplicity of selves or personas that individuals switch among as they go about their lives" (701). According to Riessman (2003), people "stage performances of desirable selves to preserve 'face' in situations of difficulty" (7), and we deal with conflicting identities by "resisting one and bringing the other to the fore" (Åkerström, Burcar, and Wästerfors 2011, 104).

In one example, Betty recounted her desire to present a particular image of herself in regard to her role as the mother of a child with a disability. She stated that she did not want to be "Mrs. Retarded Mother of the Year," which, in her estimation, would have meant surrendering "my own life, in the style I wanted." The intense commitment she believed this entailed was not "how I wanted to spend the next ten years." At first glance, this mother's self-narrative seems to be about the preservation of a particular identity in order to protect her social position and to justify their decision to place their child in an institution. The institutionalization of her daughter Nora fit the narrative of Betty's performative self, of the role that she felt compelled to construct for herself – the wife and mother who successfully fulfils her social obligations yet is unencumbered by the demands of a child with a disability and the community of which she is a part. Betty was also clear that her daughter's institutionalization prevented an undesirable role from emerging – that of "Mrs. Retarded Kid's Mother, who make it their profession almost."

Although unsettling, Betty's assertion can also be interpreted as a counter-statement to the normative expectations of mothers during this era. Making a claim against being "Mrs. Retarded Mother of the Year" can be understood as one woman's stance against being pushed into what she felt would be an all-consuming role, and as a desire to carve space for herself in a demanding domestic environment. Indeed, her assertion appears more reasonable when one considers the need for mothers to assume most of their children's physical, social, and educative needs. What is difficult in her assertion, of course, is that her understanding of the compulsory nature of this role (Butler 1990) and her unwillingness to assume it had profound, negative, and long-lasting effects on her daughter. Betty's desired self and lifestyle, in combination with a lack of support, could not include Nora; Nora was extraneous to her mother's desired life, and had to leave.

Further, Åkerström et al. (2011, 104) suggest that some "cultural identities ... constitute parallel discourses, visible during the same conversation ... as they go about making sense of their experiences." Two parents, Bertram and Susan,[8] each provided an example of this, by presenting parallel yet contradictory identities in a seeming effort to make sense of the decision to institutionalize their children.

Bertram, who became heavily involved in his local parents' association, described the work they did in efforts to improve conditions in institutions around the province. "We decided in the Association that we should be visiting as many of these places as possible as a group. And we used to go up to Orillia ... So, anyhow, they [parents' association] started raising the dust, saying – this is absolutely atrocious ... When we got to the parts of Orillia they didn't want you to see, it was absolutely disgusting. Oh geez. My wife and the women got into, I think it was E block. The windows were broken and it was wintertime. The kids were sitting against the wall, just an undershirt on. And the snow's coming in and blowing across them ... but Martin wasn't in Orillia; he was never in Orillia."

The poor conditions that Bertram observed in the institutions he visited did not alter his opinion that they had made the best possible decision for his son. Rather, he used what he knew of the other institutions in the province and their reputations for poor care as evidence that they had indeed made a good choice by sending Martin to a different facility. When asked if he thought that Orillia was worse than the other institutions, he answered, "Oh, it was. Oh, yeah." Åkerström et al. (2011) might describe Bertram's stance – believing (rightly) that conditions were 'atrocious' at Huronia, yet assuming that his son was not subject to similar conditions in his institution, even though it was run by the same government, with the same mandate – as a "performance of conflicting identities ... [occurring when] non-preferred identities for some reason cannot be hidden or subordinated" (104). Perhaps brought forward because of the research questions, Bertram's statements seemed to be a performative balancing act (ibid.), wherein he had to explain their decision to institutionalize by exposing other possibilities that appeared much worse.

A similar contradiction was expressed by Susan, who spoke of her work to improve the living conditions at the institution where her daughter Beatrice[9] lived. "It was an institution. There were a few, well, many snags. I have a letter here that I wrote in 1965 – *I'm writing to you in support of other parents who have recently been helping to publicize the gross overcrowding of patients.*" Despite Susan's awareness of the poor conditions at the institution where her daughter lived, Susan was clear that this was the right decision for Beatrice and the rest of her family: "when Beatrice was eight, we made the decision to enrol her there, and never looked back." Bertram and Susan's coming-to-terms with the decision to institutionalize seemed to include the establishment of a "situated and accomplished" (Riessman 2003, 7) identity, that of an advocate who worked on behalf of their institutionalized child, an identity which negated a parallel yet damning self-narrative.

Despite these examples of parents' performance of "two or more situationally actualized identities in parallel" (Åkerström et al. 2011, 120), none of the parents in this study referred to the idea of a secretive or conflicting family narrative, a theme that had emerged with significant impetus from the siblings.

Family Considerations

It is striking that incongruent family narratives, a theme that had carried such importance in the sibling group, barely surfaced with the parents. This suggests that parents and siblings had different understandings of how family narratives were presented, and that each group experienced these presentations differently. In brief, parents in this study seemed to experience the effects of 'double' narratives – that is, narratives that differed depending on the situation – less keenly than their children, who referred to this differentiation with some angst. The parents reported little distress regarding presentations of family that might contradict the 'real' picture. For the most part, parents indicated that they felt they had let sufficient numbers of friends and families know of their 'missing' child, and did not dwell on the possibility that people might have had inaccurate impressions of their family. Owen stated, "We just … assumed it was normal. I don't remember going to any great lengths to explain to the kids. I don't remember that." Susan noted, "If a family is sufficiently open about their child … it benefits everybody who comes in contact. All my friends, all my neighbours knew about Bea and accepted her." When asked about the impact that Beatrice's removal had on her two brothers and whether or not they ever challenged their parents on their decision, Susan added, "Oh, no, no, they never did. Never, never. No, no. It was simply accepted."

As discussed in the foregoing chapter, however, several of the siblings described the negative experience of having to navigate around the sometimes-unvoiced existence of a disabled brother or sister, both in the community and in the family home. The difficulty that siblings experienced in this regard – not telling their friends about their institutionalized sibling, for example, or knowing they were not to speak about him or her in conversation – could be reflective of the powerlessness siblings felt as children in these situations, and are remembered as a stressful part of their formative years. For the parents, the family 'secret' might not have been an equivalent stressor owing to the greater control they had in social situations.

Beyond family narratives, parents spoke about decision-making concerning their child with a disability and on the impact these decisions had on the rest of the family. First, some of the parents, particularly mothers, indicated that the removal of the child with disabilities met a need for order in the home. Betty, Nora's mother, describes her decision to celebrate Christmas in advance, to avoid including Nora in the family celebration: "I thought – I can't have Nora home *over* Christmas, you know, the actual days … we had three kids at home and a large family connection, and it seemed to me that we were the ones who held things, you know, celebrations and so on took place at our house. And we did some entertaining as well, with Owen's jobs, so between the jigs and the reels, I didn't really feel I could do it all." Susan also referred to the disruption that Beatrice caused in the home as grounds for her removal: "By now Bea had two younger brothers, and she was becoming disruptive … the boys would perhaps have something spread out carefully on the floor, and she would come along and disrupt it, and it was difficult. It was difficult to integrate her into the household." For Susan and Betty, the need to run an ordered household and to host events in the home was important, and was eased by the removal of a potentially disruptive child.

Second, congruent with observations from some siblings, some of the parents referred to the relief they felt when their child was removed from the family home. It seems that this relief stemmed from two sources:

from the simplification of their lives through a reduction in responsibilities around personal care, supervision, and upkeep of the home; and from a lessening of the embarrassment of having a child with a disability and the need to continually address the child's anomaly when interacting with other people. Susan stated: "I think you have to be perfectly frank and say it was an enormous relief. I was sad; I remember coming home, crying buckets the night I took her and of course, yes, the answer is I did miss her, but she had become, it had made family life stressful, and we just felt very confident that we were doing the best thing." Betty echoed these sentiments: "It was hard, but I was relieved to be doing it … it was a relief for me to not have her living at home all the time … I felt I would have found that hard … I felt that a lot of people were relieved that the situation had been dealt with in a way that was acceptable."

While the relief that Betty felt upon her daughter's institutionalization is not unusual in the realm of emotions that parents described, it is worth noting some of the motivations underlying her solace. Betty described feeling enormously relieved when her daughter was discharged from the institution and went to live with another family: "She was part of a family group, and in a more normal situation, and I was greatly relieved … as far as I'm concerned, that was a wonderful thing they did for us and for Nora … I felt good about that … and she was so happy." Betty also expressed relief that Nora's death involved only a brief illness: "I was so relieved that she had a stroke and died five days later. I was so relieved that's how she went, that it wasn't going to be a physical and mental deterioration over a long, long time. I mean, partly for my own sake [*laughs*] … I must say I had a sense of relief that it had all ended and in a nice way, an acceptable way." Betty explained that the relief she felt at her daughter's death was not only in response to the brief nature of Nora's illness, but to the fact that she no longer had to grapple with her own feelings of inadequacy regarding Nora's care. Nora's death signalled an end to decades of consternation that "I would fail in my duties to her … and I couldn't live up to what I thought I should do … to me, her death was the end of all that." Thus, Betty experienced relief at various steps throughout Nora's life, including when others assumed responsibility for her and when Nora eventually died, not only because her own responsibilities would be lessened, but because Nora's death provided a reprieve from feeling inadequate in the raising of a child with a disability.

Third, a discrepancy arose between siblings' perceptions of their parents' incentives for institutionalizing a brother or sister, and what the parents described as their principal motivation. While siblings felt that their parents' decision was at least partially based on their desire to create an environment geared to the non-institutionalized children's success, this was not a topic that featured prominently with this group of parents. Rather, parents' apprehensions were focused on other factors such as their perceived inability to care for the child, disruptions in life style, and public embarrassment around the existence of a child with an intellectual disability; these factors took precedence over creating an environment conducive to the well-being of the other children. This suggests that, reminiscent of Marilyn's earlier comments regarding for whom parents cried, perhaps a good deal of parents' decision-making had as much to do with their own concerns as it did with the concerns of their other children. Further, these parents did not describe considering the possibility that keeping the child at home might have proven to be a more fruitful and mutually beneficial arrangement for all their children.

This point was brought up by Toddy, a mother who did not institutionalize her child, who felt that, in the long run, the benefits of keeping her daughter at home far outweighed the work involved: "I think it's a deep love of that child, and wanting that child to be part of the family. Because when they're in an institution – regardless of how good it is, how wonderful it is, and people will tell you it's great and everything – they still miss the love of their siblings. The siblings, I found, were totally in love with Janie, totally in love with her. They never treated her differently, never. They were proud of her. And why didn't we send her to an institution? I think we just felt that – this is it. This is her place. She's here, she's ours, we want to keep her as ours." Toddy suggests that perhaps, if institutionally minded parents had been able to take the long view and considered the entire family and its prospects for decades to come, they might have decided differently.

Toddy refers to Janie as "ours," as a member of the family. Many of the discussions that emerged from the parents and from the siblings described the child with the disability as someone distinct from the 'rest of the family.' Classifying the non-disabled children (and the parents) as 'the rest of the family' establishes a boundary, and suggests that within the family, the distinction between disabled and non-disabled is as important as the demarcation between adult and child. Yet the distinction within the family is usually assumed and unnoticed, based on acceptable universal understandings of difference. According to Young (1990, 59), "given the normality of its own cultural expressions and identity, the dominant group constructs the difference which some group exhibit as lack and negation. These groups become marked as Other." Once labelled as Other, despite cultural interpretations of disability as 'lack' and incompetence, the disabled child is paradoxically considered to have contaminative potential, the power to negatively affect 'the rest,' those in the other category (Douglas 1966). In some families, the assumed potential for the negative impact of the child on the 'dominant' group was enough justification to send the child away. Toddy's stance, that Janie was "ours," presents a contrarian view: keep the child in the family and be open to the ways in which the family will grow while incorporating her difference. Toddy did not necessarily endorse an assimilation that transcends difference, but suggests rather that keeping her daughter at home provided the opportunity to break down the distinction between her and the 'rest of the family,' and for the entire family to grow in unpredictable and fruitful ways.

Another theme which emerged concerned the use of institutionalization as a way to preserve a particular way of life, bound by class conventions. Similar to some of the siblings' reflections, parents' concern regarding their social standing was a factor in their decision to institutionalize. Betty noted, "I was getting off easily, living my own life, in the style I wanted to. I was grateful to [the institution] … to have been able to do that, to live my life more normally, what to me was a more normal life." She admits she "had my own guilty feelings about getting off easily," but considered her guilt worth it to alleviate herself of a life she admittedly did not want to assume. Her reflection, as well as those from Susan, echoes Simmons's (1982) assessment that families who petitioned their local members of government in order to gain access to institutional care during this period were primarily in the middle to upper class or were striving to be. Toddy recalled, "our lifestyle was simple. We had children, we weren't going anyplace, we certainly weren't going on vacations – and I just remember the children who were institutionalized – they were the children of people who lived at a higher level of income and status in society. You hate to classify them, but I know that some people put them away – that's what I call it – 'putting them away' – it was easier for them to live the lifestyle they wanted, without the appendage."

Susan, as well as three of the siblings (Margaret, Gregory, and Abigail), referred to the British influence within their families, which included the practice of sending one's child away to school. As previously discussed, placing a child in an institution paralleled the custom of sending one's children to boarding school, both to become an autonomous and well-rounded individual, and to strengthen the class position of the family. Margaret, one of the siblings who had one brother in an institution and another who spent the majority of his school-age years at a boarding school, noted, "It's also British. It's that whole idea … that it's okay to get rid of your kids to be educated someplace else … there's a social norm around that kind of separation." Susan described a trip to the UK, taken just prior to her daughter's institutionalization, during which they prepared their daughter for the transition that was about to take place. "We took Bea around [to some boarding schools] and we told some of the boys the situation and they'd say – *Come on, Bea. We'll show you the kind of place where you're going to live. You're going to live like we do.* And they showed her their dormitories and things like that. So, we told Bea – *you're going to a boarding school.*"

Although institutions for people with intellectual disabilities were first and foremost residences, the government of Ontario had, in the 1930s, renamed the asylum in Orillia the 'Ontario Hospital School,' a title meant to convey the institution's educational potential. Susan believed this was what the institution would offer her daughter. "I realized that it is, or was, literally, a hospital school. They had an excellent school and many other facilities of an educational nature. It was an amazing place. It had every possible facility. It had swimming pools, it had gymnasiums, it had special equipment, it had trained doctors." In addition to Susan's conviction that institutions had a great deal to offer, this was also a method with which she felt comfortable, unlike the prospect of keeping her disabled child at home, which at the time was a vast unknown with few guideposts. Susan was confident about their decision: "I certainly never had any doubts about the decision because it was so obviously benefiting her … the impact that it had, that her absence had on me, was wholly positive, given who and what she was."

Susan's favourable assessment of the institution to which she and her husband had sent their daughter contrasts sharply with Muriel's impression. Muriel, whose son Rob lived at the same facility as Susan's daughter, described it as "horrible, absolutely horrible … a snake pit, a hell hole." She reported having to stop, ill, each time on the drive home after visiting him there. Moreover, she feels that the labelling to which her son has been subjected, reinforced by the time he spent at the institution, "has had a

profound effect on his life … as it did on all the other thousands of people."
In a final damning statement, Muriel feels that the people who influenced
parents to send their children there "should be burning somewhere."

It is difficult to reconcile these two vastly divergent observations which
describe the same place. Yet this discrepancy points to a theme introduced
at the beginning of the chapter: how parents interpreted and understood
disability and people with disabilities in general had a significant influence
on their perceptions of institutions and their purpose.

Interpretations of Disability and the Role of Institutions

The majority of survivors and siblings who participated in this project
stated that government-run institutions were sites in which people with
intellectual disabilities were oppressed and mistreated, both behind institutions' walls and through people's exclusion from ordinary, mainstream
life. This contrasts with the impressions of some parents who felt that
institutionalization was of benefit to the child and to the family.

It is unlikely that parents formed contrasting impressions due to
exposure to different parts of institutions, as accounts suggest that visiting
procedures were identical for all families, or because of differences between
institutions, as the statements from the two mothers above attest. It is
probably more likely that varying interpretations can be attributed to
differences in parents' predetermined understanding of the limitations of
their children and of what institutions would offer them, in combination
with a sense of their own limits in terms of the care they could provide
for their children. I am not qualified to analyze the mechanisms through
which parents came to terms with the conditions of the institution and
were able to consistently frame them in a more favourable light, yet one
can presume that parents who spoke highly of institutions were somehow
able to reconcile damning reports of institutions with their own positive
impressions, necessary perhaps in order to manage potentially difficult
emotions regarding their decision. An inverse relationship emerged: the
more highly parents viewed institutionalization, the less damaging they
imagined the process to be for both the child who lived there and for the
rest of the family.

This inverse relationship is also evident in parents' overall understandings of disability and how it is framed in relation to the individual and
to society. For those parents who understood disability as an individual

problem contained within the child, institutionalization was a viable and reasonable way to deal with it. In these cases, disability and its interaction with society is not complex: segregation provides a solution to the problem of a less capable person in a capability-demanding world. In contrast, those parents who understood disability not as an individual problem, but as a complex interaction between an individual with some kind of impairment and the society within which he or she is located, recognized that the 'solution' lay not in institutionalization, but in a restructuring of society's understandings of disability and a recalibration of what society was willing to offer in order to support a reasonable way of life. These distinctions, ones that emerged at various points throughout this project, reveal an important theme: the way in which society chooses to interpret disability – person-centred or society-centred – has a greater bearing on how people will be treated than the extent of their impairments, thus underscoring the fragility of the premise of the need for institutionalization in the first place. Moreover, these distinctions point to the vulnerability of people with disabilities to varying interpretations and discourses of disability, created by people in authority, often for their own purposes.

At an intuitive level, what emerged from this section on family considerations was the sense that parents' decisions to institutionalize were founded on fragility. Whether it was precariousness in the limited services offered to families, or a perceived lack in parents', particularly mothers', ability to care for their children, or a fragility in the marriages that were unexpectedly thrown into situations about which they knew little and often did not wish to venture further, what surfaced in these interviews was a sense of something fragile or broken in what should have been a net of support around those families with a disabled child such that institutionalization would not be necessary. The trust upon which all sound communities are built – trust in self, trust in family, trust in the government institutions designed to protect and enable citizens – was absent or seriously compromised.

The point to consider here is where and how the fragility presented itself. Families that had *reluctantly* decided to institutionalize their child, with an awareness of the lack of services available to them and their own sense of being unable to care adequately for their child, experienced this brokenness within themselves, usually manifested in guilt, depression, and regret. These were the mothers who suffered the most; these were the fathers who became heavily involved in their local association, seemingly to assuage the guilt of having sent their child away. One father described the horrible feeling that arose when he and his wife watched their son disappear into the institution for the first time: "When the staff came and took him by the hand and walked away with him, they walked down this long hall, fading into the dark, and my wife said to me – *I can't come back here. I can't watch that again. I just can't watch it.*" Contrarily, those who were content with their decision and were confident that their child was receiving good care were much more likely to speak highly of the institution, and tended to state that it was the child's high level of need that created the problem, not the lack of support.

Audrey, one of the mothers who did not institutionalize her child, stated that the brokenness upon which many of these decisions were made rests on gaps in policy and services, on society's overall denigration of disability, and on people's unwillingness to rigorously critique problematic discourse. She stated that when she conducted workshops for new parents of children with disabilities, she "was always amazed at how little people knew about disability ... they were very much in the immediate. But the immediate was the result of that history ... the whys and what's wrong with the system." Further, she notes that "there's something fundamentally wrong in a society that people will abort – I don't have any religious prejudice here; I'm not a religious person – but people will abort a potential life, rather than fight for support." Audrey's point is that despite decades of disability rights activism, precarity still exists. Current interpretations of disability continue to define disability as a problem requiring 'disappearance' or eradication, a path simpler, in many ways, than agitating for changes in policy and attitude. And while institutions have officially closed for people with intellectual disabilities, the underlying idea of disappearance has not; we have simply moved into more sophisticated ways of dealing with unwanted difference, ways that, had they been available fifty years ago, some of the mothers in this group freely state they would have taken advantage of.

Disability and the Precarious Life

I conclude this chapter with a brief reflection on the views of disability as expressed by two of the parents in this study. While these two mothers made their decision to institutionalize decades ago, their perspectives have not altered, and they parallel current thinking regarding difference and its place in contemporary society. Their perspectives indicate that current societal trends in the treatment of people with intellectual disabilities might be considered a forward reflection of decades-old inclinations. Whereas fifty years ago, segregation was the norm, technology has created less conspicuous methods of removing difference, methods which these two mothers claim they would have made use of had they been available to them.

While discussing her and her husband's decision to place their daughter in an institution, someone whom they perceived as able to benefit from the institution's 'resources,' Susan provided a guarded estimation of the value of people with more complex intellectual and physical disabilities. And while she feels that Beatrice has had a full and happy life, she is not so convinced that all individuals should so readily be offered that opportunity: "There were wards at [the institution] that would break your heart, the children, unknowing children, little lives who, well … there are a lot of people who are alive who shouldn't be. Little lives that should never have been kept, who would have been happier in heaven than on earth, you might say."

Betty was honest in her assessment of her feelings towards her disabled daughter, and admitted that the role of parent of a child with a disability was not something she ever embraced, and that had she had the means, she would have avoided it altogether. She disclosed, "I know, and I hate to say this, that if they had had amniocentesis in those days, the way they do kind of standardly now, I think, and had that been the diagnosis, I would have aborted … I enjoyed parts of Nora, but it was not to me a great pleasure … So, no, I, to be honest, I mean, I know that sounds terrible, but if it had never happened to me, I wouldn't have missed it." Betty admitted to having "faked a lot" in her concern for her disabled daughter. She explained that "Owen was much better about it than I was; he played it more," that is, her husband played the role of the involved and concerned parent better than she did. Underscoring all of this was her admission that she would have been just as content if none of this had happened at all; institutionalization provided relief and a way back to the life that she had imagined for herself.

Toddy, one of the mothers who chose not to institutionalize, acknowledged that being the parent of a child with a disability is not something that most parents choose, and that it can radically alter the plan that parents may have laid out for themselves and their families. But she iterated that that does not mean that one won't benefit from the previously unimagined life that one has been presented with: "You have another role to play. It's not the role you planned for yourself, but it's a role that's going to help a lot of other people. I kept always thinking, the more kids I would see, the more I'd say – Yes, I was right. I'm on the right track. Go for it." About her daughter, she added, "We had her for twenty-five years. She made us all better people. She made us know what it was like to have somebody around you all the time who was just not perfect … She was a lovely, beautiful child. It was a hard thing at first, but it made me so strong." Audrey added, "Life has been for us far, far more rich than it would have been if Ian hadn't been born; there's no doubt about that whatsoever."

Toddy and Audrey also noted that institutionalization, in its inherent inflexibility, prevented parents from experiencing shifts in understandings of both disability and of their children. Once a child was placed in an institution, parents were excluded from one of the principal features and rituals of parenting: the constant exposure to the change in your children as they grow, as people who are always becoming. Parents who institution-alized their children experienced them through the restrictive lens of the institution and the system that advocated their being there; it was more difficult for parents of institutionalized children to imagine their child as anything other than the impaired child whom they sent away, as someone who might change and surprise them, and to imagine an alternate and creative living situation. Parents who chose to institutionalize were also more likely to hold on to the definition of disability which had guided their decision, as they were less likely to be involved with other parents who questioned perspectives and interpretations of disability. While there were groups of parents who worked to improve the conditions inside institutions, even these groups tended to remain committed to the notion that institutions were necessary and that their children continued to benefit from living there.

Last, parents' perspectives also had an impact on their level of com-munity involvement and their faith in the belief that such engagement might effect change. Parents who saw disability as a problem residing in the child, and who had decided that the problem was best solved via the institutional offerings of the state, had less reason to try and alter the bigger political and social structures which prevented them from meeting their child's needs in the home or community. Those parents who kept their child at home attempted to understand their children at a level other than that of a problem, and generally worked to alter the way society interpreted and interacted with them. These definitional differences were fundamental in parents' varied responses to their situation. Audrey, a mother who kept her son at home, stated that the work she committed herself to was worth it, as it attempted to dismantle oppressive structures from the root and create a more inclusive world in general: "Right from the beginning, institutionalization didn't seem to me to be a solution. You don't send your kid away … it's always been big issues, and you can't do it just for him. If you fix the big things, he gets fixed, but then so does everybody else. And that's the way it should be in any society, in my opinion."

The tension between varying interpretations of disability, its location in relation to the person or society, and disagreement regarding societal responsibility towards people whose needs exceed the boundaries of 'normal' have been recurring themes in the foregoing three chapters. While the discussion now moves to the reflections of former institutional staff and key informants, thus moving outside those who experienced institutionalization directly, these tensions remain a constant feature.

Former Staff and Key Informants

The reflections from survivors, siblings, and parents are an indication of what it meant to have one's life or one's immediate relationships directly affected by institutionalization. We turn now to reflections from former staff and key informants who participated in this project, people who were connected to, but one step removed from, institutionalization as a personal process. Each group provides reflections on the functions of institutions and their impact on families, but contains widely divergent perspectives. Former staff, embedded in the structures and practices of institutions as employees, convey their experiences as people who claimed a deep commitment to the institution as well as to those who resided there. Key informants, those who know a great deal about institutions through their advocacy and activism on behalf of people with intellectual disabilities yet do not themselves have a relative who lived there, provide an alternate interpretation of how institutions functioned and of their impact on families. It proved challenging to me, as researcher, to sustain the belief that I was listening to narratives about the same phenomena, so divergent were these two interpretations.

What became clear during the analytical phase of the research was the importance of proximity to the functioning of institutions in one's framing of it. Former staff, considered 'front-line' people in the care of institutional residents, were deeply situated within the institutional environment, and the majority were not part of the highest decision-making levels of administration. Their embeddedness in the institutional model did not allow for much consideration of alternate ways of caring for people with intellectual disabilities and facilitated a conviction of its effectiveness. Key informants, on the other hand, are those who, despite decades-long advocacy on behalf of people with intellectual disabilities, have fostered a long and relatively more distant view of the situations surrounding people with intellectual disabilities, and have maintained a visionary and lengthy perspective on other, non-institutional possibilities. As a result, some interesting juxtapositions emerge between the observations of these two groups of participants: while they frequently describe identical institutional features – 'amenities,' for example – each group provides a radically different interpretation of their purpose and value.

This chapter presents, in turn, reflections from former staff and key informants, with some analytical insertions. Some effort is made to reveal the differences that emerge when contrasting narratives are laid side by side, both between these two groups, and with the narratives from previous chapters. In particular, I aim to reveal what these differences suggest about the unjust nature of institutionalization and its inherent imbalances of power.

Former Staff

Four former staff from one of Ontario's institutions for the feebleminded, two men and two women, were interviewed for this project. Combined, they had ninety-two years of experience; their longevity within the system lends credibility to their observations, despite the small sample size. All of the participants in this group reside in the town in which the institution was located; three of the participants grew up there. Hence, they feel a strong connection to the institution, both as a place of long-term employment and as a historical and geo-political landmark that has played a significant role in the life of their home community.

Two principal thematic areas emerge from former staff reflections. The first, staff perspectives on the role of families, provides observations about the complex relationships between staff and family members and the attendant power dynamics, as well as their own feelings about the meaning of 'family' and how it was constituted within institutions. The second theme concerns staff feelings about institutions in general, including the view of deinstitutionalization as a contentious issue, as opposed to the more widely held view that it was an important step towards a better life for people with intellectual disabilities.

In general, former staff referred to their experience at the institution in positive terms. All four of them described their work as the 'best job they had ever had' and stated they would have remained there had the institution remained open. Their willingness to speak with me, despite (or perhaps because of) the public criticism being directed at institutions at the time of the research, suggests an unambiguous position regarding what they perceive to be the benefits of institutional care. In general, they expressed a strong commitment to the institution and to the people who lived there, painting a complex picture in which their expressed fidelity to residents was interwoven with personal concerns about their careers as caregivers and their roles as employees. Accordingly, many of the staff expressed a sense of loss as a result of institutional closure, a theme which emerged, sometimes intensely, in all four accounts.

Observations of Families: Institutions' Changing Nature

The duration of this group's employment provides a view of several decades' worth of institutional life and of the shifting nature of policies enacted during particular time periods. For example, all of the staff noted that, in their opinion, there were residents in the institution who 'should not have been there.' These were the older residents who had been sent to an institution due to social welfare authorities' classist and eugenic concerns (discussed in previous chapters) regarding families' perceived inability to raise their children on their own, and the need to segregate potentially problematic individuals. The four former staff recognized the disjuncture between current understandings of intellectual disability and what was previously a guaranteed entry to long-term custodial care. Don, who had access to residents' files dating back decades, recalled reading "*Doctor at Sick Children's Hospital in Toronto recommended – 'institutionalize immediately; institutionalize immediately'* – that happened over and over and over again. [But] as resources changed and improved and became available, families said – *Well, geez, why can't he live in a group home?*"

Jill, who worked at the institution for over thirty years, and whose father had worked at the institution before her,[1] described what her father knew about a train from Toronto that ran directly onto the grounds of the then-named Orillia Asylum for Idiots, depositing young, sometimes parentless, and lower-income youth and children. "He said he [knew of] trainloads coming up of children that were misplaced; they didn't have anywhere else to go. And it wasn't like they were, they might have been slow, or economically, they couldn't afford to be on their own, but … there just wasn't any place to put them, so they sent them there." Jill's description echoes the sentiments expressed several decades earlier by Downey, a supervisor at the institution, who referred to the Orillia Asylum as the place where the "flotsam and jetsam" of society were being dumped (Simmons 1982, 77).

The staff noted that the period during which residents were admitted to the institution had a direct bearing on the amount of contact residents had with their families and on the nature of the contact between families and staff. Residents who had been admitted as young children and had lived in the institution for decades were much less likely to have surviving relatives or to have any contact with their families. Don explained: "Some of the older people had been there for fifty or sixty years … they were put there through the CAS [Children's Aid Society] years ago, because they were Crown wards, so they might have had no contact with family members."

These residents, the ones who had been admitted as children to the institution wherein they lived out the remainder of their lives, sometimes as long as sixty or more years, were of particular concern to the staff in this study, one of whom referred to them as the 'lost generation.' Staff felt that as institutions closed, the older generation of institutional residents who had no family to claim them would flounder without the people or structures to which they had become accustomed and would end up getting 'lost' in new systems of support. While the divergent perspectives on deinstitutionalization are discussed in greater detail below, it is interesting to note here that families' lack of presence was, to staff, an indicator of aloneness in the world that reappeared when institutions began to close. Families had been encouraged to send their children to institutions and, in those early years, were not encouraged to maintain contact. Decades later, expectations resurfaced from those same authorities that families would reclaim familial ties; if this did not happen, residents were considered vulnerable within the new, community-based landscape. While staff concerns regarding the future of some of the more isolated residents were appreciable, many advocates felt that these were not sufficient justification for keeping institutions open; they were reflective, rather, of a painful history of miscalculated needs, and the plan going forward would necessarily have to include supports for those people whose families were no longer involved.

Staff also referred to the changing nature of relationships with family members over time. Don described the loosening of bureaucratic boundaries as the decades passed, allowing families to have more contact with their institutionalized child: "Initially ... they had to write a letter to the superintendent if they wanted to come and visit. Because it was a very rigid organization, the families fit into the rules that the facility decided upon around visiting ... as time went on, it shifted where the families would just call directly to the living area ... or not even call, just show up, and that was okay, too." Don also suggested that the gradual release of hierarchy within the institution led to a more equitable sharing of responsibilities between staff and families. However, despite greater ease in communication and more frequent opportunities for shared decision-making, the overall authority for residents' care remained with the institution, as families had relinquished their child to the state when he or she was admitted (Simmons 1982). This led to sometimes complicated relationships between institutional staff and families regarding who held power and influence and who should make decisions.

Secrets and Guilt

One of the features of these complex webs of authority was the expression of deference by families towards the staff. Don suggested that many families felt "beholden" to the institution because of the care it was providing, and all of the staff in this project reported a general sense of appreciation from families. However, they also noted that this deference was complicated, expressed as a mix of guilt, gratitude, and embarrassment, particularly when families realized that the staff seemed to know their family member better than they did. Tracy felt that parents' effusive demonstrations of gratitude were indicative of a pervasive sense of guilt, yet she consistently framed their guilt as something that had been transformed, over the years, into something positive and endearing: "People who were very demonstrative of the gratitude, maybe that was an indicator that there was maybe some guilt; maybe it started out as guilt but the negative shifts into the positive ... initially there's guilt but there's gratitude attached." All of the staff remarked that part of their role included providing reassurance to parents, to ensure them that their children were receiving the best possible care.

An interesting juxtaposition to staff recollections of deference and gratitude were those parents whom staff described as 'difficult.' Don stated, "They knew best because they were the parents and they made sure we knew that every single time we dealt with them." Doug noted, "You'd hear about the difficult parents ... [they] could be very demanding ... they were not necessarily the ones who visited a lot, but you'd hear stories." 'Difficult' parents were those who made demands, or who advocated with persistence on behalf of their child. While staff's framing of parents' complaints as an unpleasant and unwelcome aspect of their work is understandable, parents' concerns must be contextualized within the inevitable tension that they must have experienced in seconding the responsibility of caring for their child to someone else, a tension that remained irresolvable as long as their child remained in the institution.

One of the more difficult tasks that staff referred to, and one that echoes some of the findings in foregoing chapters, was the maintenance of family secrets concerning institutionalized family members. The staff's constant yet seemingly neutral position within the family's emotional history meant that they frequently acted as receptacles for difficult family information, and they were sometimes asked to hold, in confidence, details that were not common knowledge within the family. Participants reported the not-uncommon occurrence of adult siblings learning of the existence of their institutionalized brother or sister much later in life, often when parents passed away, or as deinstitutionalization gained momentum and living relatives needed to be contacted regarding upcoming community placements of institutional residents. In heartbreaking anecdotes, staff recalled encounters with family members who had never known about a sibling or relative in the institution. These were often awkward moments for staff, as they involved being present to conflicted, emotional reactions. Jill noted: "it was after the parents died that they found out ... How did they feel? ... Boy, I don't know. I suppose surprise and a little bit of horror that the parents would have done that ... you know, just kind of disowned them, almost. Because there were a lot of people that parents never visited; it was like a closed chapter for them."

Don, who carried an administrative position later in his career and thus communicated with large numbers of family members during the deinstitutionalization period, described one difficult situation: "A family had placed their son there, and only by the grace of God, things worked out and they were always available, because they never told their other daughter. They told their daughter that her brother had died at birth. He didn't die; they admitted him to the facility. Forty years later, her parents died, and she was going through their papers and came across a document that said she had a brother at the facility. So, she called me ... they had listed her as a secondary contact without telling her ... So, anyway, she came to see me and she had a ton of tears … [in the end] it worked out okay. That's an example of someone who had no idea."

He went on to give another example in which staff were asked to hold in secrecy one family's story that for decades did not go beyond the institution: "There were a few like that, those secrets. We had a case where the mother wasn't married, and she never told her family she'd even had a baby. And for her whole life until she died, she came to visit him once a month, and she had never married … finally, when she got very elderly, she told a nephew that she had a son in the institution, because he called me when she died and came to visit me, and brought me her will, and explained to me who he was, and then he carried on the relationship. But he was the only person in her whole family who knew she had a son, because – Oh my God, he was illegitimate, that couldn't happen. So, she admitted him and then she came faithfully every month. The family had no clue."

Thus, staff were participants, albeit with little control over that participation, in the perpetuation of many families' secrets about an institutionalized family member. Willing or not, they were often exposed to painful family stories and were obliged to hold them in confidence, an awkward position reflective simultaneously of their role and their powerlessness in the overall workings of the institution.

Staff as Family

One of the more notable findings from the project concerned former staff's description of their relationships with residents as 'family.' Because staff acted as reservoirs for intimate family details and were responsible for all aspects of residents' care, their claims are understandable. The institution necessitated interdependence between staff and residents: residents were, quite literally, dependent on staff for their survival, and staff were dependent on residents for their livelihood and status. This paved the way for a redefining of 'family,' such that the characterization of relationships between staff and residents as family was normalized. As Tracy described, "It was just like a family, except the parents were staff members … their family was where they lived … we knew the client better than anybody." According to Tracy, staff's emotional connection to residents, which included a "sense of pride" in their accomplishments, was "family; that's family stuff."

This sentiment is reasonable in light of the intensity of life in a closed facility and the shared nature of institutional life. Yet from an observer's perspective, these statements are troubling and point to issues of power and control which are embedded in the foundation of institutionalization. As much as staff might have felt that the nature of their relationships with residents allowed them to categorize them as 'family,' the metaphor is disturbing, as it suggests an assumption of one of the most intimate of human relationships when only one party (staff) has consented to be there. While staff could forge what they perceived as 'family' relationships, they had the authority to define and characterize those relationships as they wished, an option not available to residents. Dependent on staff for their survival, residents were vulnerable in relationships they could neither define nor escape. While staff could intensify or walk away from relationships, or, in the worst cases, abuse residents in their interactions with them, institutional survivors were only and always subjected to the relationships being imposed upon them. Indeed, the characterization of relations between staff and residents as 'family' is one that never emerged from survivor accounts. The survivors in this study all articulated their removal from their homes and families as an irrevocable loss, one which was never replaced by relationships that were formed within the institution.

Moreover, there are implications regarding staff defining institutional relationships in this way. Tracy was visibly moved over the loss of her work in the institution and her 'family' there. She was deeply saddened by the closure of the institution, and she mourned in particular the 'lost generation' of older residents. While genuine, it seemed that her sadness and the intensity of her feelings towards residents were preventing her from seeing beyond her immediate experience to a view of the possibility of new, organic relationships that might be forged outside of the institution. Closed to the outside world for decades, it was difficult for staff to imagine another world for institutional residents, an oppressive perspective that limits how people with intellectual disabilities are portrayed and understood within the public imagination.

Observations of Institutions: Institutionalization as Abundance; Deinstitutionalization as Loss

One of the more notable features of staff narratives was their characterization of institutions as sites of abundance. As some of the staff had been employed at the institution for several decades, they had observed, and conveyed this with some amount of pride, an increase in the number of services and amenities available to residents. In addition, facilities and activities had shifted in emphasis and scope, depending on the philosophical underpinnings of programming considered necessary for residents' long-term rehabilitation and development. For example, in the mid-1930s, the names of the major institutions for the feebleminded were changed from 'Asylum' to 'Ontario Hospital Schools,'[2] suggesting that these were not merely residences for people with intellectual disabilities, but were educational facilities which provided a basic curriculum and skills training with qualified instructors. Further, as professional roles in institutions became increasingly prolific and specialized throughout the second half of the twentieth century, amenities were added to their list of offerings. For example, each of the three largest Schedule One[3] facilities had a pool, exercise programmes, walkways, and various activities, all of which purportedly met the physical, social, and cultural needs of its residents. Former staff saw these as positive features of institutional life. As one of them stated, "The residents lacked for nothing … there were so many options for them."

Survivors' divergent interpretation of institutional amenities is striking. One of the residents said she attended school in the institution as "an escape from the abuse." Another described singing in the institutional choir as a relief from what he experienced as a consistently violent atmosphere. Three others described their labour within the institution, historically considered to have therapeutic benefits, not as rehabilitative work, but as imposed labour which helped to keep the institution running and for which they were not compensated. Yet no survivors mentioned the pool or other programmes which the staff held in such high regard. This omission is not necessarily evidence that these services were not available to this group of survivors, nor that their use was not enjoyable, but it is indicative of the lack of centrality that these amenities held in the survivors' depictions of their institutional experience. For survivors, one of the central characterizations of institutional life was not the services offered, but rather, the fact that they had no choice regarding how and on whose terms they used them.

Moreover, staff portrayed institutional grounds as spaces within which residents could exercise freedom. Don proposed that people who use wheelchairs generally had more freedom within institutional boundaries than they do in current community settings: "We had a number of gentlemen who had electric wheelchairs, and one man had one he operated with his chin. He had full run of the property … They had free run; they could go anywhere they wanted … So, then, we're going to take those same people and move them to a street ... and are they going to be able to go all over the place? I'm not so sure."

Contrarily, survivors' principal characterization of the institution was that it was a place over which they had no control and which they could not leave. Institutional life reminded survivors daily of their exclusion from decision-making concerning their own lives, from the smallest, seemingly insignificant decisions such as choosing what clothes to wear each day and what time to get up in the morning, to life-altering ones such as where to live and what dreams to follow. Thus, while Don claimed that residents "could go wherever they wanted," this was only true insofar as they did not go beyond the gates or the mandate of the institution. Residents' desire for freedom, had they been able to act on it, was always less of a priority than maintaining the institution's efficiencies. Further, Don's claim that people now living in the community may not have as much "free rein" as they did previously must be qualified. When institutions continue to function, society's absconding of responsibility is allowed to continue. Although wheelchair users still experience limits in terms of their ability to access society freely and without barriers, institutions are not the way to address those limits. It is through the dissolution of sites such as institutions that society is forced into creating new ways to ensure inclusion and freedom, and to establish new ways of reckoning with the existence of vast yet absolutely human ranges in ability.

It can be tempting, from the perspective of a researcher endeavouring to 'hear' each of the narratives in the project with equal care and attention, to view the discrepancies between the responses of staff and residents simply as different interpretations of what was offered at the institution, based on people's variant opinions and preferences. Reflections from key informants, however, suggest otherwise. The key informants in this project suggest that we must resist the temptation to view amenities in a positive light, consider them with suspicion, and invert our initial understandings in order to see the injustice of the system within which they were embedded. Key informants point out that it was not in spite of those services that institutionalization was fundamentally unjust, but because of them. Indeed, if residents could learn in a classroom setting, then why did they have to come to an institution, spending years away from their families, in order to have access to one? Why was it that the one place where people with intellectual disabilities could learn to swim, for example, was not in their home communities, but in a segregated, isolated facility? Further, what became clear as the research project unfolded was the extent to which staff, entrenched as they were in institutional life, did not recognize these contradictions. Staff observations that residents "lacked for nothing" suggest that their proximity to the perspective of the 'institution as abundance' made it difficult for them to acknowledge that most people prefer to engage with the world on their own terms rather than live a life in which all those decisions are made on their behalf.

These perspectives were attendant on their view of deinstitutionalization as loss. They described a climate of fear surrounding institutional closure, particularly from parents, but also purportedly from residents themselves. According to staff, many families were frightened of the prospect of a new and unknown situation for their child and themselves after several decades of a government-directed, seemingly secure arrangement. Don described some parents feeling a sense of betrayal from the government: "For the past twenty-five, thirty, forty years, the government took care of their family member. All of a sudden they were worried the government wasn't going to do that anymore." Don noted that families' opposition to closure created difficulties for the staff responsible for residents' community placements. Staff were faced with complicated negotiations with families who believed that if they remained firm in their commitment to institutional care, the government might relent and allow institutions to remain open. They did not, of course, despite one family, for example, who "dug in their heels and held out to the last minute," keeping their family member at the institution until the day before the last of the government-run institutions for people with intellectual disabilities closed on 31 March 2009.

Staff also suggested that some families were opposed to institutional closure because they were frightened of the prospect of living in close proximity to their relative and would perhaps be coerced into caring for them. Doug noted that some families were concerned that community placement would mean an acknowledgment of the existence of disability in their family, which for many remained a shameful connection, and that they would be left responsible for someone's care, a task they thought they had safely buried when they had chosen to institutionalize.

Most notably, staff observed that many families felt threatened by the prospect of institutional closure as they felt this suggested that they were responsible for a decision now considered badly informed and misguided. Don noted, "I had families say to me – *Now, just a minute. Are you telling me I made a mistake thirty-seven years ago?*" Families were being forced to confront their commitment to the ideology that had informed their decision to institutionalize decades earlier. They had done the right thing, or so they had thought, and their decision was being challenged by the very people they had trusted in their decision-making about their child.

Staff observations of parents' consternation regarding changes in public understandings indicate the power of discourse regarding families' decisions, as well as its influence in parents' re-evaluation of their actions many years later. While parents might have felt secure in the knowledge that they had "done the right thing" by placing their child in an institution decades earlier, this security was deeply shaken as public opinion and government policy began to lean towards models of inclusion and community acceptance. As public debate emerged regarding preferable models of care, parents were forced to reconcile long-held perspectives of intellectual disability with suggestions that their understandings had been misguided and were dependent on socially constructed interpretations. People who had been relegated to institutions in the postwar period were now considered no different from those the government was now indicating would be better served in the community. Thus, parents who had chosen to institutionalize had to grapple with interpretations of their son or daughter now considered erroneous and were being challenged to reframe their understandings of ability and disability.

Staff also relayed their impression of a fear of institutional closure from residents themselves. They noted that many of the residents who had lived in an institution for most of their lives were fearful of moving to an environment to which they had had almost no exposure and with which they had no connection. After decades of living in one place, with a predictable if restrictive routine, concerns about moving to a new situation with unfamiliar people is understandable. In this context, the staff who participated in this study stated that they felt that their role was to act as 'advocates' on behalf of the residents, which included taking a stand against the inevitable closure of the institution. One staff in particular described the "tension" between staff who felt that institutions should remain open and the government, which was taking irretrievable steps towards closure; she described helping one resident to write a letter to the government, requesting the option of returning to the institution should things in the community "not work out." What is striking here is not that a resident expressed anxiety about the forthcoming change in living arrangements, nor that he wrote a letter in defense of what he felt was best for himself, but that the staff person felt that her role as advocate meant facilitating his actions as opposed to supporting him to prepare himself for the inevitable changes about to occur. Rather than using deinstitutionalization as an opportunity to work with residents to re-imagine a new life and to ensure proper supports were established in the community, she felt that her energies were better used fighting the government's position. This is understandable from the perspective of a staff person who had worked in close proximity with institutional residents for decades, someone who had an intimate view of the daily workings of the institution but was not exposed, or perhaps not open, to the longer view of what might be possible for people with intellectual disabilities outside the institution.

However, the fear that staff expressed regarding the closure of institutions goes beyond what this would mean to residents and the communities now being called upon to support them. It became clear that for staff, the closure of institutions was profoundly personal and represented a loss of relationship and vocational purpose. Staff noted that a twenty-five-year closure plan had been instituted in 1987, and that from that point on, anyone employed at one of the large institutions worked under the threat of eventual institutional closure, such that "your job was always in jeopardy." This was exacerbated in 2004, when the government announced that all the institutions would be closing by 31 March 2009, three years sooner than the twenty-five-year plan had called for. Notably, staff stated they were upset that the government was not honouring what they had understood to be a life-long commitment to stable employment. They noted that "staff-wise, there was great fear," and there was a sense of having been betrayed. Don stated, "When they [staff] signed on, rightly or wrongly, they felt they had a career for life." Staff concerns about the losses that deinstitutionalization would incur on residents and families must therefore be considered in conjunction with their own fears about their impending loss of employment, status, and security. It is difficult to differentiate between staff's varying motivations to oppose institutional closure, as their articulated concerns for residents were interwoven with disquiet about their own future.

Government action towards institutional closure gave rise to further considerations for staff. All of the former staff were aware that institutional closure had as much to do with saving money as it did with implementing a new model of living for people with intellectual disabilities. Two of the participants described feeling surprised when they learned this. Tracy, for example, described being saddened by learning, through an overheard conversation, that government officials determined how much it cost to maintain a facility by estimating the number of dollars needed per resident.

While admirable, her concern regarding the measurement of people's worth is also indicative of her limited exposure to the financial reasons underlying institutions, both in their development and in their closure one hundred and fifty years later. She was an active participant in a huge and bureaucratic undertaking, yet seemed surprised to learn that one of the principal impetuses behind policy direction had to do with money.

Other participants expressed more realism in their assessment. Doug, for example, noted, "I think everything came down to money and taking away the government's responsibility ... government does not want to be front-line." Don agreed that deinstitutionalization was "all about money" and added that it was a "shift in the way we did business at the facility," thus referring to the changes in Ontario's institutional history as changes in business models, as opposed to changes in how people were cared for.

In several of these observations, it is important to note the effect of power differentials between staff on their understandings of the running of the institution and the reasons for their eventual closure. The two staff who expressed the most consternation about institutional closure were both 'front-line' workers, involved in the daily care and routines of the residents, and both were women. Low down in the institutional hierarchy, their realm of decision-making did not extend past the daily concerns of residents and they had little authority in the overall running of the institution. The limitations to their authority and their lack of exposure to the bigger picture regarding policy changes might explain their difficulty envisioning alternatives to institutionalization, as well as the protection of their own positions of power in their relationships between themselves and residents. Based on hierarchies of power, inequality was felt at all levels of the system, and this is an example in which staff were both subjected to and instigated uneven power relations.

The staff reflections presented here contrast with those expressed by key informants. Before embarking on a more involved discussion of the variances and overlaps between these two groups, however, I address a more difficult area of concern, that of mistreatment and abuse. As discussed in the final sections of chapter 4, the abuse that survivors experienced was a significant and traumatic piece of their institutional experience. Yet the picture painted by former staff differs significantly. In the section that follows, I draw attention to these differences, and suggest that deeper analysis may assist in understanding their implications, particularly in regard to preventing mistreatment from occurring in the future.

Narrative Differences as a Nexus of Oppression

All of the staff who participated in this study, although few in number, held the facility and their roles within it in high regard. All of them reported that working in the institution was "the best job I ever had." Tracy tearfully stated, "It's one of the best things that ever happened in my life. It really, really was. And I wouldn't have missed it for the world." Doug noted, "it was a good place. If they hadn't closed it, I would still be there." Based on what they shared, working at the institution was a positive experience, full of community, companionship, fulfilment, and job security. It is difficult, then, to reconcile this portrait of a loving and vibrant community with accounts from survivors that paint a vastly different picture. Staff accounts contrast distinctly with survivors' narratives of oppression and abuse and of the institution as a place of confinement.

When asked about accounts of abuse that have emerged since institutions closed in 2009, all of the staff acknowledged that mistreatment likely happened in institutions at some points in their history. They acknowledge that institutions' hierarchical administration, and in their earlier years, their military-like environment, contributed to an environment of regimentation and discipline. Don and Tracy referred to encounters with other employees who had been overly rough with residents and had been reprimanded accordingly. Tracy commented, "there were people working there who shouldn't have worked there," suggesting she was aware of staff whose behaviour towards residents was questionable. However, staff also stated that incidents of abuse were not part of their direct experience. Doug stated, "Most people had a really good attitude. Really good ... I never saw anybody abuse anybody. I'm not saying it didn't happen, I don't know, but not on my watch, not that I ever saw."

Further, as Tracy jokingly observed in reference to current criticisms from the broader community towards people who had worked in institutions, "you're blackened and damned because of the actions of a few." It is these "actions of a few," however, that are the crux of survivors' accounts of mistreatment. Despite staff claims that they neither participated in nor witnessed the mistreatment of institutional residents, survivors assert that it happened, and that it defined their experiences of institutional life.

These discrepancies raise important questions, not only in terms of what actually happened in institutions, but in regard to considering the conditions that would have allowed such divergent stories to emerge in the first place, even while ostensibly describing the same phenomenon. Thus, while narrative differences raise questions about staff's willingness to acknowledge the darker parts of institutions' history, their understandings of what constitutes abuse, and the level at which they were willing to believe survivors' assertions, they also draw attention to bigger questions concerning the ways in which power has been constituted throughout institutions' histories that would have led to such divergent accounts. Specifically, what is at stake when people who possess vastly different amounts of power refer to the same phenomenon with such variant interpretations? Does it matter that participants' stories are different? And if so, how can these narrative gaps inform the redressing of historic imbalances in the presentation of 'facts' and begin to forge a more just way forward in the treatment of historically marginalized peoples?

While this kind of analysis is always marked with some degree of uncertainty (that is, which story is the 'right' one?), and the power differentials between staff add complexity to the analysis, one constant is the difference between survivor and staff narratives. Barad (2007), in her work on the "ethics of mattering," cautions that "difference is tied up with responsibility" (36), suggesting it is not enough to claim that differences exist, or to present alternate perspectives and simply accept them as different sides to the same story. Rather, the analysis must go further and attempt to unravel the reasons underlying the divergences, and to interrogate the text that emerges when the gap between the two interpretations is exposed. In such an interrogation, what are the implications for those involved, and for those who uncover the differences?

It is important to acknowledge that discrepancies between narratives do not necessarily provide evidence of injustice. Indeed, in this era of postmodern interpretation, marked by "uncertainty about what constitutes an adequate depiction of social 'reality'" (Lather 1991, 21), in which, within academic communities at least, there is general consensus that a story's multiple 'truths' are worth considering (Mabry 2002), qualitative researchers are encouraged to 'hear' all sides of the story and to listen to different interpretations with equal attention. The temptation, and indeed the easier analytical route, is to leave the narratives where they are, allowing each to provide a unique contribution to our overall understanding of, in this case, experiences of institutionalization.

However, recent revelations from the survivor community, who attest that the pain they experience in the retelling of their history is worth it insofar as it may bring justice, in combination with known power differentials in institutions' histories, suggest that oppression has informed and allowed these vastly different presentations to emerge. Moreover, the advocacy lens I assumed for this work leads me to suggest that institutions' uneven power structure rendered the residents of institutions more vulnerable, more exposed to prejudices held by those to whom they were entrusted, and more likely to suffer should their opinions or behaviours displease those in control. Despite warnings from postmodern interpretation that "consensus cannot be expected and rationales cannot be protected from challenge" (Mabry 2002, 152), this project's commitment to expose the workings of institutionalization from a relational perspective encourages me to suggest that injustice was a primary contributing factor to the divergences in the narratives I heard. Thus, narrative differences are not only indicators of different perspectives, but are prompts to investigate the unequal conditions that would have given rise to such differences in the first place.

There are a few implications to this stance. First, the priority becomes an examination of the nexus of oppression and the conditions that give rise to it, rather than the 'reliability' or 'unreliability' of the speaker. This minimizes the need to try and ascertain the 'right' story, and instead prioritizes an interrogation of "how some meanings have emerged as normative and others have been eclipsed or disappeared" (Scott 1988, 35). Attending to the disquiet of conflicting narratives is a step towards revealing the social meanings and power imbued within them. Moreover, it grants validity to the stories of people with intellectual disabilities, despite the long historical tendency to discredit them when they oppose the accepted narrative.

Second, attending to divergent narratives can act as a tool to unravel the historic injustices that underlie institutional practices. Despite emerging from those who have historically held no power in social and political circles, stories from the less powerful can challenge the assumed validity and hegemony of those who have voice, authority, and prestige. Bringing previously unheard stories to the foreground in public and academic circles gives equal voice to the historically voiceless, and can contribute to the cessation of the oppressive structures, governmental and otherwise, that have supported institutionalization throughout its history.

Moreover, a full examination of the workings of this oppression must extend beyond narratives and examine the larger socio-economic and political factors which allowed such different stories to evolve. To this end, institutionalization must be considered one facet in a system which supports 'great jobs' and horrible existences simultaneously. Simply put, the uneven power relations and social capital displayed here are the foundations upon which the larger capitalist system, of which institutionalization is one part, relies. As Ignatieff (1983, 96) claims, the reproduction of capitalist society depends upon the "constant interposition of state ... controls and repression ... penal sanction is essential to the reproduction of the unequal and exploitative social relations of the capitalist system." The narrative imbalance in this project, therefore, is a reflection of the larger mechanisms of exploitation and control that are essential for the smooth functioning of institutions and the capitalist state which they support. In brief, the success of institutions depends on injustice.

Last, it is important to acknowledge the implications of this stance on qualitative research in general, and on the notion of bias in particular. Rather than succumb to the investigative trap of not disclosing findings due to their seeming lack of clarity or consistency, or of allowing their arbitrariness to direct the analysis, thus falling into the "bottomless skepticism of extreme postmodernism" (Mabry 2002, 152), I suggest that it is necessary to claim allegiance to some of the narratives presented in order that imbalances might be righted. Perhaps this can contribute to a redefinition of 'bias,' not as a restrictive limitation within research, but as an instrument that allows us to assert where oppression exists and to identify where our efforts for righting the imbalances of history are best directed. As Breuer and Roth (2003) suggest, knowledge production elicited from situations which carry "traces of the epistemic subject" (1) offers "a production opportunity, an *epistemic window* and a possibility for *methodological innovation*" (2, original emphasis). Seen in this way, claiming bias can forge a new way forward and allow research to break free of the inaction that 'objectivity' insists upon. Thus, at risk of exposing myself to criticism from the "audit and accountability" camp (St Pierre 2011, 611), I disclose here my inclination to hear some of the stories relayed to me in my research as "more justifiable than others" (Mabry 2002, 152), and to acknowledge the political implications inherent to that claim (Lather 1991, as cited in Davison 2006).

The irresolvability of the findings from this chapter, in combination with those found in survivors' accounts, presents not merely a conundrum to the researcher, but an opportunity to not be tethered by that irresolvability in order to move forward. Claiming my bias and maintaining that survivor narratives are the means by which to dismantle oppression does not mean that I disbelieve the stories of former staff. Perhaps this was "the best job they ever had"; perhaps they really did see residents as "family." Their stories do hold a place in the findings of this research. However, while staff accounts might be 'true,' this does not mean that residents did not suffer. The fact that staff looked back positively on their experiences does not mean that residents did not experience abuse at their hands. Institutional workers' positive recollections do not mean that the system was exempt from the perpetuation of long-standing oppression. While I recognize it is possible to hold two conflicting 'truths' simultaneously, what becomes clear is the need to not become encumbered by this aspect of the conflict. Rather than grapple in a fruitless struggle to determine which elements of which story are 'true,' the way forward is to acknowledge that vast narrative discrepancies exist, that they emerged from a situation marked by significant power differentials, and that the more painful side of the story originates from those who had no power in the situation at all – all evidence of the existence of oppression and injustice, and all reason enough to work towards preventing the re-creation of the situation which gave rise to discrepant narratives in the first place – that is, to prevent the re-emergence of institutionalization and incarceration for those considered different.

Key Informants

Four key informants were interviewed for this project: one man and three women. Three of the key informants, Thelma Wheatley, Orville Endicott, and Annie Stafford, have been involved in various aspects of advocacy work for several decades; another, Paula Kilcoyne, had direct experience with one of the waves of deinstitutionalization that occurred in the late 1990s. Their cumulative involvement with people with intellectual disabilities, deinstitutionalization, and other areas of advocacy work totals well over one hundred years; this is due in large part to Annie Stafford, who has been involved in her local Association for the Mentally Retarded for more than sixty years. This lengthy participation in the community living movement means that they hold a unique position from which to reflect on Ontario's institutional history and its impact. Due to their long involvement, yet without the more intimate connection of being in a family in which one member was institutionalized, they possess a lengthy and critical view of institutionalization, of government policies that informed it, as well as people's individual situations, a perspective not necessarily gained by those who experienced institutionalization more directly. They have a deep understanding of the shifts in discourse and policy that have influenced decision-making in and around the community of people with intellectual disabilities and their families since the middle of the twentieth century.

Another important feature of this group is their strong bias in support of deinstitutionalization and community living for people with intellectual disabilities. This was not unexpected in a group composed of such long-standing advocates, but is also an indication of where support for this project lay. As support for segregation and institutionalization has faded from the public arena, it is no longer favourable, either in public opinion or in political spheres, to advocate on behalf of non-inclusion. Those who support these options tend to currently occupy marginal positions in the care of people with intellectual disabilities, and other than the former staff I interviewed, I did not encounter, nor was I approached by, any key informants in favour of institutionalization, perhaps due to a purposeful avoidance of this project on account of its presentation as one with a non-institutional bias.

One last feature of this group worth noting is their willingness to take risks on behalf of the people for whom they have acted as advocates. Stafford shared some particularly powerful stories about schemes she employed, sometimes in attempts to convince families to keep their son or daughter at home, sometimes to assist mothers in gaining access to their children if they were already institutionalized. For example, she spoke about her strategy of trying to 'strike deals' with families when she learned that they were considering institutionalizing their child – agreements that involved her supporting the family as best she could while the family kept the child at home for an agreed-upon length of time before considering institutionalization. In another example, she recalled taking parents to the Huronia Regional Centre in Orillia when unscheduled visits were not allowed, and distracting security guards by spilling a bushel of apples in the doorway so that mothers could run past and up to the wards to see their children. She reported that as a result, she was not very well liked by administrators and staff alike, but "I didn't care. They were scared of me [*laughs*]. It took me a good number of years to get to walk in and out of there without staff being nervous." Stafford realized that she occupied a privileged position: she could take risks on behalf of parents of children with disabilities, as she knew that administrators could not retaliate: "I was never afraid because I never had a child with a disability. I knew they couldn't get at me through my child. I was safe."

While insightful, and certainly helpful to the families she was trying to assist, Stafford's strategy is also indicative of the extent of the fear that families had of institutional authorities. She was aware that parents feared suffering, or feared their children suffering, the consequences of being too forthright in their demands, an indication of the mistrust and poor communication that characterized relationships between families and institutional staff in institutions' earlier history. This theme of risk-taking was a common one within the key informant group: all recounted stories of bending the rules on behalf of people with intellectual disabilities, as they knew they had less at stake in their relationships with authorities, and they believed that ensuring the rights of people with disabilities took precedence over pleasing decision-makers.

Key Informants' Observations of Families

Key informants' observations of families reflect the complexity of institutionalization and suggest that clear patterns of familial traits are not easily discerned. One point on which all of the key informants agreed concerned the social and cultural separation between families who had chosen to institutionalize, and those who had not. Paula Kilcoyne noted that although parents of children with intellectual disabilities, mothers in particular, were peers in terms of life experience, as they had all given birth to a child with a disability, their circles did not intersect, so different were the outcomes of their decision-making. She recalled the sadness of one mother who had decided to keep her child at home who, when asked to speak with a group of parents who would soon be welcoming their institutionalized child back into the community, reported feeling that she had little to say to them. Their vastly different parenting experiences acted as a barrier to sharing common experiences which might have served as a resource had there been more common ground.

These differences were particularly evident in the way that parents understood their children. Kilcoyne noted that parents who had institutionalized their child used a medical framework to mark their child's milestones, as they had no other means to understand his or her development towards adulthood. Change was noted through the measurement and history of the body. "Parents would say – this year they had this test done, and they had this surgery done," as compared to the social milestones that other parents might use such as beginning school, graduating, and so on. Parents of institutionalized children had limited opportunity to come to know their children in social, emotional, or spiritual terms and to consider milestones as something other than physical changes.

Parents' limited opportunity to know their children as complex beings bore direct consequences. Key informants noted that parents often continued to see their institutionalized children as 'children,' regardless of age. While some literature indicates that this is not an uncommon phenomenon for parents of children with disabilities (Bailey et al. 2006; Reichman, Corman, and Noonan 2008), the physical and emotional distance that institutionalization necessitated contributed to parents' limited understanding of their child as someone who would grow into maturity and who would develop some capacity to make decisions about his or her future. In this regard, key informants noted that some parents saw their child's dependent status as a guarantee that they would always have legal and decision-making rights over them. Endicott, for example, described the opposition he encountered when attempting to ensure that the rights of people with intellectual disabilities were respected: "This particular lawyer came to me with a list of offences I had committed, like advocating against parents who wanted their children to be dead ... I was acting contrary to their wishes, contrary to their interests, contrary to their rights over their children, by saying that they should be in regular classrooms with other children, all manner of things." Endicott also noted that although the location and focus of his work has shifted – "Once, our main theme was to get people out of institutions; now, it is to support people to make their own decisions" – his role as advocate, at its core, remains the same, to ensure that people have decision-making authority in their own lives.

Kilcoyne further noted that she felt that animosity existed between parents who had chosen differently for their children. She felt that those who had not institutionalized their child "felt deserving and looked negatively towards those families who had put their child in an institution." This sentiment was echoed by Muriel, a mother who had reluctantly placed her son in an institution for one year. She felt that she had been judged for that decision, and that it took sustained effort on her part in the community living movement to re-establish herself as a genuine advocate on behalf of her son.

Endicott, while agreeing that there was indeed some cultural separation between families who had chosen differently, noted a further distinction. He suggested that parents who advocated for institutional closure included those who had never placed their child in an institution, and those who had done so reluctantly. He noted, "Each group had their own unique contribution to the argument in favour of deinstitutionalization. I think there was more emotion among those who had yielded to the pressure than there was among those [who had not]. The ones who opposed institutionalization because they had made a decision against it were naturally more gravitating towards the theory of why it's wrong, than the lived experience of the wrongfulness." He suggested, through his decades-long participation in the deinstitutionalization movement, that the two different groups of parents "weren't at odds with one another; they had just come from different perspectives." He feels that, together, "they were essentially the backbone of the community living movement." Thus, while it may be tempting from an analytical perspective to group parents according to whether they did or didn't institutionalize, Endicott's observations are a reminder that the situation that many parents faced was complex, and that there were probably as many reasons for institutionalizing (or not institutionalizing) as there were families.

The key informants thus made the observation that the long journey towards deinstitutionalization was not as straightforward as current perspectives might suggest. For example, although Endicott did not characterize the differences between different groups of parents as hostile, he nonetheless did describe a time in the movement towards deinstitutionalization when "some people were saying – *We've got to fix these places up* – And then other people were whispering in my ear – *No, no, no. We have to tear these places down.*" He noted that there was a distinct period when deinstitutionalization began to be understood by families as a real possibility, during which different opinions emerged about what might be best for their children. As discussed in foregoing chapters, some parents never let go of the conviction that institutional living was the best for their child, and that energies were best spent trying to improve the conditions there.

Further, during this transitional period, some who advocated on behalf of keeping institutions open were just as likely to cite the 'wrong-doings' of community living advocates, as were other advocates in pointing out the human rights abuses inherent in the institutional model. Endicott explained that while he "became exposed early on to the issue of institutional wrongs," he also became exposed to the 'wrongs' that others felt he was committing in his work on behalf of people with intellectual disabilities. Arguments which favoured the wishes of parents over the rights of their children remained potent features in discussions around deinstitutionalization, based on long-held assumptions concerning the correlation between arbitrary measurements of 'intellect' and access to one's own moral and legal authority. Endicott's experience is a reminder that perspectives which are essentially unjust can still gain traction in the public arena, particularly in situations in which power differentials between the two parties are significant – in this case, between parents who wished to maintain authority and their much less powerful children, even if that included a definition of human rights that differed from that used by the non-disabled population.

The key informants in this study did the majority of their advocacy work at the pivotal juncture between institutionalization as a primary response to people with intellectual disabilities and the acknowledgment that it was possible for community living to be successful. By the end of the twentieth century, enough families had kept their children at home and had successfully integrated them into community and family life that there was now a valid counterpoint to the assumed role of institutional care. As Kilcoyne pointed out, "Families had been successful in the community. There were now people grown up in the community … and the people in the community had relationships, they were well, and in terms of the needs they might have had for support, they could look exactly like someone who was living at Huronia. And they were fine. They were doing well. And they had the benefit of their family around them, and a neighbourhood, and lots of people in their lives." From their perspective, the key informants could see the benefits and successes of community living that families who had institutionalized would not have had exposure to; they used that knowledge to reassure families who were about to enter the unknown territory of deinstitutionalization. As Endicott pointed out, it is striking that the name chosen for the advocacy movement by and for people with intellectual disabilities in Canada is 'Community Living,' demonstrating the key position that deinstitutionalization played in the group's early years. Despite earlier disagreements about where the group's priorities should lie, Endicott noted that advocacy eventually "pointed in the direction of closure" and that it became "unthinkable" by the late 1970s for Associations for Community Living to consider any resolutions that called for conciliatory measures or reinvestment in institutional upkeep.

Key informants' unique perspective, their willingness to employ alternate interpretations of disability when institutionalization was at its peak, and their ability to construct discourse which countered the hegemony of intellectual disability as a family tragedy allowed them to invert some of the most predominant fears of deinstitutionalization and to promote its potential. In response to fears from institutional staff that people would lose too much of their lives upon leaving the institution, Endicott stated, "I guess all we could say was – Let's believe [people who have lived in institutions] can form new relationships. Let's believe [they] will do so with more variety and richness than has been the case for fifty years." Calling people to trust that the feared 'risks' of deinstitutionalization would never outweigh its potential benefits was a key role played by advocates, and serves as a reminder of the importance of including people who have experience and critical perspective in movements for social justice.

Key Informants' Perspectives on Institutions

In addition to their observations of families, the key informants in this study also offered observations concerning the relationship between institutions and funding for people with intellectual disabilities, the most effective ways to convince policy-makers to close them down, as well as an alternate perspective on the 'offerings' of institutional life.

In the first instance, the four key informants had a solid understanding of the economic rationale for institutionalization. While all of them had strong moral and ethical concerns regarding the use of institutions, they were also aware that the reasons for institutional development, and for their eventual closure, were closely connected to fiscal concerns. Without the naiveté that some of the former staff expressed, key informants were aware that most of the decisions that were made in Ontario regarding institutionalization were based on the premise of providing guardianship with as little cost as possible. They pointed out that although the 'care' provided in institutions was questionable – and, according to survivors, frequently abusive – from an economic perspective, any money concerning people with intellectual disabilities in the province was tied up with institutions. In the early years, those families who chose to keep their children at home received almost nothing from the government. This injustice appears even more pronounced when one considers the paucity of services and supports available to people with disabilities attempting to live and thrive in the community at the time. As Kilcoyne noted, "Families were looking for money and there was no money. All the money was stuck in the institutions ... People living in institutions were getting thousands more dollars of support versus the people who were in the community ... I think the thinking was – *we've got to even this out. We can only do that if we spread the money around, and we'll be able to do that if we close down the institutions.*"

Moreover, key informants recognized, in a way that was not brought forward by the parents or the former staff, that the decades-long history of centralizing money for people with intellectual disabilities in the institutions had a direct impact on families' decisions to institutionalize. As Endicott noted: "I think we all tend to be very influenced in the direction of our lives by where the dollars are ... The dollars were in the facilities. The dollars were not in the community ... Public funds were allocated other than on the basis of need, and on a per person basis, the allocation was primarily in favour of institutionalization ... People in the community were getting either nothing or very little to be with their families." Economically speaking, it simply made more sense for many families to place their child where the money was; when families chose to keep their child at home, they received a "pittance" from the government, with constraints and "hoops" attached, and with accountability imposed upon them when they were likely "already exhausted by providing personal care."

Further, the imbalance in funding was not immediately resolved when institutions shut down. An example of how it can take the government years to implement policy that is in alignment with the needs of the population, the funding that travelled with people who moved from institutions to community placements after institutional closure meant that an imbalance in funding remained: families who had supported their children in the community for decades continued to experience shortages in financial support.

Key informants also provided perspective on the methods used by community living activists to ensure that institutions closed, and on the ways in which advocates must continue to apply pressure. In Ontario, large institutions for people with intellectual disabilities were closed via legislation as opposed to litigation. Endicott suggested that this was the more effective approach, that "a government decision is a better way to go than a judicial decision to force the hands of government. It's more planful and tends to be supported by more community-based service development." While the closure of institutions in Ontario eventually happened via government decision, and thus is enshrined in law, the class-action lawsuit that followed is evidence from survivors that institutional closure was inadequate compensation for their years of confinement. Survivors have indicated that closure alone was not enough to make up for those lost years nor for the abuse they encountered. Moreover, the outcome of the class action – an out-of-court financial settlement as well as other conciliatory measures – allowed the government to maintain control over the proceedings: survivors were not given opportunity to provide testimonies, and the claims process was prohibitive for those who did not have adequate support, resulting in not all of the monies earmarked for compensation being disbursed.[4] Further, there are indications that despite the government's commitment to closing large residential facilities, institutional existence remains a distinct possibility, with adults with intellectual disabilities who have no alternatives being sent to live in long-term care facilities designed for the elderly, and residences with up to twelve beds being permitted under current Ontario law, a size which prohibits a sense of typical community-based living. Thus, despite closure, the work for advocates remains. Muriel, one of the parents who participated in this study, expressed fears that reinstitutionalization will return in different guises: "What's happening now is so upsetting. Because things are getting worse; they're not an improvement for people."

Last, key informants provided a counter-narrative to the reflections on institutional life offered by former staff. As discussed in preceding sections, key informants encourage analyses which overturn the 'promise' of institutions as sites with multiple amenities and vast spaces, and urge consideration in the context of the oppressive system in which they were embedded. Key informants were unanimous in their stance that the existence of amenities in institutions constituted oppression as opposed to examples of a rich life.

For example, during her tenure as a social worker responsible for facilitating the move of institutional residents to the community as Huronia prepared for closure, Kilcoyne was encouraged to participate in a 'beach day' with staff and residents.[5] She experienced a disjuncture between her observations of a day at the beach on the institution's property, which confirmed her impressions of the institution as an oppressive and regimented place, and the interpretations offered by staff of a day of leisure. "They said – *we're going to have a beach day; why don't you come?* – I had never seen the lake, so I went to the beach day. I was mortified ... I couldn't see the water. Nobody could see the water ... The whole of Huronia was there that day, but people were grouped according to cottage. And the guys who were 'violent' had on jumpsuits; they were tied at the back ... they just had to stay in their little area. They weren't eating when I was there. They were just pacing around, and the staff were just hanging around. And that was the beach day. It was really awful ... There were hundreds of people in that situation. There would have been maybe sixty staff. There were hundreds of people with disabilities; it was just normal ... And it was so not normal, so not right in my mind."

Key informants' observations are a reminder that disabled people's participation in activities to which non-disabled people have unencumbered access have historically been conditional on a surrendering of their autonomy, of their connections with family, and of possibilities for work and relationships of their choosing. Only by conceding their freedom could people with intellectual disabilities participate in daily life activities that non-disabled members of the community have historically been able to take for granted.

It could be argued that key informants have held privileged positions. In their roles as observers and advocates, their income did not depend on the functioning of the institution, nor was their family life personally affected by institutionalization. Perhaps it is not reasonable to juxtapose their reflections with those of former staff, people who were dependent on the institution for their livelihood and whose perspectives were limited by a hierarchical system that discouraged internal critique or change. Examining these diverse perspectives together, however, allows the shortcomings and injustice of institutionalization to be exposed. Contrasting staff's perceptions of the benefits of institutional life and the 'dangers' of community living with the experience-based reflections from survivors and the rights-infused perspective of key informants provides a more robust view of what institutions meant in the lives of many different groups of people, and, in particular, allows an estimation of what institutionalization has meant for those who have been voiceless throughout its long history.

In the narratives presented in the foregoing chapters, institutionalization is the fixed, central point of experience. Whether by living there, by being closely connected to someone who did, or by working within its systems, the institution was the common, inanimate, yet powerful site of experience shared by those who contributed their stories. Yet due to varying points of reference, the lived experience of institutionalization and its impact on people's lives and relationships has been felt by participants in radically different ways. The task remaining is to address the experiences of institutionalization presented here and to connect them to broader systemic factors that have emerged at various points in this text. These include power and its distribution, the role that institutions have played in the larger scheme of the provincial economy, and the vulnerability of 'disability' to shifts in political discourse and cultural meaning. These, and other thematic concerns brought forward through participants' narratives, provide the starting point for these stories' final consideration, and point to where ongoing work in creating spaces in which everyone can find meaning must be directed.

PART THREE

CONCLUSIONS

Power, Governance, and the Construction of Intellectual Disability

Introduction

The foregoing chapters present several accounts of lived experiences of institutionalization. These are the stories of the spaces created between family members, between institutionalized individuals and the rest of society, and between lived experiences of disability and the meanings assigned to it. These narratives provide a window into the personal, yet they also encourage a re-reckoning with theories of institutionalization and larger systemic factors that were addressed in earlier parts of the text. The intention of this chapter is to re-examine some of the theoretical perspectives introduced earlier in light of participants' personal revelations. Where do people's narratives concur with what political and cultural theorists have observed and predicted about institutions, and in what ways are they contrarian? How do these narratives contribute to a more robust understanding of the implications of segregation of 'the different' in society, and how do these inform more just ways forward? In the sections that follow, three principal areas of theoretical and systemic concern are addressed: power and the "government of disability" (Tremain 2005), the relationship between institutions and economic forces, and the construction of intellectual disability. All of these have had influence on institutions' long and contentious presence throughout history and have played a role in people's personal and day-to-day experiences of institutionalization.

Power and Governmentality

Foucault's theories of surveillance, the relationship between knowledge and power, and the creation of the 'docile' subject have made significant contributions to current understandings of the historical ontology of institutions and their role in the felt need for segregation. All of these theoretical elements emerged in participants' narratives: from survivors' comments regarding the institutional culture of constant observation, control, and lack of privacy; to the ways in which power over people's futures was held by those with intellectual and moral authority, such as doctors, educational and government authorities, and parents; to key informants' comments regarding institutions' role in crushing residents' spirits. Foucault's (1995) poetic depiction of the making of the disciplined subject provides a linguistic and visual bridge to understanding the process of subjection in the evolution of the modern institution. I quote at length: "What was then being formed was a policy of coercions that acts upon the body, a calculated manipulation of its elements, its gestures, its behaviour. The human body was entering a machinery of power that explores it, breaks it down, and rearranges it. A 'political anatomy,' which was also a 'mechanics of power,' was being born; it defined how one may have a hold over others' bodies, not only so that they may do as one wishes, but so that they may operate as one wished, with the techniques, the speed, and the efficiency that one determines. Thus, discipline produces subjected and practised bodies, 'docile' bodies" (138).

Yet for Foucault, the more dangerous element here is the way in which this power was exercised: not as a "constant, total, massive, non-analytical, unlimited relation of domination, established in the individual will of the master" (137), but through the extensive hand of coercion. Power, therefore, becomes "more a question of the direction of conduct than it is of confrontation between adversaries" (Tremain 2005, 8).

In light of what we have heard from institutional survivors and their families, Foucault's theory of power's coercive nature both concurs with, and lies in contradiction to, the experiences of those who were institutionalized against their will and of the families who made the decision to place them there. His suggestion that the institution's discipline simultaneously "increases the forces of the body (in economic terms of utility) and diminishes those same forces (in political terms of obedience) ... and turns [power] into a relation of strict subjection" (1995, 138) paints a picture of powerlessness that concurs with that given by survivors. Moreover, Foucault's notion of the "conduct of conduct" is in close alignment with parents' accounts of their decisions regarding institutionalization, as they testified that the overriding public sentiment was that families should participate in the socially sanctioned route of segregation as opposed to striking out on their own. Indeed, the evolution of the modern institution is not known for being met by swathes of resistance; unlike other sites of injustice occurring during the same time period as that encapsulated in this study, the ongoing use of institutions for people with intellectual disabilities carried on, relatively unopposed and, for the most part, unknown.

However, there are points in the narratives that offer resistance to Foucault's notion of subjection. Sadly, survivors have indicated, and have done so in even greater numbers since the initial research was carried out, that the disciplinary regime experienced in institutions went far beyond the practice of coercion and included explicit harassment and abuse, "confrontations between adversaries" that had frequent opportunity to erupt. Moreover, survivors' recollections of rebellious behaviour on their part to ensure at least minimum standards of living, as well as some acknowledgment of their existence, trouble Foucault's notion of the docile body, which, according to Hughes (2005, 80), "underestimates the body's role as subject, as an agent of self- and social transformation." Indeed, one of the strongest lines of resistance that emerged from the narratives came from those survivors who were institutionalized for 'intersectional' reasons – that is, not only because of arbitrary assessments of intellectual (in)capacity, but due to other socially prescribed reasons such as class, gender, and Indigeneity. It was these survivors – those who were best able to articulate and act against the oppression they were experiencing, and who were most aware of the arbitrary nature of the measurements that had landed them there – who spoke out against the overall injustice of institutional life, and, not unexpectedly, told stories of the most severe and unwarranted punishment.

Similarly, not all parents of children with intellectual disabilities experienced power's subtle exertion in the same way. In equal measure to those parents who chose to institutionalize their son or daughter were those who resisted the predominant discourse and kept their child at home, again troubling Foucault's notion of the extent of power's reach and suggesting that Foucault's theories do not go far enough in accounting for the counter-force of familial connection and fidelity. Despite these points of resistance, however, Foucault's work is an important tool in understanding how such a huge system, dependent on human suffering for its enactment, was allowed to function so silently, for so long, and with so little resistance.

Bourdieu is another theorist whose work contributes to and is enriched by the narratives in this text. Bourdieu's notion of the *habitus* is a useful framework for examining the relationship between large socio-political forces and the individual decisions that families made, or as regards our purposes here, how power played out within families and homes as they discerned 'what to do with' a child born with a disability.

The *habitus*, a central element of Bourdieu's (1990) work, refers to engrained habits and inclinations which we use to perceive and interact with the social world. The *habitus* is a "product of history, [consisting of] individual and collective practices ... in accordance with the schemes generated by history" (54). Bourdieu acknowledges the role of history and the historical accumulation of individual and collective practices as precursors to our engagement with the social. He further suggests that this historical accumulation is embodied: "[The *habitus*] ensures the active presence of past experiences, which, deposited in each organism in the forms of schemes of perception, thought and action, tend to guarantee the 'correctness' of practices and their constancy over time" (ibid.). Thus, the *habitus* "guarantees all the 'reasonable', 'common-sense' behaviours (and only these) which are possible within the limits of [social] regularities" (55).

Bourdieu's acknowledgment of the accumulation and embodiment of historical practices and their influence on thought and action makes the *habitus* a useful analytical device, as it incorporates both the micro level – "an actor's bodily and cognitive habits" – and the macro level – "the actors, practices, and institutions with which he or she interacts" (Ignatow 2009, 103). The *habitus* therefore acknowledges the influence of social expectations and representations of intellectual disability, as well as families' internal negotiations with those representations in their decisions to institutionalize. Bourdieu's theories suggest that actions taken by families to place their child in an institution can be explained by the confines of historical practices, already constituted and deeply embedded in social systems, felt at the level of the individual.

Testimonies from families who participated in this study, in particular siblings and parents, resonate with this analysis. All of the parents acknowledged some degree of tension between the influence of external pressures and internal belief systems when discerning whether or not to institutionalize. Theirs was not an isolated decision when the social world is taken into account, even though for many parents it might have felt that way. In addition, a certain amount of irony emerges: once the decision to institutionalize had been made, regardless of the level of social elements involved, parents were left to grapple alone with its personal aftermath.

Further, Bourdieu posits the idea of a "quasi-contract" (67), an agreement between players (i.e. social actors) and "the field," an arbitrary, socially constructed "pitch" upon which social rules and practices are enacted. The amount of power and influence one holds on the field is directly related to one's "social capital," which in turn stems from the "chances being objectively offered to him by the social world" (64). The social spaces within which families discerned the future of their disabled child, and indeed the future of their entire family, can be imagined as just such a "pitch," from which the players with the least amount of social capital were being excluded, and for which those with authority were determining the rules.

Last, Bourdieu's work describes limits to the *habitus*, which in turn reveal a paradox regarding the amount of freedom experienced by families once they had made the decision to institutionalize. While he suggests that the *habitus* encompasses seemingly endless possibilities for action (55), he also indicates its boundaries: "The *habitus* makes possible the free production of all the thoughts, perceptions and actions inherent in the particular conditions of its production – and only those ... [there is an] infinite *yet strictly limited generative capacity*" for our actions (ibid., emphasis added). Despite families' anticipation that institutional placement might garner them greater freedom, in particular from the demands of caring for their child and creating opportunities for him or her in the community, reflections from participants suggest that many families were never released from the emotional hold of their child and the decision they had made. Indeed, in several cases, removing the child from the home resulted in a life-long burden of questioning and self-recrimination, and in some mothers' cases, long bouts of depression, a far cry from the freedom they might have imagined. It appears that some of those who placed their child experienced these "limits of our capacities" at an embodied level; the physical freedom of the institution did not offer them the emotional or social freedom they had anticipated. Indeed, I would suggest that institutionalization as a whole did more to limit the freedoms of all parties involved, despite its promise to the contrary: while institutional residents suffered the most blatant curbing of their fundamental rights, other family members, and even those in authority and society in general, also experienced loss in the form of lost possibilities for potential relationships, and lost opportunities to imagine and create a more inclusive society.

Another observation in regard to the connection between experiences of institutionalization and the distribution of power concerns the internalization of socially sanctioned rankings of power, or processes in which the political becomes personal (Maybee 2011, 245–59). Narratives from participants suggest that all of the parties involved in these stories absorbed the "devalued bodily capital" (255) of the disabled individual, particularly when authorities claimed that the situation was dire enough to warrant institutionalization, and felt the effects of this devaluing in a deeply personal and embodied way. This was, of course, experienced most intensely by institutional survivors, as evidenced in the psychological, emotional, and physical marks they endured and continue to carry, many years after leaving the institution. Former residents indeed bear the marks of their incarceration, becoming what Grosz (1994, 23) refers to as "sites of political, cultural, and geographical inscriptions." Yet, as already discussed, other family members also experienced institutionalization not only as a political and bureaucratic undertaking, but as a personal and corporeal phenomenon in the form of bodily and psychological distress, indicating the level to which institutionalization worked its way into the heart of affected people's lives.

Last, the idea of the governance of disability in the context of this study necessarily involves acknowledgment of the distribution of power within the family and how this affected people's experience of institutionalization. As discussed at the conclusion of the chapter devoted to siblings, what seemed to emerge from this particular group of participants was an inverse relationship between the amount of power one held within the family and the level of distress one experienced throughout the process. A deeper critical analysis, however, points to the need to examine how people's responses were structured and shaped by the social conditions surrounding them. That is, the fathers and brothers in this group seemed to carry less of an emotional burden around the phenomenon of institutionalization in their family than the mothers and sisters. This is not surprising when one takes the obligatory strength of male roles, especially during the postwar period encapsulated by this study, into account. Conversely, nurturing and care of others was expected of women; one could argue, therefore, that the emotional distress experienced by many of the mothers and sisters was the normative and approved response within the gender-specific boundaries of the current social and political milieux.

Institutions and the Economies of Difference

Foregoing chapters have described the historical connection between the development of institutions and market-based economies, and recent scholarship suggests that the focus of government intervention in the lives of people with disabilities continues to rely on capitalist imperatives and their attendant financial priorities (Erevelles 2014; Russell and Malhotra 2002). Historically, the economic efficiencies that institutions offered within the larger economy justified their use, and despite recent rhetoric which has increasingly framed government support for people with disabilities within a human rights framework, this fiscal relationship has only strengthened as governments have linked deinstitutionalization to neoliberal policies defined primarily by fiscal restraint (Carpenter 2007).

In light of this association, it is interesting to note the range of responses from participants regarding the connection between their own experiences, or those of their loved ones, and institutions' economic foundations. What emerges is a pattern reliant on one's distance from the immediacy of the institutional experience. Former staff and key informants, those who were most removed from the direct effect of institutionalization on their personal and family lives, were most likely to discuss the connection between the government's policy directions for people with intellectual disabilities and the financial direction of the province. Both of these groups offered a longer perspective on the impact of government fiscal priorities on decisions concerning institutionalization. However, and as noted in chapter 7, staff's awareness of the extent to which residents represented a certain dollar value in the overall ministerial budget was directly related to the amount of power and authority they held in the institution. Those staff who performed front-line work but did not have decision-making authority expressed surprise when they learned that most of the decisions in the institution were made according to their financial implications. These staff had maintained the position, sometimes through decades of work in the institution, that "it was all about family," all about caring for people with disabilities, and thus were disconcerted when presented with an alternate perspective, that institutions were more about managing an unwanted population in the most efficient way possible. Those in more administrative positions, however, were more comfortable with this information and indeed felt that the economic benefits of institutions were reason enough to keep them open.

In their narratives, survivors gave indication of the link between their own incarceration and the functioning of the institution, including its economic efficiencies. Through their stories of doing laundry, working in the storage department, tending to the garden, and caring for residents with more complex impairments, survivors provided evidence of their essential roles in the institutions' upkeep. Further, those who became politically active after their discharge from the institution (for example, the two litigants in the class-action lawsuit, as well as other survivors who have played active roles in the advocacy movement) described becoming cognizant of the ways in which their labour was being used to support their facility and the institutional system more broadly.

In addition, while some of the siblings and parents were aware of the financial relationship between the province and the provision of services – one mother, for example, thought that institutions were marvellously efficient, as they provided for her daughter's educational, vocational, and daily needs all under one roof – the focus of their discussions centred much more around their family member's designation as 'different,' the lack of resources directed towards community living and engagement, and the familial consequences of social discourse and institutionalization. This was probably due, in part, to the focus of the study and the nature of the questions being asked, but it also demonstrates the greater importance that reflection on the personal impact of institutionalization has played in many people's coming to terms with the experience, as opposed to a broader picture of institutions' connections with economic and political forces.

A second area of consideration regarding the link between institutions and larger economic forces was the inequitable funding arrangement between the provincial government and families who had a member with a disability. Institutions for the feebleminded in Ontario, throughout their entire 150-year history, were fully and consistently publicly funded. This meant that institutions were closed to outside influences, and that the government was perpetually attempting to keep their running costs as low as possible (Simmons 1982). This also meant that during the eugenic period in the early part of the twentieth century, 'progressives' who worked in such fields as public health and education (Dr Helen MacMurchy of Toronto Public Health is one example) claimed that it was a government responsibility to ensure that feeblemindedness did not spread throughout the population. Framing feeblemindedness as a public health concern legitimized the use of institutions and their funding through the auspices of the Ministry of Health. One possible corollary of this "medically necessary" reasoning included the thinking that aggressive eugenic policy, such as segregation and sterilization, might eventually eliminate feebleminded-ness in its entirety, minimizing concerns about how non-institutionalized disabled people would be cared for. The fervent idealism which guided many progressives' quest to build a utopian society may have prevented the implementation of more inclusive and equitable policy, so determined were they to eradicate feeblemindedness as their first priority (McLaren 1990).

Accordingly, families who admitted their child to an Ontario institution had their child's care fully covered from 'cradle to grave.' This remained true until the end of the institutional era; as people began to be transferred from institutional to community care, financial compensation was granted to those agencies welcoming the previously institutionalized individuals. Those families who chose to keep their child at home, on the other hand, throughout the majority of the institutional era, received nothing in com-pensation from the government. The government's reluctance to provide financial support for people with intellectual disabilities in the community and their families who were attempting to forge a way for them can also be explained in part by the principally conservative ideology that dominated the Ontario political scene throughout the twentieth century. Successive conservative governments were reluctant to allow their funding platforms to move into areas of social welfare or concern, political practices to which they were ideologically opposed. This began to shift slowly beginning in 1974, when policy concerning people with intellectual disabilities was transferred from the Ministry of Health to the Ministry of Community and Social Services. Even with this change in philosophy and direction, it was not until institutions began to be closed more deliberately by the government near the end of the twentieth century that the imbalance in the way funds were distributed to families was reconsidered and made more equitable.[1]

This economic imbalance appears even more pronounced when the kinds of families who were historically lobbying to have their children admitted to institutions are considered. As discussed previously, socio-economic status and social positioning were strong predictors of which families desired to have their child admitted. Those families who were higher on the social ladder, or who desired to be regarded as such, were more likely to pursue admission of their own volition. At institutions' peak in the 1960s and 1970s, wait lists for admission were long, and Members of Provincial

Parliament were regularly approached by families desiring that their son or daughter be considered. It is more likely that families with sufficient navigational skills and social means would have undertaken such requests.

The practical implications of the maldistribution of financial resources are not difficult to discern. As pointed out in the previous chapter, the human tendency is to make our decisions "based on where the dollars are," and many of the families in this study were no exception. For some families, working tirelessly on behalf of their son or daughter in a vacuum of resources did not make sense when the alternative of allowing the government to provide for all of their child's needs already existed. Further, at the time, much about the care of a child with an intellectual disability was unknown, or was considered daunting; thus, the tendency to lean towards someone else taking on that responsibility is not surprising.

Yet, as always, the pursuit of institutionalization by those families searching for a higher rung on the ladder of social success must be juxtaposed with the forced institutionalization of many hundreds of people due to their families' lack of social status and the resultant scrutiny by child welfare officers. While many families actively sought institutionalization as a way to ensure a more secure social presentation, others, designated by markers such as race, class, and gender, had no choice in the matter and were directed to send their child to an institution whether they wanted to or not (Strong-Boag 2007). Despite variations in admission routes, economic considerations remained omnipresent; amid fears that 'degenerate' families would become unpredictable drains on the public purse, institutions offered a way for the government to deal with this population with a certain amount of predictability. Thus, whether families decided to institutionalize their son or daughter to save face or were forced to send their children due to public health and educational authorities' fears that they were not skilled enough to raise their children, how much it would cost to care for these children, and who would pay for it, were always the government's driving considerations.

Disability studies scholars have addressed the connection between financial concerns and societal limitations for people with disabilities (Barton 2001; Oliver 1990; Thomas 2002). Russell and Malhotra (2002, 212) state that "disability is a socially-created category derived from labour relations, a product of the exploitative economic structure of capitalist society: one which creates (and then oppresses) the so-called 'disabled' body as one of the conditions that allow the capitalist class to accumulate wealth." As discussed in chapter 1, capitalism is reliant on sites of segregation and the oppression enacted through them by means of exploitative labour and forced banishment from sites of meaningful and human engagement (Ignatieff 1983). Thus, a complete understanding of the oppression experienced via institutionalization cannot be undertaken without acknowledging its connection to human labour, production, and the market. While social and identity models of disability have challenged predominant perspectives of disability as an individual and personal tragedy in which society plays little part, Russell and Malhotra iterate the importance of "reconceptualising disability as an outcome of the political economy" (211). Thus, while the closure of institutions has predominantly been seen as a decision based on increased awareness of human rights and a desire to end sanctioned oppression against people with intellectual disabilities, the role of provincial finances cannot be ignored. The financial savings accrued due to the secondment of care to community agencies, families, and private enterprises was as much a part of the government's decision to deinstitutionalize as were concerns regarding people's care and well-being.

Deinstitutionalization was a major victory for the disability community. However, the seemingly unabated progression of neoliberalism and capitalism necessitates ongoing analysis of the financial reasoning which underscores most if not all of the decisions being made on behalf of people with disabilities. Attention to fears of difference and shunning due to aesthetic (Hahn 1989) and ontological anxieties (Shildrick 2002) is vital, yet the work of creating true inclusion cannot be completed without an interrogation of the link between government economic prosperity and the rigid protection of the residual welfare system, in which both disability and need must be proven and wherein the state intervenes only when all other means have been exhausted. Current government claims of the need for austerity mean that families continue to go to extraordinary lengths to find meaningful homes and work for their children; government priorities appear to centre on cutting as closely as possible to the financial line at which families' survival hovers, while still being able to claim that movement towards inclusion is taking place. As long as government priorities remain embedded within a capitalist, neoliberal model, an effective approach by academics and activists must include incisive critique of the role of finances in decisions concerning people with disabilities and the extent of the care and opportunities made available to them.

Sandra Carpenter (2007) makes this connection explicit in her essay on the "neo-asylum era," or the ways in which institutionalization as a process continues to "descend" (1) on people with disabilities despite the physical closure of buildings such as Huronia. In her paper, Carpenter states that trends such as the regionalization of health care in Ontario as well as larger trade agreements are facilitating the reinstitutionalization of people with disabilities due to regional authorities' contractual agreements with private long-term healthcare providers (7), agreements that tend to "disadvantage small statistical groups such as people with disabilities" (8), and due to trade partnerships such as NAFTA that "make it impossible to go back" (7). She encourages, therefore, a wary eye towards government policy that promises to improve the lives of people with disabilities.

While analyses which include economic considerations do not change the outcome of this study, nor do they change the fact that not all participants reflected on these factors, they do encourage realistic cynicism and scepticism in the face of government promises for reform. While governments have learned well the benefits of couching economic necessities in the language of treating people better, the past several decades have demonstrated the need for a culture of critique which is mindful always of the link between promises and budgetary concerns. The retrospective view offered in this study reveals the constancy of economic factors throughout institutionalization and deinstitutionalization's long history in Ontario, even when government promises would like us to believe otherwise.

Construction of Intellectual Disability

One of the most consistent themes emerging from this project concerns the construction of intellectual disability. Shifting political and moral rationales defending the need for institutionalization throughout history, as well as family narratives that reveal the changing nature of interpretations and understandings, demonstrate the produced and arbitrary nature of classifications of disability. In the sections that follow, I address two elements of the construction of disability relevant to this project: first, the construction of intellectual disability as a category and the arbitrariness of 'intellect'; and second, the impact that the construction of disability had on families who chose to institutionalize a family member.

Intellect as a Category and a Classification

As discussed in chapter 1, significant scholarly work has challenged the notion of a reified, immutable, and inherited intelligence (Gould 1996). Foucault's genealogical work which traces the rise of the "tyranny of reason and the silencing of unreason" (Carlson 2005, 134) has been instrumental in current understandings of the designation and classification of those considered intellectually inferior. In the same way that disability scholars have pointed to the designation of the 'marked' and disabled body to ensure the viability of the non-disabled (Garland Thomson 1997; McRuer 2006), so too have scholars indicated that the emergence of a discourse of reason in the late fifteenth and sixteenth centuries allowed a "parallel discourse of unreason, reason's *Other* to materialize" (Stainton 2004, 225). In her detailed analysis of the emergence of the modern institution based on both quantitative and qualitative reasoning, Carlson (2010) "problematizes" the notion of intellectual disability as a category and explores the "discriminatory and erroneous assumptions" that present intellectual disability as a "self-evident and unproblematic 'natural kind'" (12). She outlines the need to interrogate carefully the "history and status of mental retardation as a *classification*" (Carlson 2005, 133, original emphasis), and to expose the history of intellectual disability, as opposed to its categorization as a medically defined condition. She notes that institutions, and the tests designed to ensure particular people were placed there, allowed the "emergence of a new kind of individual" (137–8), discursively produced through the mechanisms designed to discipline and control them.

Moreover, scholars note that classifications of intellectual capacity and inferiority have historically been informed by racist, classist, and colonialist notions that gained prominence in the middle of the nineteenth century. Borthwick (1996), for example, notes that Darwin-inspired explanations of intellectual disability suggested that 'inferior' forms of intelligence were part of the natural order of the biological universe: "these people were different not because they were like us, but because they were intact and complete specimens of a lower order of being" (406). Likewise, Chapman, Carey, and Ben-Moshe (2014) note that the emergence of scientific explanations for human progress comfortably incorporated "racist hierarchies" (8) in the classification of certain 'typologies' of intellectual disability. According to Wright (2011), John Langdon Down's initial descriptions of Down syndrome were based on "ethnic and racial classifications typical of the anthropological discussions of the mid-Victorian period" (12), later leading to the medical term "mongolism." Quoting Down (1866) from one of his earliest observations, "It is difficult to realize he is the child of Europeans, but so frequently are these characters presented that there can be no doubt that these ethnic features are the result of degeneration."

Classifications of intellect, in combination with intersecting factors with degenerative assumptions such as race, class, and Indigeneity, have historically undergone transformations in order to meet the administrative needs of governments during specific time periods. Particularly during periods of intense anxiety regarding the propagation of 'unfit' citizens, such as the eugenic period, boundaries regarding designations of intellect were flexible and mutable, allowing those in positions of authority to justify the use of institutions to segregate those considered threatening to the rest of the population. Moreover, as discussed in chapters 1 and 2, the mutually constitutive relationship between eugenics, intellectual classification, and statistics (Mackenzie 1981) suggests that statistical information did not simply confirm eugenic fears, but that eugenic thinking has, during different time periods, informed how data is gathered and formulated, influencing the results and subsequently enabling eugenic thinking and practices to continue unquestioned.

The construction of categories of intellect and its organizational fallout in the form of segregated institutions takes on phenomenological significance when re-examined in light of survivors' comments. All of the survivors questioned, to varying degrees, how they ended up living in an institution. Although many of them knew the story of their institutionalization, survivors continued to question the fundamental reason why they, of all the members of their family, were made to go there. Rather than this being an indication of poor family communication (although that played a part in many cases), or a lack of insight on the part of survivors, survivors' questioning converges, rather, with Carlson's work regarding the intentional and discursive production of intellectual disability. Survivors' awareness that the reasons for their incarceration could be challenged indicates an understanding that these reasons were contingent on particular understandings of ability and disability, and that the institution itself played a role in their development as a 'person with a disability.' As one of the survivors noted, he was not 'disabled' until he went to the institution: "I was a normal person before I went there." These comments are living evidence of theories concerning the discursive production of intellectual incapacity. While I do not claim that differences in capability in some areas do not exist, what survivors challenge here are the societal "values and meanings that we attach" to intellectual ability (Rembis 2014, 143), values that have been the driving force in determining people's futures, where they live, and the level of influence they have been able to exercise in determining their own futures.

We might wish that the deinstitutionalization of thousands of people and the recent closure of the large, government-run institutions in Ontario is indicative of a movement towards the 'de-classification' of intellectual disability, towards its deconstruction as a firm and immutable category. Yet despite their closure, as well as the work of postmodern, feminist, and critical disability scholarship, the notion of a measurable and hierarch-ically arranged intelligence remains influential in scholarly and popular discourse, and standardized measures of intellect continue to be used as tools to predict individuals' potential for successful integration into modern society (Kliewer and Drake 1998). More dangerously, arguments from the utilitarian bioethicist tradition (see, for example, Singer 2011, Kuhse 1995, and Rachels 1986) continue to play a central role in debates in which people's inherent value is assessed according to demonstrable skill and intellect, the assumed indicators of the potential for a "'normal' and 'full human existence'" (Vehmas 1999, 43). While measures of intellect might not currently lead to visible manifestations of incarceration to the same scale as the mass institutionalization of previous eras, examples of their impact in the lives of people with intellectual disabilities remain, as evidenced by the obstructed access to and exercise of rights (Carey 2009), limits on reproduction (Tilley et al. 2012), segregated work arrangements (Galer 2014), nominal 'community living' situations (Ben-Moshe 2011), and neoliberal arrangements that make it increasingly difficult, financially and otherwise, for people with disabilities to access the services to which they are entitled (Carpenter 2007).

"We had no relationship with him at all. I mean, none."

For families who participated in this project, the construction of dis-ability was a principal factor in the way in which family relationships were lived and understood. This impact was most often felt through two significant transitions. The first concerns survivors' brothers and sisters. Many siblings described a process of adjustment in their understanding of their institutionalized family member. They describe a progression, either through their own individual encounters with their sibling later in life, or through personal reflection on their family and what had transpired there, during which their initial understandings of their brother or sister changed as they grew older, arriving at an interpretation different from the one they had grown up with. Some siblings also described the personal distress they experienced when the understandings of their sibling that they gained later in life began to conflict with the language, interpretations, and expectations that they had used or had been instructed to use when they were children. Michelle described growing up in a household with demeaning attitudes towards intellectual disability, a perspective that was deeply challenged by her own journey of understanding around disability, in part due to her involvement, almost five decades after her sister had been institutionalized, with a creative arts group consisting of people of varying abilities. "I never thought my sister could be creative. But I know now she could have been; she probably was." Carmen, too, described her transition from her role as family facilitator in the face of her mother's ongoing distress about having given birth to a child with a disability, to a sister who desired to establish some understanding, however belated, of her sister. These and other siblings describe an increasing awareness that the definitions of intellectual disability to which they had originally been exposed were not as fixed as their original understandings would have had them believe.

This recalibration of understandings and relationships, while brought to light by the siblings of survivors, also often meant a recalibration of how the entire family understood itself, and was frequently manifested as a point of significant tension. Conflict emerged within some families when parents were challenged by their non-disabled children about the 'story' of the disabled child that had been presented to them and by the decisions that had been made about them.

In most of the families that participated in this study, contestations in understandings of what or who the disabled family member actually consisted of were most often dealt with through silence. A few siblings, however, described more successful attempts to re-open the family conversation about the decision to institutionalize; in these cases, while parents weren't necessarily opposed to discussing it, they remained convinced of the appropriateness of their decision and were not able, according to siblings, to see their son or daughter as someone other than one who had required full-time custodial care. In light of the significant moral compromises that some parents had gone through in their decision to institutionalize, as well as the numerous social pressures to which they would have been exposed, this defensiveness is understandable; however, this does not diminish attempts by their non-disabled children to suggest that perhaps the definitions that had been used to describe and categorize their brother or sister were contestable.

The second trend from the research which brings to light the constructedness of disability concerns the deinstitutionalization process, during which family members began to re-establish relationships with each other, often after decades of separation. For many families, this reconfiguration of family in which they were obliged to participate was a difficult reckoning, one that brought to light the potential for disability to be seen as something mutable and as something that can be built from medical and social discourse. Former staff, frequently bearers of the news to families that processes were underway for their child to be released from the institution and that a community placement was being sought, described witnessing parents' confusion in light of the alternate presentation being given for their son or daughter, that he or she might actually be capable of community living and not only institutionalized care. The deinstitutionalization process, similar to siblings' adjustment of their understandings of disability, allowed the cracks in the limited definitions of intellectual disability to be revealed.

Parents' understandings of institutions as locations wherein all of their child's needs would be met also had to be reconsidered through the deinstitutionalization process. Whether or not parents considered their decision to institutionalize a 'mistake,' throughout the deinstitutionalization process, the spectrum of ways of living and being with people with intellectual disabilities began to widen. No longer were parents being presented with the two options of decades past: institutionalized care, or raising one's child at home with minimal support. Through increasing numbers of advocacy, self-advocacy, and parent organizations, as well as increasing government support towards community living, more alternatives were emerging, and for many of the parents who had chosen to institutionalize, these alternatives introduced the theoretical possibility of doing things differently. Yet for the parents in this study who had chosen to institutionalize, this did not change their conviction that they had done the right thing for their child and for their family. Further, all these parents were elderly and had made these decisions decades earlier. In their twilight years, it is likely they did not want to revisit their earlier decision and complicate it with revised understandings of disability and the need for institutionalization. Parents were aware that there was nothing they could do to alter the life path they had chosen for their son or daughter many years earlier, and most chose to live that decision without regret, even in the face of increasing public criticism being directed at institutions. Indeed, one of the more interesting, and perhaps more cautionary, findings from this research is the fact that even when parents knew of the difficulties that existed in institutions, including the possibility of abuse and mistreatment, those who were supportive of institutionalization in general did not believe that their son or daughter was affected, or that those abuses were happening in the place where their son or daughter lived.

Last, the constructedness of disability must be considered in con- junction with the constructed nature of the systems designed to house people so labelled. Those parents and siblings who expressed discomfort with reified and fixed definitions of disability were also more likely to question the immutable and beneficial role of the institution. Indeed, when parents were informed that institutions would be closing, the bene- fits of institutionalization were thrown into doubt, much the same way the extent of their child's disability was thrown into doubt. Despite the historical confidence invested in institutions by authorities and the public, the gradual re-entry into the community of hundreds of institutionalized individuals, for the most part without serious consequences, indicated the instability of institutionalization as a system.

While it is easy as observers to be dismissive of parents who sent their children away to be institutionalized, perhaps their steadfast conviction in the rightness of their decision is instead indicative of the depth of what was at stake for them. Rather than interpreting parents' determination to believe that they had made the right choice as stubbornness or a lack of openness to alternate possibilities, this could perhaps also be seen as a sign of something to which all parents are prone: the need to believe that you have done the best thing for your child and that you did not err in their upbringing. For most of these parents, the possibility, introduced late in life, that they had made a poor choice in one of their principal life tasks raised an area of self-reflection with which they did not wish to engage. Further, it is important to consider how social conditions made it difficult for parents to imagine possibilities other than institutionalization, and how it created the need for parents to remain convinced of their decision. While it is tempting to blame parents for their child's institutionalization and to criticize them for their stubbornness and their conviction that their child's disability was the root of the problem, to do so individualizes the problem and prevents examination at the level of social responsibility. Blaming parents in isolation situates the problem at the personal level, instead of broadening the analysis to include other players and historical conditions. Phrased as a question, in what ways does society perpetuate the conditions that make it difficult for parents and other caregivers to imagine new and alternate ways of supporting people with disabilities? What are the conditions that make it difficult for parents, caregivers, and political authorities to admit that mistakes have been made? How is it that governments and professional bodies have so much at stake in the care and treatment of people with disabilities that intransigence tends to be the preferred course of action? And what have we learned from the experiences of the families here in order to map a future less dependent on such limiting conditions?

Finally, the ongoing historical process of the construction of disability has perpetuated the framing of people with intellectual disabilities as Other. Although boundaries between classifications of people have blurred, such that notions of race, gender, and ability no longer hold the strict distinctions they once did, people with intellectual disabilities remain an entity, a group categorized and named, faulty and limited. One of the key informants noted that whereas the earlier trajectory of advocacy work concerned the movement from institutions to community living, the concern now is to assist people to move towards positions of self-advocacy and decision-making. In the same way that the nature of advocacy work has moved, so too, must there be a change in what is perceived as its desired endpoint. The importance lies not only in new understandings of what people are capable of, but in a recalibration and dissolution of disability's boundaries, boundaries that have historically justified people's oppression and segregation.

Conclusion

The narratives presented in this text provide a body of material from which the effects of institutionalization can begin to be discerned. It is a beginning in that, as with other forms of institutionalized trauma, carried through generations and with diffuse effects throughout various communities, its full emotional and cultural significance has yet to be realized. The "ghosts of forced confinement" (Chapman, Carey, and Ben-Moshe 2014, 18) to which many of these narratives refer – broken relationships, recovery from trauma, long processes of reconciliation, reconfigurations of family histories – are surfacing; "these are the hauntings that need to inform politics, policies, activism, and scholarship" (ibid.). What have we learned from the unfinished trajectory of institutionalization, and how do these stories inform the way forward? How can we, in the words of historian David Rothman (1971, 295), "not remain trapped in inherited answers"?

One starting point is the creation of forums in which the stories of survivors and others affected by institutionalization can be shared and believed. Many of the participants commented that this was the first time that they had ever spoken of their institutional experience. In most families, once the decision to institutionalize had been made, the life of the institutionalized person remained hidden, as did the stories of the families who had placed them there. For decades, the 'problem' of the person with intellectual disabilities did not constitute a presence on the Canadian socio-political landscape, and thus appeared resolved; people were unseen and unheard, and, other than the staff who worked there, few people had any contact with institutions at all. As siblings in particular attest, there was little room in the normative Canadian social landscape of the 1950s, 1960s, and 1970s for families to discuss their decision to institutionalize, the impact this was having on their personal and public lives, or that they had had a child with a disability in the first place. Thus, until very recently, people who experienced institutionalization, either directly or through their families, have borne this formative piece of their personal and family history in silence and alone. Despite institutions' vast geographic presence in Ontario, exemplified by fortress-like buildings on large tracts of land strategically placed to ensure maximum geographic coverage, institutions have occupied a silent position in the history of the province.

Further, this invisibility and silence did not necessarily end when institutions began to close. Once this period ended in people's lives, either though death or deinstitutionalization, there were few avenues to discuss or share experiences. Even while hundreds of people moved into the community, the shared chapter of institutionalization was not addressed, and for many years the history remained 'theirs' with which to contend. Not until two institutional survivors launched a class-action lawsuit against the Ontario government in 2010 for abuse and mistreatment while under government care was there any movement towards a public accounting for what had happened. Indeed, survivors and advocates have pointed out that had these two litigants not brought their case forward, the government might not have felt compelled to issue a public apology nor to begin to address institutionalization's aftermath. Emerging from the actions of these two litigants, projects addressing the repercussions of institutionalization, often through creative and arts-based methods, have begun to emerge. Further, the breaking open of the story of the institutionalization of people considered intellectually disabled has, in Canada, been contemporaneous with the emergence of other stories of mass incarceration in our history, such as those from Indigenous people forced to live in residential schools. These beginnings of historical acknowledgment have the potential to create a common space within which stories can be held. Yet for many survivors from institutions for the 'feebleminded,' residential schools, and other sites of confinement, the past and the stories that contain it remain painful and difficult, despite an increased awareness of and sensitivity to the atrocities people have lived through.

The concern that materializes from these axes of silence is that the re-emergence of incarcerative systems is more easily achieved. Canada's historical foundation of segregated treatment of marginalized peoples increases particular groups' vulnerability to this re-emergence, including people with intellectual disabilities. Although the People First community in Canada is strong and tireless in its advocacy work, there remain many thousands of people with complex impairments who are at risk of being absorbed into currently accepted forms of institutionalized care, new forms of incarceration that continue to propagate the limitations of eras past, but with new "rationalizations that allow the rest of us to live with them" (Carey, Ben-Moshe, and Chapman 2014, ix). People with more comprehensive needs continue to be considered a concern to be 'dealt with,' and, in many cases, are not provided with ways of making their desires known, making it less likely that their wishes concerning where and how they would like to live will be listened to or understood. Moreover, in the current era of austerity, the redesigning of welfare systems, including the regionalization of services and the threat of the expansion of privatized health care, means that the systemic constraints placed upon people with disabilities have not really disappeared, but have shifted, rather, into less visible, income-dependent locations (Carpenter 2007).

These redesignings, or the submersion of segregation into more hidden and acceptable forms, are supported by another axis underlying the variant narratives in this text: the ubiquitous assumption that people with intellectual disabilities may only possess a certain amount of self-determination. Despite the removal of many physical barriers to an autonomous life, legal structures within Canada continue to favour substitute decision-making on behalf of people with intellectual disabilities, thus utilizing a guardianship model, as opposed to supporting people to make their own decisions (Stainton 2016). This "implicit lack of recognition of a person's right to decide" (10) means that in most cases, the final determination of where one's future might lie remains external to the person of concern. Thus, in day-to-day decisions, those which "define personhood" (ibid.), as well as ones concerning living arrangements, work, and personal relationships, authority still lies, in most provinces, with those appointed to make decisions on a person's behalf, a process more often linked with administrative priorities than with the wishes of the person concerned.

Anita Silvers (1995), in her seminal reflection on "reconciling equality to difference," urges us to interrogate "whether social institutions have embraced or excluded certain kinds of selves ... [as this] alerts us to how what we take to be essential components of these excluded persons may in fact be the product of historical contingency" (50). The narratives in this text tell stories of people's exclusion from one social institution, the family and the community in which it was located, only to be moved, unwillingly, into another, a movement made natural due to its assumed necessity, a movement contingent upon historical understandings of impairment and difference. Silvers rejects the assumption, an assumption that directed the institutionalization of the survivors in this text, that "inequality follows naturally rather than artificially on disability" (32), and argues instead that an "alternate construal of justice" (33) be established which prioritizes the realization of people's individual and collective needs and desires. In such a conception of justice, people's differences are acknowledged, not to justify one's classification under the rhetoric of administrative efficiencies, but to support the realization of the life one desires for oneself. In such a moral order, precedence would be given to social arrangements – cultural, financial, educational, and otherwise – that facilitate the outcomes people need to live a fulfilling and meaningful life.

For the survivors who participated in this project, the desire most often expressed was for a home, a place of rest. Their abrupt removal from their initial place of belonging, as fraught with difficulty as it might have been, was recounted by all of the survivors as a wound from which they will never completely recover. Joe, a survivor who has thought deeply about the consequences of institutionalization, states that having a place of safety that one can call one's home is fundamental, a shared human necessity. He challenges current thinking that prioritizes certain models of home due to their efficiencies, and argues that we must consider first what homes provide to people in light of what they have lived and what they may go on to live in the future: "I think we should call them 'Peace at Last' homes, not group homes ... I think that name should be in every home ... I think it should be called 'Peace at Last,' because if you hear their stories, you'll know what they all went through." Pat, even while admitting that her home life before she entered the institution was not the happiest, described never losing her desire to leave the institution and to 'come home.' "When I went home for a visit, it just made me want to stay ... I kept asking them – when am I going to go home for good?"

This project was the recounting of the stories of many people who felt the effects of institutionalization in one way or another. And while this text cannot claim to know the precise way forward in the quest to recognize people's desire for home, survivors have provided some indication. Survivors, the only participants in this project who felt the direct effects of institutionalization against their will, were adamant that the kind of segregation they lived through should never happen again. Peter stated: "We all benefit from the fact that people aren't in institutions, and I feel that everybody can live in the community with support, whatever it happens to be." The narratives presented here suggest that many of the survivors, still coming to terms with the emotional, social, and physical consequences of years spent in an institution, are far from 'peace at last.' So, too, do many members of their families continue to reconcile the losses and personal and familial difficulties experienced through institutionalization. While it is beyond this book's mandate to provide a definitive roadmap towards those places of peace, the experiences articulated here indicate that they will never be found in large, locked facilities, nor in the forced segregation of Ontario's institutional history, nor in denigrating constructions of intellectual disability. Rather, this project has indicated that a radical reconfiguration of difference and its meanings is called for as part of the work of creating communities in which all members have a place.

APPENDICES

Appendix A

Participant	Relationship to institutionalized individual	Occupation	Details of institutionalization
Peter Park	self	One of the founders of People First; advocate for disability rights	Admitted 1960, age c. 18; duration 18 yrs
Joe Clayton	self	Advocate; artist; photographer; teacher	Admitted c. 1958, age 12; duration 6–7 yrs
Hilary[1]	self	Employed at day programme	Admitted c. 1948, age 5; duration over 30 yrs
Brian	self	Caretaker at high school	Admitted c. 1973, age 12; duration 9 yrs
Sean	self	Employed at day programme	Admitted 1955, age 8; duration 23 yrs
André	self	Retired day programme employee	Admitted 1955, age 14; duration c. 20 yrs
Patricia Seth	self	Advocate for disability rights; public speaker; principal litigant in class action	Admitted 1965, age 7; duration 13 yrs
Graham[2]	self	Retired restaurant employee	Admitted 1953, age 15; duration 23 yrs
Marie Slark	self	Advocate; public speaker; principal litigant; seamstress	Admitted 1961, age 7; duration 9 yrs

1 sister of William, indicated in Appendix B.
2 brother of Gregory and Abigail, indicated in Appendix B.

Appendix B

Participant	Relationship to institutionalized individual	Details
Colleen	Sister	10 yrs old when brother, age 5, was institutionalized
Carmen	Sister	15 yrs old when sister, age 5, was institutionalized
Marilyn Dolmage	Sister	4 yrs old when infant brother was institutionalized
William[1]	Brother	Approx 11 yrs old when sister Hilary, age c. 5, was institutionalized
Erin	Sister	4 yrs old when brother, age 2, was institutionalized
Margaret	Sister	Approx 6 yrs old when brother, age 3, was institutionalized
Gregory[2]	Brother	10 yrs old when brother, age 15, was institutionalized
Vici Clarke[3]	Sister	8 yrs old when brother, age 7, was institutionalized
Abigail[2]	Sister	13 yrs old when brother, age 15, was institutionalized
Michelle[4]	Sister	4 yrs old when sister, age 2, was institutionalized
Olivia[4]	Sister	Infant when sister, age 2, was institutionalized

1 brother of Hilary, indicated in Appendix A
2 brother and sister of Graham, indicated in Appendix A
3 daughter of Muriel Grace, indicated in Appendix C
4 sisters, daughters of Owen and Betty, indicated in Appendix C

Appendix C

Participant	Relationship to institutionalized individual	Details
Bertram	Father	Son institutionalized at age 5
Toddy Kehoe	Mother; daughter not institutionalized	Advocate; founded schools
Louise	Mother	Daughter institutionalized at age 3
Muriel Grace[1]	Mother	Son institutionalized at age 7 for one year; advocate; involved in Association
Susan	Mother	Daughter institutionalized at age 8
Betty[2]	Mother	Daughter institutionalized at age 2
Owen[2]	Father	Daughter institutionalized at age 2
Audrey Cole	Mother; son not institutionalized	Advocate; involved in Association

1 mother of Vici, indicated in Appendix B
2 married couple, parents to Michelle and Olivia, indicated in Appendix B.

Appendix D

Participant	Relationship to institution or project
Doug	Former staff at an Ontario institution
Don	Former staff at an Ontario institution
Tracy	Former staff at an Ontario institution
Jill	Former staff at an Ontario institution

Appendix E

Participant	Relationship to institutionalization / deinstitutionalization process	Comments
Paula Kilcoyne	Hired by community agency to facilitate deinstitutionalization from Ontario institution	Disability rights advocate
Annie Stafford	Volunteer and worker with local Association; advocate against institutionalization	Started nursery schools for children with disabilities in '60s, '70s, '80s; bursary in her name for people with intellectual challenges
Orville Endicott	Legal counsel to Community Living Ontario	Decades of disability rights advocacy
Thelma Wheatley	Advocate on behalf of deinstitutionalization; historical interest and knowledge	Disability rights advocate

Notes

INTRODUCTION

This chapter title is informed by the work of Carlson (2010).

1 The narratives of Marie and Pat are found in chapter 4 of the text.

2 *Gristle in the Stew*, 2012, dir. D. Gutnick; *Gristle in the Stew (Update): Revisiting the Horrors of Huronia*, 2016.

3 See, for example, "Recounting Huronia: A Participatory Art-Based Project"; and the Huronia Survivors Speakers Bureau.

4 See, for example, T. Alamenciak, "Huronia: Settled but Not Forgotten," *The Toronto Star*, 30 September 2013.

5 Premier Wynne's apology can be found at: https://www.mcss.gov.on.ca/en/mcss/programs/developmental/Premier_Apology.aspx.

6 My choice to focus here on two theoretical bodies of work does not preclude the relevance of other frameworks that can assist with this analysis. Bourdieu's theories of the habitus and Butler's work on performativity, for example, are helpful in analyses which emerge later in this text.

CHAPTER ONE

1 Chapman (2014) points out that the residential school system, established concurrently with institutions for the intellectually disabled in the mid-nineteenth century, with overlapping motivations and rationalities, is a distinct yet predictable development from the earliest sites of confinement for Indigenous peoples. As far back as 1657, "boarding schools for aboriginal boys" (33) were being established in what is now known as Canada; deaths that occurred as a result, however, were not considered an unfortunate side-effect of the training required to develop Indigenous children into white citizens, as was the rationale from the mid-nineteenth century onwards, but instead as part of the process of annihilating the "nothingness" of Indigenous peoples through "capture or killing" (35).

2 Quote from Tyor and Bell 1984, 21.

3 'Monogeny' refers to the scientific belief that human beings have descended from a single pair of ancestors; 'polygeny' refers to evolution from different ancestral groups.

4 From the title of Chapman, Carey, and Ben-Moshe 2014, "Reconsidering Confinement: Interlocking Locations and Logics of Incarceration."

5 Fournier and Crey (1997) suggest that a meeting in Orillia, Ontario, in 1846, at which government officials committed to the Indian residential system, was a key moment in the schools' historical development. The number of schools expanded rapidly, such that by the end of the 1880s, "up to a third of all aboriginal children were confined to the schools, many for the majority of their childhoods" (50). The first institution for the feebleminded was established in Orillia in 1876.

6 For further discussion of the assumed 'naturalness' of segregating those identified as having an intellectual disability, and how this tends to be remarked upon when other marginalized groups are included in that distinction, see Berubé 1996, Carlson 2010, and Piepmeier 2012.

7 Institutional survivors in Ontario, with advocates and colleagues, have initiated arts-based projects, published in academic journals, and conducted workshops and speakers' bureaus as ways to educate the public about their experience and as part of the longer project of healing and recovery. These include the Recounting Huronia Project, the Huronia Speakers Bureau, and a special issue of the *Canadian Journal of Disability Studies* (vol. 6, no. 3). Political activism includes the ongoing work of People First of Canada, a decades-old self-advocacy group, as well as the class-action lawsuit launched against the Ontario government in 2010 by two survivors of the Huronia institution.

CHAPTER TWO

1 At several points in this chapter, I use terminology that was in use during the historical period which I am describing. Thus, terms such as 'feebleminded,' 'idiot,' 'retarded,' and 'insane' appear, taken directly from the names of institutions, or from texts that were in use at the time.

2 The asylum in Orillia underwent several name changes throughout its history, reflecting attempts by the provincial government to project an increasingly benevolent image of the institution. Its latest incarnation was "The Huronia Regional Centre," or "Huronia," reflecting the region in which it was located. At different points in this chapter, I use the terms "Huronia" or simply "Orillia" to indicate the Orillia institution.

3 H.G. Simmons (1982) has, to date, written by far the most extensive and comprehensive analysis of the development of institutionalization for

people with intellectual disabilities in Ontario. As such, this chapter draws heavily from his work. While I have attempted to bring in the analyses of other authors and historical records, Simmons is my primary point of reference in analyzing the developments particular to this chapter.

4 Some of the more prominent examples include S.G. Howe's "experimental school for idiots" (Ferguson 1994, 45), founded in Boston in 1848; H.B. Wilbur's private school for the feebleminded, established in his home town of Barre in the same year (ibid.); and the Vineland Training School for Boys and Girls, established in 1888 in Vineland, New Jersey, which in 1906 became a headquarters for intelligence testing and investigations into eugenic principles. For further detail, please see Ferguson 1994, Simmons 1982, Trent 1994, and Tyor and Bell 1984.

5 See, for example, Buck 1950, Frank 1952, and Rogers 1953.

6 A substantial Roman Catholic presence in Ontario and Quebec provided opposition to sterilization legislation. Institutions were considered a more humane way to ensure segregation of the feebleminded from the rest of the population, and to separate feebleminded men and women from each other.

7 The institution at Smiths Falls, initially called the Ontario Hospital School, Smiths Falls, was originally designed to hold two thousand four hundred residents, although its ultimate capacity was slightly less than that (Radford and Park 2003). The name of the Smiths Falls institution was changed to Rideau Regional Centre in 1974. The Ontario Hospital School for Retarded Children at Cedar Springs, later called Southwestern Regional Centre, was also originally designed to hold two thousand beds; eventually, plans were modified such that the maximum population was around one thousand (Simmons 1982).

8 While most Canadian provinces have closed long-term institutions for people with intellectual disabilities, four provinces continue to have functioning custodial institutions: Nova Scotia, Quebec, Manitoba, and Alberta. In 2013, the Alberta government decided to close the Michener Institute in Red Deer, infamous for its practice of sterilizing inmates without their consent until the 1970s; however, the decision to close was reversed in 2014, and the Michener's ongoing functioning remains a contentious topic among stakeholders – current and former residents, families, advocates, government officials, and employees.

9 Carlson (2010, 36–40) points out the historical tension in categorical descriptions of intellectual disability between 'static' (in which intellectual impairments were considered unchangeable and thus impervious to intervention) and 'dynamic' (based on the assumption that people with intellectual impairments are capable of improvement).

10 Ferguson (1994) suggests that for people considered the most 'unteach-able,' with the most severe impairments, the 'slide' from an educative

model to a custodial one is not completely accurate, as from the beginning of the institutional era, custodialism was the assumed model of care, and that they never benefited from Séguin's model of therapeutic intervention.

11 It is notable that for the first fifty years of its history, the asylum in Orillia had only two superintendents, A.H. Beaton and J.P. Downey. This suggests that their particular regard for people with intellectual disabilities, and the policies to which they adhered, remained firmly in place for almost five decades. Knowing the close working relationship that these men had with the provincial governments at the time (Simmons 1982) helps to explain the lack of movement in government policy around people with disabilities and institutionalization processes throughout the first third of Orillia's existence.

12 P. Berton, "What's Wrong at Orillia; Out of Sight, Out of Mind," *Toronto Daily Star*, 6 January 1960.

CHAPTER THREE

1 The term 'postwar' is used throughout the text to denote the years following World War II.

2 While research from professional disciplines such as nursing and psychology continues to prioritize the impact of the disabled child on the remainder of the family (see, for example, Blacher et al. 2005, Jones and Passey 2004, and Reichman, Corman, and Noonan 2008), notable exceptions have emerged in the last thirty years from the disability studies literature, wherein accounts written by people with disabilities have begun to recalibrate perceptions of the 'effect' of disability on the home and family life. (See, for example, Jones 2007 and Odell 2011.)

3 Beyond the lure of abundance and space that such arrangements offered, May (2008) suggests that political leaders also saw suburban neighbourhoods as another way to minimize the potentially devastating impact of a nuclear attack, as they decentralized urban cores, preventing the "concentration of residences or industries [which might act as] potential targets" (161).

4 This is not to suggest that racialized families during this era did not aspire to the same goals; in terms of admissions to institutions for intellectually disabled children, however, records suggest that the majority of children admitted were of Euro-Canadian descent.

5 However, as earlier discussion suggests, many children were institutionalized under the auspices of Children's Aid agencies or other forms of state intervention, often for reasons of low socio-economic status and presumptions of parental incompetence.

6 Carey (2009, 29–30) suggests that some parents during this era might have viewed the decision to institutionalize as a custodial 'right' that best served

their interests, despite this being a restriction of the individual rights of the person with intellectual disabilities.

7   The class-action lawsuit launched against the Ontario government in 2010 by Marie Slark and Patricia Seth is a good example of this. The survivor community, as well as a strong advocacy group, continues to work to ensure the Ontario government adheres to promises made at the time of the public apology (December 2013), including securing financial compensation owed to survivors, and for accountability in regard to the cemetery on HRC grounds.

8   Beginning in 2014, the Orillia-based Huronia Cultural Campus Foundation has been proposing to convert the site of the former Huronia Regional Centre into an arts and culture centre. Their proposal has been met with resistance from within the institutional survivor community, who state they have not been included in the planning process. Several survivors have indicated that they do not want the site of the former institution to be used as a cultural site; some are advocating for the buildings' demolition.

The former Rideau Regional Centre in Smiths Falls has been converted into a retirement community. Southwest Regional Centre near Chatham was purchased by a private developer in 2012 and has since been demolished, and plans exist to convert the site into hobby farms.

9   Many survivors have articulated that, at the least, they need to be consulted regarding the proposed projects.

CHAPTER FOUR

1   A combination of pseudonyms and real names (at the request of participants) is used in the text; only pseudonyms are indicated. The name used in the title of this chapter, Sean, is a pseudonym.

2   Details of participants are given in the appendices.

3   Two of the survivors noted that they have Indigenous status. In both cases, social welfare agencies were involved in their placement at a government institution for people with intellectual disabilities. As both survivors were sharing their experiences of institutionalization and its effects on their family relationships, an in-depth exploration of their overlapping stigmatized identities was not undertaken. It is worth noting that, while they occupied multiple identities (Aylward 2010) perceived as requiring intervention from the state (i.e. Indigeneity and intellectual disability), for reasons these two survivors were not able or chose not to articulate, intellectual disability became the identity for which the state intervened, indicative perhaps of government priorities, or simply convenience.

4   Pseudonym.

5 Pseudonym.

6 Pseudonym.

7 Pseudonym.

8 Pseudonym.

9 Formal government attention was brought to the problem of people attempting to escape from the institutional system after two incidents involving two men who had been on 'supervised' foster placements based out of Rideau Regional Centre near Smiths Falls: one man committed suicide; another suffered severe frostbite after attempting to leave his placement. A public enquiry headed by Williston in 1971, and his report in favour of deinstitutionalization that followed, assisted in facilitating a shift in opinion from the problem being located in the person attempting to escape, to that of the institutional system in general.

CHAPTER FIVE

1 Some of the parents interviewed for this project indicated that, while they may not have been 'forced' to institutionalize their child, the lack of community supports, in conjunction with pressure from medical doctors and other figures of authority, resulted in a felt pressure to institutionalize.

2 Pseudonym.

3 Pseudonym.

4 Pseudonym.

5 Pseudonym.

6 Pseudonym.

7 Their sister is Nora, the centre of Nora's Christmas of the previous chapter.

8 Pseudonym.

9 Pseudonym.

10 Pseudonym.

11 The institution in Orillia, most recently called the Huronia Regional Centre, is located in an area of Ontario that is popular with cottagers.

12 Marilyn's brother Robert died in the institution of treatable pneumonia when he was eight years old.

13 Pseudonym.

14 For more on mothers' responses to having a child with an intellectual disability, see Panitch 2008.

15 Vici and Rob's mother, Muriel, is included in the chapter on parents. Notably different from other parents in this study who chose to institutionalize, Muriel is openly critical of institutions, and regrets her decision to place her son there.

CHAPTER SIX

1 This is particularly interesting in light of the three parent-child pairings represented in the parent-sibling groups.
2 Pseudonym.
3 In attempts to create services for their children, some parents in urban areas began to establish small, parent-run co-operative nurseries and schools in order to provide programming for their children and to provide respite and support to each other. Many of these were precursors to local Associations for the Mentally Retarded. In their earliest days, they did not receive government funding, and parent groups lobbied to bring these schools into the mainstream educational system. For more on the parent movement and its influence on the development of services for children with intellectual disabilities, please see Simmons 1982 and Panitch 2008.
4 Pseudonym.
5 Pseudonym.
6 Pseudonym.
7 Pseudonym.
8 Pseudonym.
9 Pseudonym.

CHAPTER SEVEN

In this chapter, pseudonyms are used for former staff; real names are used for key informants.
1 Simmons (1982) notes that it was common for more than one generation of families to work at the same institution. This was particularly true when institutions were located in small towns or rural settings.
2 A complete history of the name changes undergone by Ontario institutions can be found at the Government of Ontario website: http://www.mcss.gov.on.ca/en/mcss/programs/developmental/HRC_history.aspx.
3 Schedule One facilities were residential facilities for people designated as having intellectual disabilities that were fully funded by the government of Ontario. At their peak in the 1960s, there were sixteen such institutions in Ontario. The three largest were the Huronia Regional Centre in Orillia, the Rideau Regional Centre in Smiths Falls, and Cedar Springs Regional Centre near Chatham.
4 The Ontario government has since attempted to address undistributed money from the class-action settlement by instituting a Strategic Program Investment Fund to which survivors and advocates could apply for funding to initiate community-based, survivor-led projects dealing with the lived experience and aftermath of institutionalization.

5   Huronia Regional Centre was located on the shores of Lake Simcoe, near Orillia, Ontario.

CHAPTER EIGHT

1   The Ontario government has implemented 'Passport' funding, a 'client-directed' funding program based on articulated need: http://www.mcss.gov.on.ca/documents/en/mcss/publications/developmental/passport/passport_guidelines_en.pdf.

References

Accessibility for Manitobans Act (2013). S.M. 2013 c. 40, CCSM c A1.7 [AMA]. https://web2.gov.mb.ca/bills/40-2/b026e.php.

Accessibility for Ontarians with Disabilities Act (2005). S.O. 2005, c. 11. https://www.ontario.ca/laws/statute/05a11.

Affleck, W., K.C. Glass, and M. MacDonald. 2013. "The Limitations of Language: Male Participants, Stoicism, and the Qualitative Research Interview." *American Journal of Men's Health* 7 (2): 155–62.

Åkerström, M., V. Burcar, and D. Wästerfors. 2011. "Balancing Contradictory Identities: Performing Masculinity in Victim Narratives." *Sociological Perspectives* 54 (1): 103–24.

Allen, G. 1997. "The Social and Economic Origins of Genetic Determinism: A Case History of the American Eugenics Movement, 1900–1940 and Its Lessons for Today." *Genetica* 99: 77–88.

Aylward, C. 2010. "Intersectionality: Crossing the Theoretical and Praxis Divide." *Journal of Critical Race Inquiry* 1 (1): 1–48.

Bailey, D., M. Bruder, K. Hebbeler, J. Carta, M. Defosset, C. Greenwood, L. Kahn, S. Mallik, J. Markowitz, D. Spiker, D. Walker, and L. Barton. 2006. "Recommended Outcomes for Families of Young Children with Disabilities." *Journal of Early Intervention* 28 (4): 227–51.

Barad, K. 2007. *Meeting the Universe Halfway: Quantum Physics and the Entanglement of Matter and Meaning*. Durham, NC: Duke University Press.

Barton, L. 2001. "Disability, Struggle, and the Politics of Hope." In *Disability Politics and the Struggle for Change*, edited by L. Barton, 1–10. London: David Fulton Publishers.

Beckwith, R.M. 2016. *Disability Servitude: From Peonage to Poverty*. London / New York: Palgrave Macmillan.

Ben-Moshe, L. 2011. "The Contested Meaning of 'Community' in Discourses of Deinstitutionalization and Community Living in the Field of Developmental Disability." In *Disability and Community: Research in Social*

Science and Disability, vol. 6, edited by A. Carey and R. Scotch, 241–64. Bingley, UK: Emerald.

Berton, P. 1960. "What's Wrong at Orillia: Out of Sight; Out of Mind." *The Toronto Daily Star* (6 January 1960).

Berubé, M. 1996. *Life as We Know It: A Father, a Family, and an Exceptional Child*. New York: Pantheon Books.

Borsay, A. 2002. "History, Power, and Identity." In *Disability Studies Today*, edited by C. Barnes, M. Oliver, and L. Barton, 98–119. Cambridge: Polity.

Borthwick, C. 1996. "Racism, IQ and Down's Syndrome." *Disability & Society* 11 (3): 403–10.

Bourdieu, P. 1990. *The Logic of Practice*. Translated by R. Nice. Stanford, CA: Stanford University Press.

Braybrooke, D., and C. Lindblom. 1970 [1963]. *A Strategy for Decision: Policy Evaluation as a Social Process*. New York: The Free Press.

Brookfield, T. 2012. *Cold War Comforts: Canadian Women, Child Safety, and Global Insecurity*. Waterloo, ON: Wilfred Laurier University Press.

Breuer, F., and W. Roth. 2003. "Subjectivity and Reflexivity in the Social Sciences: Epistemic Windows and Methodological Consequences." *Forum: Qualitative Social Research* 4 (2): Art 25.

Buck, P. 1950. *The Child Who Never Grew*. New York: J. Day Co.

Buell, M., and I. Brown. 2003. "Lifestyles of Adults with Developmental Disabilities in Ontario." In *Developmental Disabilities in Ontario, Second Edition*, edited by I. Brown and M. Pierce, 639–61. Toronto: Ontario Association on Developmental Disabilities.

Burghardt, M. 2017. "Institutional Survivorship: Abandonment and the 'Machinery of the Establishment.'" *Canadian Journal of Disability Studies* 6 (3): 118–148.

– 2016. "Containment, Conformity: Families, Institutions, and the Limits of Imagination." *Canadian Journal of Disability Studies* 5 (1): 42–72.

– 2015. "'He Was a Secret': Family Narratives and the Institutionalization of People with Intellectual Disabilities." *Disability & Society* 30 (7): 1071–86. http://dx.doi.org/10.1080/09687599.2015.1076718.

Butler, J. 1990. *Gender Trouble: Feminism and the Subversion of Identity*. New York: Routledge.

Carey, A. 2009. *On the Margins of Citizenship: Intellectual Disability and Civil Rights in Twentieth-Century America*. Philadelphia, PA: Temple University Press.

– 2003. "Beyond the Medical Model: A Reconsideration of 'Feeblemindedness', Citizenship, and Eugenic Restrictions." *Disability & Society* 18 (4): 411–30.

Carey, A., L. Ben-Moshe, and C. Chapman. 2014. "Preface: An Overview of *Disability Incarcerated*." In *Disability Incarcerated: Imprisonment and*

Disability in the United States and Canada, edited by L. Ben-Moshe,
C. Chapman, and A. Carey, ix–xiv. New York: Palgrave MacMillan.

Carlson, L. 2010. *The Faces of Intellectual Disability: Philosophical Reflections.*
Bloomington, IN: Indiana University Press.

– 2005. "Docile Bodies, Docile Minds: Foucauldian Reflections on Mental
Retardation." In *Foucault and the Government of Disability*, edited by
S. Tremain, 133–52. Ann Arbor, MI: University of Michigan Press.

Carpenter, S. 2007. *Neo-Asylum Era: Institutions without Walls.*
http://cilt.operitel.net/Documents%20of%20the%20CILT%20Website/
Final-Neo%20Asylum%20Era%20OutlineREV3.txt.

Cavell, R. 2004. "Introduction: The Cultural Production of Canada's Cold
War." In *Love, Hate, and Fear in Canada's Cold War*, edited by R. Cavell,
3–32. Toronto: University of Toronto Press.

Chadha, E. 2008. "'Mentally Defectives' Not Welcome: Mental Disability in
Canadian Immigration Law 1859–1927." *Disability Studies Quarterly* 28 (1).
http://dsq-sds.org/article/view/67/67.

Chapman, C. 2014. "Five Centuries' Material Reforms and Ethical
Reformulations of Social Elimination." In *Disability Incarcerated:
Imprisonment and Disability in the United States and Canada*, edited by
L. Ben-Moshe, C. Chapman, and A. Carey, 25–44. New York: Palgrave
Macmillan.

Chapman, C., A. Carey, and L. Ben-Moshe. 2014. "Reconsidering
Confinement: Interlocking Locations and Logics of Incarceration."
In *Disability Incarcerated: Imprisonment and Disability in the United States
and Canada*, edited by L. Ben-Moshe, C. Chapman, and A. Carey, 3–24.
New York: Palgrave Macmillan.

Chappell, A.L. 1998. "Still Out in the Cold: People with Learning Difficulties
and the Social Model of Disability." In *The Disability Reader: Social Science
Perspectives*, edited by T. Shakespeare, 212–20. London: Continuum.

Chupik, J., and D. Wright. 2006. "Training the 'Idiot' Child in Early
Twentieth-Century Ontario." *Disability & Society* 21 (1): 77–90.

Churchill, W. 2004. *Kill the Indian; Save the Man: The Genocidal Impact of
American Indian Residential Schools.* San Francisco, CA: City Lights.

Clark, L., and C. Marsh. 2002. *Patriarchy in the UK: The Language of Disability.*
http://pf7d7vi404s1dxh27mla5569.wpengine.netdna-cdn.com/files/library/
Clark-Laurence-language.pdf (accessed 19 April 2017).

Clarke, C., M. Lhussier, C. Minto, C. Gibb, and T. Perini. 2005. "Paradoxes,
Locations, and the Need for Social Coherence: A Qualitative Study of
Living with a Learning Difficulty." *Disability & Society* 20 (4): 405–19.

Davis, L. 2010. "Constructing Normalcy." In *The Disability Studies Reader,
3rd ed.*, edited by L. Davis, 3–19. New York: Routledge.

Davison, K. 2006. "Dialectical Imagery and Postmodern Research." *International Journal of Qualitative Studies in Education* 19 (2): 133–46.

Dorn, M. 1999. "The Moral Topography of Intemperance." In *Mind and Body Spaces: Geographies of Illness, Impairment, and Disability*, edited by R. Butler and H. Parr, 46–69. London: Routledge.

Douglas, M. 1966. *Purity and Danger: An Analysis of Concepts of Pollution and Taboo.* London: Routledge and Kegan Paul.

Down, J.L.H. 1866. "Observations on an Ethnic Classification of Idiots." *Clinical Lecture Reports, London Hospital* 3: 259–62.

Duffin, J. 2009. *Medical Miracles: Doctors, Saints, and Healing in the Modern World.* Oxford, UK: Oxford University Press.

Egerton, G. 2004. "Entering the Age of Human Rights: Religion, Politics, and Canadian Liberalism, 1945–1950." *The Canadian Historical Review* 85 (3): 451–79.

Ellis, J., and J. Simons. 2002. "Max Weber (1864–1920)." In *From Kant to Levi-Strauss: The Background to Contemporary Critical Theory*, edited by J. Simons, 81–96. Edinburgh, UK: Edinburgh University Press.

Enns, R. 1999. *A Voice Unheard: The Latimer Case and People with Disabilities.* Halifax, NS: Fernwood Publishing.

Erevelles, N. 2014. "Thinking with Disability Studies." *Disability Studies Quarterly* 34 (2). http://dsq-sds.org/article/view/4248/3587.

Esping-Andersen, G. 1990. *The Three Worlds of Welfare Capitalism.* Princeton, NJ: Princeton University Press.

Farber, B. 1959. "Effects of a Severely Mentally Retarded Child on Family Integration." *Monographs of the Society for Research in Child Development*, Serial #71, 24 (2): 1–112.

Ferguson, P. 1994. *Abandoned to Their Fate: Social Policy and Practice towards Severely Retarded People in America, 1820–1920.* Philadelphia, PA: Temple University Press.

Finkelstein, V. 1980. *Attitudes and Disabled People: Issues for Discussion.* New York: World Rehabilitation Fund: International Exchange of Information in Rehabilitation, Monograph #5. https://disability-studies.leeds.ac.uk/wp-content/uploads/sites/40/library/finkelstein-attitudes.pdf.

Fischer, D.H. 1970. *Historians' Fallacies: Toward a Logic of Historical Thought.* New York: Harper & Row.

Ford, C.A. 2017. "Trauma from the Past." *Canadian Journal of Disability Studies* 6 (3): 13–19.

Foucault, M. 2006. *Madness and Civilization: A History of Insanity in the Age of Reason.* Translated by R. Howard. New York: Pantheon Books.

– 1995. *Discipline and Punish: The Birth of the Prison.* Translated by A. Sheridan. New York: Vintage.

– 1994. "What Is Enlightenment?" In *Ethics: Subjectivity & Truth*, edited by P. Rabinow, 303–19. New York: The New Press.

– 1984. "Truth and Power." In *The Foucault Reader*, edited by P. Rabinow, 51–75. New York: Pantheon.

– 1980. "Two Lectures." In *Power / Knowledge: Selected Interviews and Other Writings, 1972–1977*, edited by C. Gordon, 78–108. Translated by C. Gordon, L. Marshall, J. Mepham, and K. Soper. New York: Pantheon Books.

– 1972. *The Archaeology of Knowledge*. Translated by A.M. Sheridan Smith. New York: Pantheon Books.

Fournier, S., and E. Crey. 1997. *Stolen from Our Embrace: The Abduction of First Nations Children and the Restoration of Aboriginal Communities*. Vancouver, BC, and Toronto: Douglas & McIntyre.

Frank, J.P. 1952. *My Son's Story*. London: Sidgwick & Jackson.

Galer, D. 2014. "'A Place to Work Like Any Other?' Sheltered Workshops in Canada, 1970–1985." *Canadian Journal of Disability Studies* 3 (2): 1–30.

Garland Thomson, R. 1997. *Extraordinary Bodies: Figuring Physical Disability in American Culture and Literature*. New York: Columbia University Press.

Gelb, S. 1996. "Social Deviance and the 'Discovery' of the Moron." *Disability, Handicap & Society* 2 (3): 247–57.

Gentile, P. 2000. "'Government Girls' and 'Ottawa Men': Cold War Management of Gender Relations in the Civil Service." In *Whose National Security? Canadian State Surveillance and the Creation of Enemies*, edited by G. Kinsman, D. Buse, and M. Steadman, 131–41. Toronto: Between the Lines Press.

Gibson, B. 2006. "Disability, Connectivity and Transgressing the Autonomous Body." *Journal of Medicine in the Humanities* 27: 187–96.

Girard, R. 2001. *I See Satan Fall like Lightening*. Translated by J.G. Williams. Maryknoll, NY: Orbis Books.

Gleason, M. 1999a. *Normalizing the Ideal: Psychology, Schooling, and the Family in Postwar Canada*. Toronto: University of Toronto Press.

– 1999b. "Embodied Negotiations: Children's Bodies and Historical Change in Canada, 1930 to 1960." *Journal of Canadian Studies* 34 (1): 112–38.

– 1997. "Psychology and the Construction of the 'Normal' Family in Postwar Canada, 1945–1960." *The Canadian Historical Review* 78 (3): 442–77.

Goffman, E. 1961. *Asylums*. Chicago, IL: Aldine Publishing.

Goodall, H.L. 2005. "Narrative Inheritance: A Nuclear Family with Toxic Secrets." *Qualitative Inquiry* 11 (4): 492–513.

Goodey, C.F. 2011. *A History of Intelligence and "Intellectual Disability": The Shaping of Psychology in Early Modern Europe*. Farnham, UK: Ashgate.

Goodley, D. 1996. "Locating Self-Advocacy in Models of Disability: Understanding Disability in the Support of Self-Advocates with Learning Disabilities." *Disability & Society* 12 (3): 367–79.

Gould, S.J. 1996. *The Mismeasure of Man*. Revised and expanded edition. New York: W.W. Norton & Company.

Grosz, E. 1994. *Volatile Bodies: Towards a Corporeal Feminism*. Bloomington, IN: Indiana University Press.

Guest, D. 1997. *The Emergence of Social Security in Canada, 3rd ed.* Vancouver, BC: University of British Columbia Press.

Hacking, I. 2002. *Historical Ontology*. Cambridge, MA: Harvard University Press.

Hahn, H. 1989. "Disability and the Reproduction of Bodily Images: The Dynamics of Human Appearances." In *The Power of Geography: How Territory Shapes Social Life*, edited by J. Wolch and M. Dear, 370–88. Boston: Unwin Hyman.

Harris, J. 2002. "One Principle and Three Fallacies of Disability Studies." *Journal of Medical Ethics* 28 (3): 204.

Harvey, D. 2005. *A Brief History of Neoliberalism*. Oxford, UK: Oxford University Press.

Helleiner, J. 2001. "'The Right Kind of Children': Childhood, Gender and 'Race' in Canadian Postwar Political Discourse." *Anthropologica* 43 (2): 143–52.

Helps, L. 2007. "Body, Power, Desire: Mapping Canadian Body History." *Journal of Canadian Studies* 41 (1): 126–50.

Holt, K.S. 1958. "The Influence of a Retarded Child upon Family Limitation." *Journal of Mental Deficiency Research* 2 (1): 28–36.

Hughes, B. 2007. "Being Disabled: Towards a Critical Social Ontology for Disability Studies." *Disability & Society* 22 (7): 673–84.

– 2005. "What Can a Foucauldian Analysis Contribute to Disability Theory?" In *Foucault and the Government of Disability*, edited by S. Tremain, 78–92. Ann Arbor, MI: University of Michigan Press.

Hughes, B., and K. Paterson. 1997. "The Social Model of Disability and the Disappearing Body: Towards a Sociology of Impairment." *Disability & Society* 12 (3): 325–40.

Hutton, S., P. Park, M. Levine, S. Johnson, and K. Bramesfeld. 2017. "Self-Advocacy from the Ashes of the Institution." *Canadian Journal of Disability Studies* 6 (3): 30–59.

Iacovetta, F. 2006. *Gatekeepers: Reshaping Immigrant Lives in Cold War Canada*. Toronto: Between the Lines Press.

– 2004. "Freedom Lovers, Sex Deviates, and Damaged Women: Iron Curtain Refugee Discourses in Cold War Canada." In *Love, Hate and Fear in Canada's Cold War*, edited by R. Cavell, 77–107. Toronto: University of Toronto Press.

Ignatieff, M. 1983. "State, Civil Society and Total Institutions: A Critique of Recent Social Histories of Punishment." In *Social Control and the State: Historical and Comparative Essays*, edited by S. Cohen and A. Scull, 75–105. Oxford, UK: Basil Blackwell.

Ignatow, G. 2009. "Why the Sociology of Morality Needs Bourdieu's *Habitus.*" *Sociological Inquiry* 79 (1): 98–114.

Ingleby, D. 1983. "Mental Health and Social Order." In *Social Control and the State: Historical and Comparative Essays,* edited by S. Cohen and A. Scull, 141–88. Oxford, UK: Basil Blackwell.

Inglis, P. 2013. "Reinterpreting Learning Difficulty: A Professional and Personal Challenge?" *Disability & Society* 28 (3): 423–26.

Jacobs, L., B. De Costa, and V. Cino. 2016. "The Accessibility for Manitobans Act: Ambitions and Achievements in Antidiscrimination and Citizen Participation." *Canadian Journal of Disability Studies* 5 (4): 1–24.

Jonsen, A. 2000. *A Short History of Medical Ethics.* New York: Oxford University Press.

Jordan, T. 1961. *The Mentally Retarded, 2nd ed.* Columbus: Charles E. Merrill Books, Inc.

Kelm, M.E. 2005. "Diagnosing the Discursive Indian: Medicine, Gender, and the 'Dying Race.'" *Ethnohistory* 52 (2): 371–406.

Kennan, G.F. 2012 [1951]. *American Diplomacy.* Chicago, IL: University of Chicago Press.

Kennedy, A. 2008. "Eugenics, 'Degenerate Girls', and Social Workers during the Progressive Era." *Affilia: Journal of Women and Social Work* 23 (1): 22–37.

Kinsman, G. 2004. "The Canadian Cold War on Queers: Sexual Regulation and Resistance." In *Love, Hate and Fear in Canada's Cold War,* edited by R. Cavell, 108–32. Toronto: University of Toronto Press.

Kliewer, C., and S. Drake. 1998. "Disability, Eugenics and the Current Ideology of Segregation: A Modern Moral Tale." *Disability & Society* 13 (1): 95–111.

Kristeva, J. 1982. *Powers of Horror: An Essay on Abjection.* New York: Columbia University Press.

Kuhse, H. 1995. "Quality of Life as a Decision-Making Criterion II." In *Ethics and Perinatology,* edited by A. Goldworth, W. Silverman, D.K. Stevenson, E.W.D. Young, and R. Rivers, 105–19. New York: Oxford University Press.

Lamp, S. 2006. "'It Is for the Mother': Feminists' Rhetorics of Disability during the American Eugenics Period." *Disability Studies Quarterly* 26 (4). http://dsq-sds.org/article/view/807/982.

Lather, P. 1991. *Getting Smart: Feminist Research and Pedagogy with/in the Postmodern.* New York: Routledge.

Levitz, M. 2003. "Voices of Self-Advocates." In *The Human Rights of Persons with Intellectual Disabilities: Different but Equal,* edited by S. Herr, L. Gostin, and H.H. Koh, 453–65. Oxford, UK: Oxford University Press.

Lobato, D. 1983. "Siblings of Handicapped Children: A Review." *Journal of Autism and Developmental Disorders* 13 (4): 347–64.

Longmore, P. 2010. "Conspicuous Contribution and American Cultural
    Dilemmas: Telethon Rituals of Cleansing and Renewal." In *Rethinking
    Normalcy: A Disability Studies Reader*, edited by T. Titchkosky and R.
    Michalko, 137–57. Toronto: Canadian Scholars' Press.

Mabry, L. 2002. "Postmodern Evaluation – Or Not?" *American Journal of
    Evaluation* 23 (2): 141–57.

Mackenzie, D.A. 1981. *Statistics in Britain, 1865–1930: The Social Construction
    of Scientific Knowledge*. Edinburgh, UK: Edinburgh University Press.

Malacrida, C. 2015. *A Special Hell: Institutional Life in Alberta's Eugenic Years*.
    Toronto: University of Toronto Press.

Marks, D. 1999. *Disability: Controversial Debates and Psycho-Social Perspectives*.
    London: Routledge.

Marzano-Parisoli, M.M. 2001. "Disability, Wrongful Life Lawsuits, and
    Human Difference: An Exercise in Ethical Perplexity." *Social Theory and
    Practice* 27 (4): 637.

May, E.T. 2008 [1988]. *Homeward Bound: American Families in the Cold War
    Era*. New York: Basic Books.

Maybee, J. 2011. "The Political Is Personal: Mothering at the Intersection
    of Acquired Disability, Gender, and Race." In *Disability and Mothering:
    Liminal Spaces of Embodied Knowledge*, edited by C. Lewiecki-Wilson and
    J. Cellio, 245–59. Syracuse, NY: Syracuse University Press.

McLaren, A. 1990. *Our Own Master Race: Eugenics in Canada, 1885–1945*.
    Toronto: McLelland & Stewart.

McLaren, M. 2002. *Feminism, Foucault, and Embodied Subjectivity*. Albany:
    State University of New York Press.

McNay, L. 1994. *Foucault: A Critical Introduction*. Cambridge: Polity Press.

McPhail, D. 2009. "What to Do with the 'Tubby Hubby'? Obesity, the
    Crisis of Masculinity, and the Nuclear Family in Early Cold War Canada."
    Antipode 41 (5): 1021–50.

McRuer, R. 2006. *Crip Theory: Cultural Signs of Queerness and Disability*.
    New York: New York University Press.

Menzies, R. 1998. "Governing Mentalities: The Deportation of 'Insane' and
    'Feebleminded' Immigrants out of British Columbia from Confederation to
    World War II." *Canadian Journal of Law & Society* 13 (2): 135–73.

Metzler, I. 2006. *Disability in Medieval Europe: Thinking about Physical
    Impairment during the High Middle Ages, c. 1100–1400*. London: Routledge.

Mosoff, J. 2000. "Is the Human Rights Paradigm Able to Include Disability:
    Who's In? Who Wins? What? Why?" *Queen's Law Journal* 26: 225–76.

Odell, T. 2011. "Not Your Average Childhood: Lived Experiences of Children
    with Physical Disabilities Raised in Bloorview Hospital, Home and School
    from 1960 to 1989." *Disability & Society* 26 (1): 49–63.

Oliver, M. 1990. *The Politics of Disablement.* London: MacMillan.

Panitch, M. 2008. *Disability, Mothers, and Organization: Accidental Activists.* New York: Routledge.

Park, D. 1990. *Changing Shadows: The Huronia Regional Centre, 1876–1934.* Toronto: Unpublished Master's thesis, York University.

Park, D., and J. Radford. 1998. "From the Case Files: Reconstructing a History of Involuntary Sterilisation." *Disability & Society* 13 (3): 317–42.

Pelias, R. 2008. "H.L. Goodall's *A Need to Know* and the Stories We Tell Ourselves." *Qualitative Inquiry* 14 (7): 1309–13.

Philo, C. 1989. "'Enough to Drive One Mad': The Organization of Space in 19th-Century Lunatic Asylums." In *The Power of Geography: How Territory Shapes Social Life,* edited by J. Wolch and M. Dear, 258–90. Winchester, MA: Unwin Hyman.

Piepmeier, A. 2012. "Saints, Sages, and Victims: Endorsement of and Resistance to Cultural Stereotypes in Memoirs by Parents of Children with Disabilities." *Disability Studies Quarterly* 32 (1). http://dsq-sds.org/article/view/3031/3058.

Polit, D.F., and T.C. Beck. 2008. "Is There a Gender Bias in Nursing Research?" *Research in Nursing and Health* 31: 417–27.

Porter, R. 1997. *The Greatest Benefit to Mankind: A Medical History of Humanity.* New York: W.W. Norton.

Porter, T.M. 1996. *The Rise of Statistical Thinking 1820–1900.* Princeton, NJ: Princeton University Press.

Price, J., and M. Shildrick. 2002. "Bodies Together: Touch, Ethics, and Disability." In *Disability / Postmodernity: Embodying Disability Theory,* edited by M. Corker and T. Shakespeare, 62–75. London: Continuum.

Race, D., K. Boxall, and I. Carson. 2005. "Towards a Dialogue for Practice: Reconciling Social Role Valorization and the Social Model of Disability." *Disability & Society* 20 (5): 507–21.

Rachels, J. 1986. *The End of Life: Euthanasia and Morality.* Oxford, UK: Oxford University Press.

Radford, J. 1991. "Sterilization versus Segregation: Control of the 'Feebleminded,' 1900–1938." *Social Science in Medicine* 33 (4): 449–58.

Radford, J., and D. Park. 2003. "Historical Overview of Developmental Disabilities in Ontario." In *Developmental Disability in Ontario, 2nd ed.,* edited by I. Brown and M. Percy, 3–18. Toronto: Ontario Association for Developmental Disabilities.

– 1993. "'A Convenient Means of Riddance': Institutionalization of People Diagnosed 'Mentally Deficient' in Ontario, 1876–1934." *Health and Canadian Society* 1 (2): 369–92.

Reaume, G. 2006. "Patients at Work: Insane Asylum Inmates' Labour in Ontario, 1841–1900." In *Mental Health and Canadian Society: Historical*

Perspectives, edited by J. Moran and D. Wright, 69–96. Montreal, QC: McGill-Queen's University Press.

– 2004. "No Profits, Just a Pittance: Work, Compensation, and People Defined as Mentally Disabled in Ontario, 1964–1990." In *Mental Retardation in America: A Historical Reader*, edited by S. Noll and J.W. Trent, 466–93. New York: New York University Press.

– 2000. *Remembrance of Patients Past: Patient Life at the Toronto Hospital for the Insane, 1870–1940*. Toronto: University of Toronto Press.

Reichman, N., H. Corman, and K. Noonan. 2008. "Impact of Child Disability on the Family." *Maternal & Child Health* 12 (6): 679–83.

Rembis, M. 2014. "The New Asylums: Madness and Mass Incarceration in the Neoliberal Era." In *Disability Incarcerated: Imprisonment and Disability in the United States and Canada*, edited by L. Ben-Moshe, C. Chapman, and A. Carey, 139–59. New York: Palgrave Macmillan.

Riessman, C.K. 2003. "Performing Identities in Illness Narrative: Masculinity and Multiple Sclerosis." *Qualitative Research* 3 (1): 5–33.

– 2002. "Analysis of Personal Narratives." In *Handbook of Interview Research*, edited by J. Gubrium and J. Holstein, 695–710. London: Sage.

Rhodes, L. 2001. "Toward an Anthology of Prisons." *Annual Review of Anthropology* 30: 65–83.

Roberts, B. 1989. "Women's Peace Activism in Canada." In *Beyond the Vote: Canadian Women and Politics*, edited by L. Kealey and J. Sangster, 276–308. Toronto: University of Toronto Press.

Rogers, D.E. 1953. *Angel Unaware*. Westwood, NJ: Revell.

Rothman, D. 1983. "Social Control: The Uses and Abuses of the Concept in the History of Incarceration." In *Social Control and the State*, edited by S. Cohen and A. Scull, 106–17. Oxford, UK: Basil Blackwell.

– 1971. *The Discovery of the Asylum: Social Order and Disorder in the New Republic, Revised Edition*. Boston: Little, Brown, & Company.

Runté, M., and A. Mills. 2006. "Cold War, Chilly Climate: Exploring the Roots of Gendered Discourse in Organization and Management Theory." *Human Relations* 59 (5): 695–720.

Russell, M., and R. Malhotra. 2002. "Capitalism and Disability." *The Socialist Register* 38: 211–28.

Schwalbe, M.L., and M. Wolkomir. 2003. "Interviewing Men." In *Inside Interviewing: New Lenses, New Concerns*, edited by J.A. Holstein and J.F. Gubrium, 55–72. Thousand Oaks, CA: Sage.

Scott, C. 2017. "That's My Story and I'm Sticking to It." *Canadian Journal of Disability Studies* 6 (3): 20–9.

Scott, J. 1988. "Deconstructing Equality-versus-Difference: Or, the Uses of Poststructural Theory for Feminism." *Feminist Studies* 14 (1): 32–50.

Scull, A. 1983. "Humanitarianism or Control? Some Observations on the Historiography of Anglo-American Psychiatry." In *Social Control and the State*, edited by S. Cohen and A. Scull, 118–40. Oxford, UK: Basil Blackwell.

– 1979. *Museums of Madness: The Social Organization of Insanity in Nineteenth-Century England*. London: Allen Lane.

Scully, J. 2002. "A Postmodern Disorder: Moral Encounters with Molecular Models of Disability." In *Disability / Postmodernity: Embodying Disability Theory*, edited by M. Corker and T. Shakespeare, 48–61. London: Continuum.

Shakespeare, T. 2006. *Disability Rights and Wrongs*. London: Routledge.

Sherman, B., and J. Cocozza. 1984. "Stress in Families of the Developmentally Disabled: A Literature Review of Factors Affecting the Decision to Seek Out-of-Home Placements." *Family Relations* 33 (1): 95–103.

Shildrick, M. 2009. *Dangerous Discourses of Disability, Subjectivity, and Sexuality*. London: Palgrave MacMillan.

– 2002. *Embodying the Monster*. London: Sage.

Silvers, A. 1995. "Reconciling Equality to Difference: Caring (f)or Justice for People with Disabilities." *Hypatia* 10 (1): 30–55.

Simmons, H.G. 1982. *From Asylum to Welfare: The Evolution of Mental Retardation Policy in Ontario from 1831 to 1980*. Toronto: National Institute on Mental Retardation.

Simons, J. 2002. "Immanuel Kant (1724–1804)." In *From Kant to Levi-Strauss: The Background to Contemporary Critical Theory*, edited by J. Simons, 17–32. Edinburgh, UK: Edinburgh University Press.

Simpson, M. 2011. "Othering Intellectual Disability: Two Models of Classification from the 19th Century." *Theory & Psychology* 22 (5): 541–55.

Singer, P. 2011. *Practical Ethics, 3rd ed.* Cambridge: Cambridge University Press.

St Pierre, E.A. 2011. "Post Qualitative Research: The Critique and the Coming After." In *The SAGE Handbook of Qualitative Research, 4th ed.*, edited by N. Denzin and Y.S. Lincoln, 611–25. Los Angeles, CA: Sage.

Stainton, T. 2016. "Supported Decision-Making in Canada: Principles, Policy, and Practice." *Research and Practice in Intellectual and Developmental Disabilities* 3 (1): 1–11.

– 2004. "Reason's Other: The Emergence of the Disabled Subject in the Northern Renaissance." *Disability & Society* 19 (3): 225–42.

Stefan, S. 1993. "Silencing the Different Voice: Competence, Feminist Theory, and Law." *University of Miami Law Review* 4: 763–815.

Stiker, H.J. 1999. *A History of Disability*. Translated by W. Sayers. Ann Arbor, MI: University of Michigan Press.

Strong-Boag, V. 2011. *Fostering Nation? Canada Confronts Its History of Childhood Disadvantage*. Waterloo, ON: Wilfrid Laurier University Press.

– 2007. "'Children of Adversity': Disabilities and Child Welfare in Canada from the Nineteenth to the Twenty-First Century." *Journal of Family History* 32 (4): 413–32.

Thobani, S. 2007. *Exalted Subjects: Studies in the Making of Race and Nation in Canada.* Toronto: University of Toronto Press.

Thomas, C. 2002. "Disability Theory: Key Ideas, Issues and Thinkers." In *Disability Studies Today*, edited by C. Barnes, M. Oliver, and L. Barton, 38–57. Cambridge: Polity Press.

– 1999. *Female Forms: Experiencing and Understanding Disability.* Buckingham, UK: Open University Press.

Thorn, B. 2009. "'Healthy Activity and Worthwhile Ideas': Left- and Right-Wing Women Confront Juvenile Delinquency in Post-World-War-II Canada." *Histoire Sociale / Social History* 42 (84): 327–59.

Tilley, E., J. Walmsley, S. Earle, and D. Atkinson. 2012. "'The Silence Is Roaring': Sterilization, Reproductive Rights, and Women with Intellectual Disabilities." *Disability & Society* 27 (3): 413–26.

Tormey, S. 2002. "Karl Marx (1818–83)." In *From Kant to Levi-Strauss: The Background to Contemporary Critical Theory*, edited by J. Simons, 50–64. Edinburgh, UK: Edinburgh University Press.

Tremain, S. 2005. "Foucault, Governmentality, and Critical Disability Theory: An Introduction." In *Foucault and the Government of Disability*, edited by S. Tremain, 1–24. Ann Arbor, MI: University of Michigan Press.

– 2002. "On the Subject of Impairment." In *Disability / Postmodernity: Embodying Disability Theory*, edited by M. Corker and T. Shakespeare, 32–47. London: Continuum.

Trent, J. 1994. *Inventing the Feeble Mind: A History of Mental Retardation in the United States.* Berkeley, CA: University of California Press.

Tyor, P., and L. Bell. 1984. *Caring for the Retarded in America: A History.* Westport, CT: Greenwood Press.

Union of the Physically Impaired against Segregation. 1976. *Fundamental Principles of Disability.* London: UPIAS. https://tonybaldwinson.files. wordpress.com/2014/06/1975-11-22-upias-and-disability-alliance-fundamental-principles-of-disability.pdf.

Vehmas, S. 1999. "Discriminative Assumptions of Utilitarian Bioethics Regarding Individuals with Intellectual Disabilities." *Disability & Society* 14 (1): 37–52.

Ward, T., and C. Stewart. 2008. "Putting Human Rights into Practice with People with an Intellectual Disability." *Journal of Developmental and Physical Disabilities* 20 (3): 297–311.

Wendell, S. 1996. *The Rejected Body: Feminist Philosophical Reflections on Disability.* New York: Routledge.

Whitaker, R. 2004. "'We Know They're Out There': Canada and Its Others, With or Without the Cold War." In *Love, Hate, and Fear in Canada's Cold War*, edited by R. Cavell, 35–56. Toronto: University of Toronto Press.

Whitaker, R., and G. Marcuse. 1994. *Cold War Canada: The Making of a National Insecurity State, 1945–1975.* Toronto: University of Toronto Press.

Williams, V., and P. Heslop. 2005. "Mental Health Support Needs of People with a Learning Difficulty: A Medical or a Social Model?" *Disability & Society* 20 (3): 231–45.

Williston, W. 1971. *Present Arrangements for the Care and Supervision of Mentally Retarded Persons in Ontario.* Toronto: The Queen's Press.

Wolfe, P. 2016. *Traces of History: Elementary Structures of Race.* Brooklyn, NY: Verso.

Wright, D. 2011. *Down's: The History of a Disability.* Oxford, UK: Oxford University Press.

Young, I.M. 1990. *Justice and the Politics of Difference.* Princeton, NJ: Princeton University Press.

Index